D0850835

CROSSING THE YARD

CROSSING THE YARD

Thirty Years as a Prison Volunteer

Richard Shelton

The University of Arizona Press   Tucson

In order to respect the privacy of the inmates and former
inmates who appear in this book, I have decided in all but
three cases to either change the names entirely or use only
first names. The three exceptions to this are former inmates
who have written extensively about their incarceration themselves and have given me permission to use their names.

The University of Arizona Press
© 2007 Richard Shelton

Library of Congress Cataloging-in-Publication Data
Shelton, Richard, 1933–
  Crossing the yard : thirty years as a prison volunteer /
Richard Shelton.
      p. cm.
   Includes bibliographical references.
   ISBN 978-0-8165-2594-2 (alk. paper) —
   ISBN 978-0-8165-2595-9 (pbk. : alk. paper)
   1. Shelton, Richard, 1933– 2. Volunteer workers in
corrections—Arizona. 3. Prisoners—Education—Arizona.
4. Prisons—Arizona. 5. Creative writing—Study and
teaching. 6. Teacher-student relationships. I. Title.
PS3569.H39367Z46 2007
365.92—dc22
[B]   2007008827

Manufactured in the United States of America on acid-free,
archival-quality paper containing a minimum of 50% post-
consumer waste and processed chlorine free.

12 11 10 09 08 07   6 5 4 3 2 1

This book is dedicated to my "partners in crime" over the years:

> Tom Cobb
> Will Clipman
> Pamela Stewart
> Peggy Shumaker
> Jay Barwell
> Chris Cannady
> Lollie Butler
> Deidre Elliott
> Mark Menlove
> Joni Wallace
> Mac Hudson
>
> and especially
> Lois Shelton

The author wishes to thank Gregory Kuykendall, Dan Barr, and Kenneth Lamberton for reading the manuscript and making valuable suggestions and the Lannan Foundation for a generous grant that helped to make this book possible.

Contents

---

1 *Getting In*

The prisons, the reformatory, and the jail have achieved only a shocking record of failure. There is overwhelming evidence that these institutions create crime rather than prevent it.

—Task Force Report on Corrections, National Advisory Commission on Criminal Justice Standards and Goals, 1973

1

When I am on an airplane trying to get some reading done and a friendly stranger sitting next to me asks, "Where are you from?" I reply, "I just got out of the state prison." Usually that takes care of that, and I can continue reading. Sometimes, if there are any unoccupied seats, the stranger moves to one of them.

Although my answer is a dodge to buy a little time for myself without being rude, it isn't a lie. Every Saturday I go into two different units of the Arizona State Prison Complex, and several hours later I come out. On Sundays I often go into two other units and come out. So I can honestly say I just got out of the state prison. For the past more than thirty years I have been going into one or more of the many units of the prison to direct a program of creative writing workshops. For me, getting in has always been more difficult than getting out. I remember the struggles I have had over the years getting into various Arizona state prisons. That's just one of the ironies that permeate all modern American prisons.

My thirty years as a volunteer teacher in the state prison system did not begin innocently. In fact, the abstract concepts of guilt and innocence have perhaps not occupied my mind as much as they should have. I have been occupied instead with the slightly less amorphous ideas of crime and punishment as our society views them. Since I have been working with convicts, I have seen the death penalty abolished by the Supreme Court and then reinstated in most states, including Arizona, suggesting that this one extremely important concept of punishment, at least, has no absolute foundation in law and is subject to the political climate of a particular time and place.

My association with convicts and former convicts began in 1970 or 1971. I can't be sure about the date. I had no idea I was entering into a world that would eventually define a large part of my life, and I have never kept very good records. I was an assistant professor in the English department at the University of Arizona in Tucson, teaching literature and poetry writing in the Creative Writing Program. I received a letter from a young man on death row in the Arizona State Prison at Florence, seventy miles north of Tucson. He had read my recently published book of poetry, and he asked if I would consider reading some of his poems and giving him critical feedback.

I recognized his name. Anybody who had been living in Arizona in the mid-1960s would have recognized his name, and often with a shudder of horror. He was Charles Schmid. He had been the charismatic ringleader of a group of Tucson teenagers and young people involved with drugs and bent upon mayhem. Three young girls, one only thirteen years old, all of whom were in some way known to this group, disappeared in 1964 and 1965. The Tucson police were baffled. The FBI was called in. Several members of the Mafia, then prominent in Tucson and evidently enlisted by family or friends of the victims, became involved in trying to extort a confession from Charles Schmid. Finally, two friends of Charles Schmid broke their silence, turned state's evidence, and admitted that they had played a tangential role in the murder of one of the girls, but that the real murderer of all three girls was Charles Schmid.

The newspapers called the murders "thrill killings" and followed the search for and arrest of Charles Schmid with daily front-page headlines and photographs. He was extremely short, good-looking, and he had been a champion gymnast in high school. At one point, when the police came to arrest him, his mother, Katharine, had blocked the front door of his house with her massive body, demanding that the police produce a search warrant, which they did not have. She delayed them long enough for Schmid to get away, although he was captured later.

As several of Schmid's friends produced damning evidence against him, the ensuing search for bodies made for more lurid headlines and photographs in the papers. National magazines called Schmid the "Pied Piper of Tucson," and referred to Speedway Boulevard, where Schmid and his friends cruised and hung out, as "the ugliest street in

America." Both his trials were major media events. He steadily denied his guilt in the murder of the second two victims, who were sisters, but finally led authorities to the remains of the first victim's body buried in a sandy arroyo in the desert. For his part in this murder he received a sentence of fifty years to life, while his two accomplices received relatively light sentences. For the murder of the other two girls, he was given a death sentence.

I had read about this as it played out on the front pages of the local newspapers for months, and remembered it somewhat vaguely when I received the letter from Charles Schmid six or seven years later. My immediate reaction was probably typical—nothing in my background had taught me to react in any other way—but I am ashamed of it now. Here was my chance, I thought, to read the poetry of a monster. Perhaps even to meet him. It was thrilling. I considered him some exotic subspecies of human I had never before encountered. He was stepping right out of a brutal murder mystery and into my quiet, academic life. Without a moment's hesitation and for all the wrong reasons, I wrote back to him that I would be willing to read and critique his poetry. If I was aware that this young man was facing the gas chamber in two years, I was not unduly concerned about it. That would make him seem even more exotic. He had, after all, been convicted of murder. Who was I to question the judicial system that had found him guilty, or the severity of the punishment that system had meted out? It was none of my business. I was excited to be involved in the process as a kind of voyeur as long as it was understood that I was not part of it.

These people, the son who had probably murdered three girls and the mother who protected him and never accepted his guilt, were not people who inhabited the world I knew, and so they were not really people. They existed only on the pages of the newspaper, and I associated them, like the newspaper, with my first cup of coffee in the morning. If anyone had told me, then, that a few years down the road I would be sitting in a hospital in Phoenix where Charles Schmid was dying, signing papers giving the necessary permission to remove first his kidney and then his eye in order to save him, or that years later I would be sitting beside his gallant mother, Katharine, holding her hand as she was dying in a Tucson hospice, or especially that I would spend the next more than thirty years working with the imprisoned, I would have said they were crazy. When I got that innocuous letter from Charles Schmid asking me to read and comment on his poetry, I didn't know it, but I was about to find out what I was made of, or at least, over the next thirty years, get some kind of notion.

Charles Schmid and I corresponded for several months. I found his poetry rough and in need of much revision, but it indicated remarkable talent. It was intense, often dark and brooding, but it had notable verbal energy and immediacy, and it showed that he understood the use of images. One of the images I remember was that of a girl's white arm sticking up out of the sand of a desert arroyo. It occurred in the context of a passionate love poem to the girl. It gave me pause.

Then in one of his letters Charles asked if I would come visit him. I was by this time beginning to realize, dimly, that I was dealing with a human being and that I could no longer think of my involvement as casual, as a form of literary slumming; but at the same time I was very curious and titillated at the thought of meeting a real monster. So I filled out the necessary forms that would clear me to visit a prisoner on death row, and when the clearance came through, I drove seventy miles north to Florence, wondering what to expect.

Florence was a small, dusty, desert town with a picturesque Victorian courthouse and not much else to recommend it. It seemed to have developed as an adjunct to the state prison, although it was actually there before the prison was constructed and the last batch of prisoners was brought from the ancient Yuma Territorial Prison in 1909. The name of the town had nothing to do with the city in Italy. It had been named either in honor of one of the daughters of its founding father, or after the wife of a territorial governor—Arizona was still a territory when the prison was built.

When I first visited the prison in the early 1970s, I could not think of anything with which to compare it. There was a very high wall around much of it, but the approach was gracious, down a drive lined with palm trees with an architecturally awkward, vaguely Moorish, large building at its end. Behind this building and beyond the high wall was a collection of many buildings ranging from what appeared to be military barracks to a huge neoclassical structure with impressive lines and dimensions.

At the entrance to the palm-lined drive was a large sign listing the many things it was illegal to bring into the prison. Among the items on this list that I might expect, like illegal drugs, booze, and firearms, one item caught my attention: *unauthorized writing*. I didn't realize at the time that I would spend the next thirty years bringing in *unauthorized writing* or that I would also carry a great deal of it out. In fact, I have never been able to figure out which writing was *authorized* and which wasn't. Was Emily Dickinson *authorized*? Was Edward Abbey? So I simply ignored the entire rule. That has proven to be the best way for me to function in regard to several prison rules, which are often meaningless and intended only to intimidate or to be enforced at the whim of the administration as needed for control or punishment. I was entering a dictatorship, and I had no idea how to behave in a dictatorship, but I would learn. In a dictatorship everyone is subversive, even the dictator.

During my first visit, I don't know which of us was more nervous, me or Charles Schmid, but I suspect he was. There were two visitation rooms for prisoners on the main yard at Florence at that time. One was for visitors to inmates in the general population and one was for visitors to inmates in segregation, protective custody, and those on death row. I noticed, even during my first visit, that Charles had a good deal of status among the inmates in the more restricted visiting room. Many of them seemed to know him, and as he walked past them they greeted him as "Smitty." It was the first of many visits, and as long as he was on death row, a guard always accompanied him and stood beside or behind his chair during every visit. Some of the guards seemed very attentive to what we were saying to each other, while others paid little attention. We sat in a long room with a heavy metal screen down the middle of it separating the inmates from the visitors. The screen and the walls were painted an ugly shade of what was supposed to be tan, I suppose, but it looked like dried mud. There was a countertop on either side of the screen, and at that level a slot in the screen large enough to pass the poems we were discussing back and forth.

I remember Charles becoming very angry during one of my visits when the guard insisted on standing so close that he stepped on Charles' foot. Charles was convinced he had done it on purpose. I could tell from this episode that he was still cocky in spite of everything and that he had a hair trigger. What I couldn't tell was how much of this outburst was genuine anger and how much was theatrics in an attempt to impress me. He was obviously a consummate actor.

I didn't mind having our conversations overheard because I realized that the technical aspects of the poems we were discussing were well over the guards' heads anyway. We might as well have been speaking Greek much of the time as far as they were concerned. But Charles chaffed under this monitoring of our conversations. It was an awkward situation in which to critique anyone's work, although Charles was eager for the advice of a published poet, especially one who taught creative writing at a university. He took criticism well and revised quickly and thoroughly, cutting the florid, overwritten passages and tightening the lines. His ability to create powerful images was remarkable from the beginning.

As well as I remember that first visit, I remember the drive back to Tucson even better. It included some of the most earnest soul-searching I had ever done. For the first time in my life I understood the biblical image of Jacob wrestling with the Angel, only in my case it felt as if I were wrestling with the Devil. I realized then that I was dealing with a real young man in desperate trouble, not some freak in a sideshow. It also hit me that this personable and very frightened young man who had tried so hard to impress me with his "cool" had probably done horrible things, not once but several times. Things so horrible that I could not even imagine them without remembering a drama or movie, things that had left the lives of several families, including his own, blighted forever. How could I justify doing anything to help such a person, even if it were only helping him write better poetry in the months he had left before he was to be executed? How could I balance any humanitarian feelings I might have for him against the dreadful weight of suffering endured by the families of his victims?

On the other hand, he was a young man facing death in the gas chamber in two years. Could he possibly be innocent of the murders he had been found guilty of? He had never really admitted that he was guilty of any of them, merely that he had witnessed and been implicated in one of them. I wanted to believe this, but finally rejected it as cop-out logic. If I were going to continue to work with him and be his friend, possibly the only one he had outside of prison except his long-suffering mother, Katharine, I would have to do it with the full knowledge of what he surely was—a mass murderer, a man who had deliberately killed three young girls. *I am, after all,* I told myself, *an educator, and all I am being asked to do is educate.*

At this point I learned the meaning of the phrase "to swallow hard." For about sixty miles on the Pinal Pioneer Parkway I swallowed hard. By the time I reached the Tucson city limits I had rationalized it out and arrived at a philosophical position that would permit me to continue to work with Tucson's most notorious killer. I was reminded of that position recently when I saw a sign in front of a church that said: YOU HAVE NO PAST HERE. ONLY A FUTURE. I would treat Charles Schmid, I said to myself, as if he were born yesterday and had no past. I would do this as long as he behaved in ways I could find acceptable. If he tried to con me or expressed attitudes I couldn't tolerate, I would have nothing further to do with him. I could not justify this position logically, but I felt that it was right for me. I felt I could take it from there, and I've been taking it from there ever since. The results, over the years, have only strengthened my belief that it was the best choice I could have made under the circumstances. Although that choice has led me to more pain than I could have imagined then, it has also enriched and enlarged my life. It has led me through bloody tragedies and terrible disappointments to a better understanding of what it means to be human and even, sometimes, to triumph.

2

Shortly after I began to visit Charles Schmid every other weekend, I also began to get letters from other inmates at Florence, most of them on death row, although some were in the general prison population. Charles had mentioned some of these men to me and told me they also wrote. Prose in some cases, but most often poetry. I was beginning to find out that many men in prison write, especially poetry and usually very bad, sentimental poetry. I was also beginning to find out that the prison grapevine works faster than the telephone and can leap the barriers between death row and the rest of the prison in seconds. The writers wanted to know if I would critique their work also. I did the best I could, but after a few months I was corresponding with so many men in prison that I was spending more time on it than I could afford while teaching full-time at the university and trying to do some of my own writing.

What I needed was some way to get them all together in one group, in a workshop like the ones I taught at the university. If I could do that, I thought, I could probably accomplish in two hours a week what it was taking me many hours to do by correspondence, and I could do a much better job of it. But I knew that even if I had some organization or church behind me to get me in, the prison administration would never permit me to have a workshop that mixed men on death row with those in the general population. And I was distracted by the ticking clock. Charles had exhausted all possibilities of appeal before I met him. A commutation from the governor was about as likely as an angel landing on the roof of the prison. I watched Charles grow more restless and terrified each week, although he tried to hide it under a bravado that fooled no one.

One Saturday early in 1972, while I was visiting Charles, he whispered to me, "Don't drive up next time. I won't be here. Tell Katharine

I love her. I won't contact her and I promise, on my honor, I won't contact you."

I don't remember how I responded. It didn't seem to matter. He had obviously made up his mind and had a plan he felt was foolproof. Perhaps, if I had thought he could do it, I might have tried to talk him out of it, but nobody escapes from maximum-security death row, I thought. It was simply more of his bravado, a gesture to bolster his tough-guy image in spite of his short stature and the fact that he was constantly told what to do by guards who towered over him.

About a week later, however, I was not totally surprised to read in the morning paper that he had escaped, although the prison authorities didn't seem to know how. Nor did I. Teams on horseback and with dogs were combing the desert in search of him. I went to see Katharine, as I had been doing after each of my visits to Charles. She sat at her kitchen table with her head in her hands, beyond the ability to cry anymore, and she said to me what I didn't have the guts to say to her: "I know they'll find him. I only hope they don't hurt him when they do. But if they kill him, it might be better than what he's facing. I think that's what he wants—to get it over with."

Her pain was palpable. I could feel it coming off her in waves as she suffered for the acts of her adopted child, acts so dreadful that she refused to admit he had done them. I learned about the victims of crime from Katharine, how violent crimes always have many victims and some of them often get little help or emotional support.

Charles did not contact me, but something peculiar happened to my home phone. The dial tone changed slightly and there were strange clicking noises. I suspected that it was bugged. Other than Charles' mother and her second husband, Maurice, I was probably the only one on his visitor's list. It figured that the cops would expect him to contact me for help.

When my son, Brad, who was then a teenager, complained that something was wrong with the phone, I foolishly told him I thought it had been bugged by the police. He told all his friends, and his status soared. He was the only teenager in their white, suburban, upper-middle-class world whose phone was bugged by the police. He would call one or the other of his friends and the two of them would take turns saying insulting things about the police. I've often wondered who was listening in on these conversations and what they thought. The only thing I really resented about it was that when they removed the bug, they did something to disrupt the phone line, and we had to call the phone company to send someone out to restore it. A minor hassle when compared to Charles' desperate situation, and Brad was enjoying himself immensely.

Charles managed to avoid capture for four days. He was recognized in a railroad yard in spite of, or possibly because of, the bizarre blond wig he had contrived, a wig that looked ridiculous above the black stubble of his jaw. Three years later, in an article he wrote for the *Tucson Citizen* (Dec. 30, 1978), he said: "The escape was futile. I couldn't function in the free world. No one would give me a job and I wasn't inclined to use violence or crime for my sustenance. I lasted four days. I was hungry and tired, and when they found me, for once, isolation seemed a welcome relief."

Then, on June 29, 1972, a miracle happened, a miracle so important that it made me a believer in miracles for life, although looking back on it now I can see that for Charles it simply meant the substitution of one kind of gruesome death for another kind of gruesome death. In *Furman v. Georgia* the U.S. Supreme Court ruled that capital punishment, as it was practiced in Georgia, was cruel and unusual punishment; and because such policies were the same in other states, they all became illegal. In this decision, which many hailed as a triumph of sanity over barbarism while others denounced it as an unmitigated disaster, the Supreme Court abolished the death penalty. Death row was dismantled by law, and in 1973 its occupants were placed in maximum security in the general prison population with life sentences, although the prison administration at Florence kept the execution chamber in case the court should change its mind. As I recall, the decision came down less than a month before Charles was scheduled for execution.

I'm sure what I felt was mild compared to what Charles and his mother felt, but I had almost never felt such relief. It was as if I had been carrying a huge stone day and night and suddenly it was gone. As relief and thankfulness flooded through me, I realized that this young man was becoming something like a son to me, in spite of everything. It felt to me as if I had been given the knowledge of this dark and troubled creature to balance the scales for the gift of my own son, Brad, who was everything a father could have asked for and more. I was even struck with the physical contrast: Brad was very tall and blonde, with a direct, untroubled gaze and an aura of complete assurance. He knew he was loved. Charles was very short, very dark, and he looked out at the world with deeply troubled eyes beneath heavy, dark brows. Except for the devotion of the woman who had adopted him, I don't think he knew what love was.

I found out from Katharine that she had adopted him immediately after he was born to an unmarried woman in the Tucson nursing home run by Katharine and her first husband. Growing up, Charles had hated his adoptive father, and ultimately Katharine divorced him. Somehow, shortly before the first of the three murders, Charles had found out who his birth mother was. By that time she was a successful attorney in Phoenix. Charles had gone to meet her, but she had thrown him out and told him not to come back. When he did go back, she hired thugs to beat him up. Then the murders began.

Late in 1972, after the Supreme Court decision abolishing capital punishment, I was serving as a member of a panel for the Arizona Commission on the Arts. Our job was to choose young writers who would go into the public schools in Arizona for short residencies, working with the students' creative writing. Several years earlier I had obtained from Betty Kray at the Academy of American Poets the initial funding for this program and had worked for more than a year to get it matched. Now, as a member of the panel, it occurred to me that the Arizona Commission on the Arts would be the ideal sponsor for a prison creative writing workshop if I could sell the idea to them. I had never heard of such a workshop in a prison, but I didn't see why it wouldn't work.

Nancy Pierce, the commission's newly chosen literature director, was enthusiastic when I approached her with the idea. She told me that she had received several letters from a young man named J. Charles Green in the prison at Florence requesting that the Arizona Commission on the Arts sponsor some kind of class in creative writing. She had been touched by the letters. J. Charles Green was one of the inmates who had been sending me his poems to critique. Now that I had volunteered to direct a workshop in the prison, Nancy promised she would approach the board of the Arizona Commission and propose it.

Not only did the commission agree to sponsor a creative writing workshop, they agreed to provide me with mileage expenses and two hundred dollars for books for members of the workshop. Nancy went to Florence and negotiated with the prison authorities, offering to provide an arts program directed by a published writer and university faculty member, and all for free. Her initial reaction to the prison authorities was disgust and dismay, and their initial reaction was distrust, but after several visits and much negotiation, she was able to convince them of the possible benefits of the program, although the negotiations dragged on into the spring of 1974. The prison administration was obviously not eager to provide a creative writing workshop for inmates.

I continued to visit Charles every other weekend. He was now in the maximum-security section of the prison, pushing hard for the workshop. One sunny Saturday morning in early 1974, Charles and I were walking along the fence in the outdoors visitation area as we often did, talking.

"I'm not going to point," Charles said, "but look at the southwest corner of the yard, where the walls meet."

"Okay, I see it."

"For several days during the year the sun sets directly behind that corner. Anyone looking in that direction at that time of day will be looking directly into the sun. Anybody going over the wall would be invisible. You were a gymnast. You know how easy it is to climb up a corner with your back against one wall and your feet against the other. Nothing to it. I could get to the top of the wall in less than three minutes. I may have to. It depends. But I promise you, like I did last time, I won't try to get in touch with you."

"No, Charles. No! No! Don't do this. You can't embarrass them again. They'll kill you this time. For Katharine's sake, don't do this. How about for my sake?"

"Maybe I won't have to. But it's an ace in the hole. I may have to play it. I'm going to try to make a deal with the devil."

"What devil?"

"The warden. Cardwell. I've got to have a little bit of freedom. Just a little bit of freedom. I'm suffocating. I'm going to ask them to give me every psychological test they've got, and if I pass them, make me an O.T. I've got to get outside these walls."

"What's an O.T.?"

"Outside trustee. They live in those barracks you go by as you drive in. Outside the walls."

"Why do you think Cardwell will go along with it? He's not exactly your greatest fan."

"Because I'm going to tell him I can break out. I've done it before, from death row, and I can do it from here much easier. I want him to know I know how to do it. If he'll make me an O.T., I'll promise to behave and never run away. If he doesn't, it's over the wall for me. Every time I go over the wall it will be headlines. He can't stand too much of that. And in case I have to go, I wanted to tell you something while I have the chance. You're the only person out there who might believe me. My friends in here do. They know it's true. I'm not the same person. I know it sounds like a cop-out, just a way to avoid taking responsibility for what I've done. But it's not that way. I'm only now beginning to realize, to understand, what I've done. Something's happened to me. Something wonderful and frightening. I can't explain it, but I feel like somebody else. And you are what made it happen."

He turned away quickly, but not before I could see that he was blushing. I was flabbergasted, both by his plan and by the glimpse of emotion I had seen. Could this be the same young man I had first met less than three years ago in the visitation room, who had tried so hard to impress me with his tough macho act and had such a fit when a guard stepped on his foot? Could this be the same young man who had probably murdered three girls? I'm no psychologist, but I could tell something weird was happening or had already happened, and I had missed the moment of its happening. Perhaps it wasn't a moment. Perhaps it was gradual, but it had reached a point, like the summit of a hill, and was moving faster and faster down the other side. I looked at Charles in amazement. He turned back and looked me straight in the eyes and I thought, *My God, he even looks different.*

From what I had heard about Warden Cardwell, I didn't think Charles had a chance, but there was much about Cardwell I didn't know. I'm willing to accept Charles' own version of it as he wrote it in the newspaper article for Ken Burton, a journalist on the staff of the *Tucson Citizen* in 1975 (not published until 1978), although I noticed in this account Charles left out the threat of embarrassing Cardwell by going over the wall. It may be that he never actually made that threat when he talked to Cardwell, or it may have been exactly that threat Cardwell responded to. I'm not in a position to know or judge. What I want to believe is that Cardwell saw the same thing I did when he looked at Charles, and he realized that something previously missing in the monster was now apparent in the man before him. Maybe it was what we call a soul, although I'm not entirely sure what that is.

In the article published in the *Tucson Citizen* in 1978, Charles said:

> In March 1974, I put it all on the line. I asked for and took every test the prison had to offer: Revised Beta, California Achievement Test, Stanford Binet, Rorshach [*sic*] and a battery of psychological tests. I passed with flying colors.
>
> Although I knew the parole board would not give a damn, I figured there was still one man it would make a difference to: Warden Harold J. Cardwell. He examined the results carefully. Then he interviewed me. When he was finished, I was placed on honor status and moved from the main wall to a dorm area in the Honor Compound.

Charles had gone from death row to outside trustee status in what looked like the shortest period of time on record. He moved into a barracks outside the main walls, coming back inside the walls for classes and the creative writing workshop. He kept his word about not trying to escape and was given a considerable amount of the freedom he so craved. He had various duties, including being a porter (janitor) in the dormitory, but the work he really enjoyed and spent much of his time doing was training and caring for the dogs. These were not the kind of dogs I currently encounter every week as I go into the various prisons, dogs trained to sniff out illegal substances, especially marijuana. In Harold Cardwell's prison of 1975, the dogs were mostly bloodhounds trained to hunt men, to chase down escapees.

Except for the hamlet of Florence on the west, the prison was surrounded by open desert. Arroyos cut through the desert, creating submerged pathways down which a man could run and generally not be seen by those outside that particular arroyo. When a prisoner escaped, the dogs would be given some piece of his clothing to smell and then turned loose to follow his tracks. Guards followed them on horseback, sometimes led by Harold Cardwell, although he was a little too paunchy and loose in the saddle to cut much of a figure.

What Harold Cardwell evidently hadn't thought of when he allowed Charles to train the dogs was that Charles had successfully escaped and knew the best routes away from the prison, the routes any escapee would probably take. The result was another of those ironies that make any prison system, if seen from a little distance, both tragic and hilarious. By hiding pieces of meat in various places, Charles trained the dogs to take off in a direction opposite to that which an escaping prisoner would most likely take. The mounted men followed them, led on by their excited barking and baying. It must have been slapstick. I would have cast Charlie Chaplin as the escapee running through the desert in one direction and Wallace Beery as Cardwell, sloshing around on a horse leading the pursuers in the opposite direction. Meanwhile, back at the ranch, Charles was stuffing socks in his mouth so the guards wouldn't hear him laughing.

That was one part of his duties with the dogs. He also had to take them in a truck to the vet in Florence from time to time. He told me that he sometimes made these outings alone, not accompanied by a guard. I didn't believe him, although as I think back on the weird ambience of that period at Florence, he might have been telling the truth. He loved these little trips and told me how exciting it was to drive by Katharine's house in Coolidge, a hamlet near Florence, or think about how shocked people would be if they knew who was driving down the street in sleepy little Florence with a truck full of dogs. He also loved to be able to walk outside the dormitory at night and look at the stars. He was settling in to the pleasures of a highly restricted amount of freedom, and his poems and letters suggested that he was responding well.

He had first published in 1972 in the "little magazine" *Inscape*, edited by Joy Harvey and Ramona Weeks, who had established Baleen Press in Phoenix. They published two poems we had worked on while I was visiting Charles on death row. While *Inscape* had an unpretentious format, it had editors with considerable taste and literary foresight. They were publishing the poems of Albert Goldbarth, Mark Doty, Vern Rutsala, Greg Pape, and other poets whose work has come to be highly valued. Baleen Press also published books, including my *Calendar* in 1972.

Publication in *Inscape* was a tiny step toward literary success, but for Charles it was a door opening, maybe only a crack, but opening nonetheless, so that he could glimpse a future far beyond anything he had dreamed of, a future that would be possible even though he remained in prison the rest of his life. Soon Ramona Weeks asked me if I thought Charles would have, within a year, enough poems of high quality to collect into a chapbook. I told her I thought he would have. He was currently working on a series of poems he called "The Ladies" and producing good work. Ramona and Joy then applied for and obtained a grant from the National Endowment for the Arts to publish several chapbooks. One of them was scheduled to be Charles Schmid's.

Charles was ecstatic. On January 2, 1974, he wrote: "About the book: I'm thrilled. Honestly, whatever you and Ramona decide is fine with me. I'm just so honored I can't think clearly. . . . Thanks almost entirely to you I have a kind of dignity."

In July of the same year, now in the trustee barracks, he wrote: "Am making some progress and am just thrilled. I have never been happier in my life. The job allows me sufficient creative time . . . just great. Feel so good I nearly explode. . . . What a beautiful feeling to work to create . . . to be happy. That in itself is a kind of poem. . . . Oh Richard, thank you for bringing me to your world. I may not ever have a very big or important place in it . . . but at least I sense I somehow belong."

3

Nancy Pierce's negotiations with the prison authorities for a creative writing workshop were at least partially successful by the summer of 1974. I had wanted a program that met for a couple of hours each week on an ongoing basis for as long as I could make it work, a program modeled after the creative writing workshops at the university, but neither the Arizona Commission on the Arts nor the prison would agree to such an open-ended affair. Evidently both of them viewed it the way some members of our government have come to view war: if they went in, they had to be sure they could get out. What they agreed to was a six-week summer pilot program that would meet for three hours one night a week. The plan was that if the pilot program proved to be successful, meaning if I didn't get into any trouble and was sufficiently docile while being patted down, patronized, and sneered at by the guards, and if enough men took part and seemed to want to continue, the program would then be folded into the regular curriculum of Central Arizona College, a two-year school that provided the regular post-GED courses for the prison, and I would continue to direct the workshop. *Well,* I thought, *we'll cross that bridge when we get there.* In the meantime I had six weeks of groundbreaking work ahead of me and as yet no idea how hard, exciting, or rewarding that work would be.

Since a large number of men expressed interest in the program, the prison had specified that two workshop directors could come in. I chose as my partner for the pilot project Tom Cobb, a fiction writer and graduate of our Master of Fine Arts program in creative writing. He had accepted a position as a member of the faculty at Eastern Arizona College in Thatcher, but he was free for the summer and his parents lived in Tucson. Tom, with his great writing and teaching ability, his enthusiasm and dedication, was the perfect choice for such work. The first workshop met on June 24, 1974, my forty-first birthday. When we arrived at the prison at 5:30 in the afternoon the temperature was 117 degrees. The twenty-one-foot prison wall trapped the heat and from the inside seemed to be undulating, as if it were a mirage.

On our way to Florence, Tom and I had stopped in Coolidge, a small town near Florence, as I often did on my trips to visit Charles. There we were treated to a barbecue dinner at the home of Katharine and her husband, Maurice. After Katharine had exhausted all her money on Charles' legal defense, and gone into debt amounting to many thousands of dollars she would never be able to repay, she and Maurice had moved to the sad, impoverished community of Coolidge so she could be near the prison and visit Charles as often as permitted. They had opened a small, ramshackle barbecue joint in order to survive. I had already sat in that little kitchen for hours discussing with Katharine Charles' desperate situation and any possible strategies to save him from execution, trying to pretend an optimism I did not feel, trying to keep her from the abyss of despair while I was falling into it myself.

Now, everything had changed. He was serving a life sentence without possibility of parole, but he was alive and she could see him every week. Perhaps after the first miracle there could be others. Who knew? So the mood was almost festive as Tom and I ate Maurice's barbecued beef and Katharine's green beans and potato salad and drank what seemed like gallons of iced tea to ward off the heat that was abated only slightly by a ratchety swamp cooler in the kitchen window. I was in awe of Katharine's absolute and appalling loyalty to an adopted child. I still am. This woman who had been nothing to me but a sad, shadowy figure in the newspapers had become, as I got to know her, the quintessential Mother, grieving for her damaged child. *There are so many different kinds and intensities of love,* I thought. *This may be one I will never see again.*

And I thought about the twisting grief of those who had lost their children, probably at her child's hands. My own son, Brad, was healthy and bright, and I was blessed with a wonderful wife and a good position as a university professor. Why had I taken on this burden when all I had to do was say "No! Leave me alone. I will not take part in your orgy of pain. I cannot bear it." I didn't realize then how few choices we have in these matters. Perhaps I took it on simply because I had blundered into it, and some part of me knew I could bear it, although there was a period later when I felt nothing but pain and doubt and a hideous guilt. There was to come a time when I regretted that I had ever met Charles Schmid, when I felt that he would have been much better off if he had never met me. When that time came, my other friends in prison steadied me and sobered me. They took me in hand and set me on the path I have followed since then, not without terrible qualms of self-doubt, but in spite of them.

The main gate at the Florence prison, which was in 1974 the only real prison in the state, was a huge archway covered with a gate of heavy bars that moved on a track and was controlled electronically. The gate itself had been brought from the old territorial prison at Yuma and installed when the new territorial prison was built at Florence in 1908–9. It made a loud, reverberating CLANG as it closed, and for those prisoners being brought in for the first time, it must have sounded like the clang of doom. It did to me when I went in for the first time, and it actually crossed my mind that I might never get out. I wondered if Tom Cobb was feeling the same thing, but neither of us showed it. This was, after all, a male institution (there were as yet no female guards and the women's prison was across the road), and the first rule for everybody was to show no fear. So we immediately began to adapt to the prison environment. We began to behave as temporary prisoners, which we were.

But standing back beyond a red line on the other side of that huge gate we could see a group of prisoners obviously waiting for us, and not very patiently. Among them, hopping and dancing about with eagerness and energy was Charles Schmid, risen almost from the dead and raring to go. With him were J. Charles Green and several others with whom I had been corresponding but had not met. It was J. Charles Green and Charles Schmid who had been instrumental in advertising the workshop and signing up others to be in it. Of the small group of inmates waiting to meet us and escort us across the yard that day, two were to be dead within a year, one butchered and one I believe may have been the victim of medical neglect. Other murders would follow inexorably. Tom and I didn't know it, but we were entering, in the words of T. S. Eliot, "Death's other kingdom."

After we were searched and passed through a metal detector where I had to take off my boots and belt and was getting worried about both my Levi's and the lead my father had convinced me was in my ass, an elderly guard rifled through every book in the large box of books we were carrying, shaking his head and muttering as if books were a curse that we would all be better off without. Finally he said, "Well, you can lead a horse to water but you can't make him drink," meaning, I suppose, that we could bring in as many books as we wanted to, but none of the men in prison would, or perhaps could, read them. When he had pronounced his final words of wisdom, the ancient guard waved us on across the red line to where our special inmate escort group was waiting.

I had never before met J. Charles Green face to face, and I had never seen Charles Schmid so excited. In one quick movement he took the box of books from me and hoisted it onto his strong shoulder, grinning with delight that he was finally able to do some small thing for me.

J. Charles Green was a frail twenty-six-year-old poet with remarkable talent and probably the best reading background of any inmate in the workshop. He had important contacts in the literary world. The COSMEP prison program run by Joe and Carol Bruchac in Greenfield, New York, had sent him dozens of books of poetry that he would share with other members of the workshop. He had been pushing hard for a creative writing workshop at Florence for a long time, during all the months I had been working with Charles Schmid. Now, to see a real fiction writer and a real poet walk through the main gate to start a workshop was almost more than he could deal with. He was speechless with excitement.

Duane Vild, the young director of education at Florence, joined us and led us to a little doorway with an iron door in the west section of the main wall. We went through this and into another yard called the Institute of Educational Rehabilitation, or the IER, or just the education yard. In spite of its fancy name, Tom and I were not much impressed with it. It was an area of fairly recently built grim and unpainted concrete-block buildings, some of them dormitories and some classrooms. The classrooms had concrete floors, no windows, and were furnished with either desk chairs or long tables with folding metal chairs. Spaced at regular intervals on the tables were gallon tin cans to be used as butt cans and spittoons.

The classroom we were led to held about thirty men, and the atmosphere was electric with anticipation, expectation, excitement. As we stepped into the room, all the noise stopped suddenly, and Tom and I were scrutinized by more than thirty pairs of eyes. I had never been so thoroughly stared at, not even by my first class of seventh graders in 1958 in Bisbee. As it turned out, one of the men in front of us in the prison classroom had been one of those seventh graders in 1958, although I did not recognize him until later when he introduced himself.

An elderly man immediately got up and approached me carrying a manuscript that was at least a foot thick. "I've been working on my novel for thirty years," he said. "Will you be able to read it and tell me what you think?"

"I don't write fiction," I answered. "Mr. Cobb is the fiction writer. You'll have to talk to him." I saw Tom flash the whites of his eyes like a horse in panic, and I was suddenly glad I had never written fiction.

It was obvious that the group was too big to handle as one workshop, and Tom and I had discussed this possibility. I introduced myself and Tom and said, "We are going to divide you into two groups. Those who are interested in working with prose will meet with Mr. Cobb in the room next door. Those who are interested in working with poetry will remain in this room and work with me." A hand shot up. "What's prose?" I heard Tom sigh audibly, but he was not discouraged. I think that I, who had already had sixteen years' experience in the classroom, was far more worried than Tom was. He was just beginning his teaching career and ready to take on anything.

Eventually we got them sorted into two groups, with the understanding that they could switch back and forth if they wanted to, and eventually poor Tom read enough of the foot-thick manuscript to determine that it was worthless. How he went about imparting this information to its writer, or whether or not he did at all, I don't remember. I was having my own struggles trying to convince my group of hotshot poets that clichés, sentimentality, and doggerel were not necessarily the best ways to go. I was learning that the process of learning in prison often consists of unlearning. Most of them were slaves to strict rhyme and wooden meter. In school, if they had been to school, they seemed to have read only Longfellow, the worst of the worst. Several of them aspired to be writers of greeting card verse. Tom was having similar problems with his group. It was obvious that we had our work cut out for us.

So it wasn't the most auspicious beginning, but it was a beginning. I had no idea then that it was the first meeting in what was to become the oldest permanent floating prison creative writing program in America, and like the floating crap game in *Guys and Dolls*, it would manage to stay one jump ahead of the cops for more than thirty years. Most of the cops then and now, although they have changed considerably over the years, would prefer not to be bothered with it.

There were many bright spots in that first workshop, and some of them were exceedingly bright and exciting enough to make the 140-mile round-trip and the hard work worthwhile. Looking back on it, I don't think I've ever had a workshop with more talent per capita. There were Charles Schmid and J. Charles Green and several others I had worked with through the mail. Then there was another one, a handsome, grinning, back-slapping, swaggering young Irishman from Boston whose every move said that he knew he was hot stuff. His name was Stephen F. X. (Francis Xavier) Dugan. I found out that he was a jailhouse lawyer with considerable knowledge and expertise, which meant that he was rich in terms of whatever commodities the prison could provide, including drugs. He was also richly talented as a writer, and he knew it, although his poetry was still self-indulgent and had a ways to go.

The struggle between me and Stephen Francis Xavier Dugan, which began that afternoon when he appeared in my workshop carrying, of all things, a tennis racket and looking as sharp in his tailored prison regulation Levi's and chambray shirt as anyone could have in tennis whites, lasted for so many years that I can't even say exactly how long it lasted. It was a struggle that, years later when Stephen began living in the free world, would exhaust and disgust me to the point that I gave up and declared him the winner, champion of his own destruction. Then my wife, Lois, who had become even more disgusted with him than I was, stepped in and took over. She refused to give him money for food because she knew he would spend it on booze. Repeatedly she picked him up in the most unsavory places and took him to the detox center where he could dry out for several days. She drove him to AA meetings even when he was drunk and belligerent. There they told him to sit down and shut up. Eventually he did, but not before he had done his best to ruin the lives of two women in Tucson, both former students of mine and dear friends. Eventually AA and another woman became the instruments that saved him.

Now Dr. Dugan (PhD in history), who has published many books of poetry and recently both fiction and nonfiction, is a teacher and administrator at a *collegio* in Mexico, where his students all but worship him. He has been there, clean and sober, for many years. He has attended Harvard University. He was undoubtedly the most talented student in the first prison workshop in 1974. While still in prison he published four books of poetry and was awarded a National Endowment for the Arts Writer's Fellowship, the first incarcerated writer ever to receive such an honor. And I came within inches of losing him during the first week of the pilot program. I had the temerity to be critical of the first poem he brought in. He was deeply offended. He didn't come back to the next session. Finally, after licking his wounds for two weeks and seeking the solace of heroin, which was readily available on the prison yard, he returned, quieter and less ebullient, but ready to learn.

A few years later he said to me wistfully, "I guess I'm not going to be able to rob any more bars when I get out."

"Why is that, Stephen?"

"I'm too famous," he said glumly. And he was.

Suddenly I realized it's as simple as that. Famous writers do not rob bars.

For all his brains, Stephen was not the smartest member of that first workshop. It took me awhile to figure it out because the smartest member of the group was also smart enough to keep his brains well hidden behind the facade of a country boy from the hills of Kentucky. He was a tall, lanky, quiet man only a few years younger than I was, shy and slow to speak, with a scar on his thin face and cool gray eyes. He reminded me of Gary Cooper. They called him Cash, and nobody messed with him. Later, while he was still in prison, Cash designed a complex mechanism to store solar energy, something that had never been done. Ultimately the mechanism didn't work, but it came so close that it attracted the attention of a solar energy contractor who employed Cash and helped get him out of prison. Cash became wildly successful in the field of solar energy. Like Stephen Dugan, he is still my friend. He lives in Texas and comes to see Lois and me fairly often. Between visits we talk on the phone. He used to fly his own plane to Tucson, but he has developed a heart condition and isn't supposed to pilot a plane anymore. His handsome young son served, and survived, in Iraq, and he and his wife also have a beautiful grown daughter.

One day in the IER yard when we were waiting for somebody to come unlock the classroom door and let us in, I asked Cash about the scar on his face.

"How'd you get that scar, Cash?"

Cash looked down at the ground and began to rub the toe of his shoe in the sand, as if to find the answer there. Finally, in his quiet, laconic way he said, "Some dude cut me."

"What did you do then?" I asked.

Again the long pause while Cash studied the dirt at his feet and moved the toe of his shoe in small circles through it. "Well, I reckon I tied him to the railroad tracks," he said in the same soft drawl.

Then there was Ronnie, one of the leaders of the black inmates. Ronnie was a thoughtful, intelligent giant and, I believe, the strongest man I had ever known. His biceps were bigger than my upper legs. I don't remember how it got started, but everyone enjoyed watching Ronnie perform feats of strength with "the Proffesuh." At first he would merely grasp me by the waist in his massive hands and hold my 160 pounds in front of him at arm's length for amazing periods of time. Then we devised a variation on the routine that made it possible for him to show his strength and me to show my trust. Again he would grasp me by the waist and hold me at arm's length, but in this case I would be upside down. We were careful never to perform these stunts when there was any danger of a guard strolling in and misinterpreting the situation.

I remember (how could I forget?) the morning when Ronnie interjected, right in the middle of our discussion of a poem that had nothing to do with sex, the completely gratuitous but serious and thoughtful comment, "I know some men don't believe in eating pussy, but I do." He wasn't trying to derail our discussion. It was simply something that had occurred to him at that moment, and he needed to express it. I was learning by experience when to let a digression prevail and when to get the discussion back on track. It's an art I have never mastered completely, but I learned most of what I know about it by teaching in prison rather than at the university.

I'm sorry I have lost track of Ronnie over the years, but I heard through the prison grapevine that he became a preacher. Somehow that didn't surprise me too much. I'm sure he's a good preacher, but I wonder if he ever interrupts his sermons to make pronouncements on acceptable sexual practices. It would probably offend some of the congregation, but it would certainly keep the rest of them awake.

Another remarkable young black man in that workshop was Calvin. The first thing I noticed when he began to turn in work was that he sometimes spelled his name "Calvin," sometimes "Calven," and sometimes "Calvan." He was extremely bright and loved to read and talk philosophy, but I suspected that his literary ability was a fairly recent acquisition.

One day I handed him two books, one by James Baldwin and one by James Weldon Johnson, and said, "Here's a couple of books by black writers I thought you might enjoy."

Calvin looked at the books with a start, as if I were handing him a snake, and then he looked at me with incredulity. "I . . . I didn't know," he stammered, "that any blacks had written any books." Then it was my turn to look at him with incredulity, but he was absolutely serious.

Later I was told his story. He was raised by an aunt in a Phoenix ghetto and was totally illiterate when he came to prison. All of his brothers were in prison. He and his friend had tried to rob a convenience store one night. His friend had the gun. The clerk resisted, and Calvin's partner panicked and shot and killed him. In Arizona, the law states that all participants in a robbery in which someone is killed are equally guilty, regardless of which of them committed the murder. Calvin was given a death sentence for first-degree murder in January 1970. He was placed on death row at the age of sixteen. When the Supreme Court abolished capital punishment in 1972, Calvin's sentence was changed to "life" and he was placed in the general population at Florence.

As soon as he landed in prison, Calvin went to work to learn to read and write through the prison's GED (high school equivalency) program. He had obtained his GED just before I arrived at the prison. Then he went for his AA degree in psychology, the highest degree he could obtain by means of the courses offered through Central Arizona College at the prison. I attended the ceremony the night he was given his diploma. His diminutive aunt was there, weeping. As I watched him receive his diploma, I remembered a conversation we had had a few days earlier.

"What's it like to be illiterate," I had asked him.

He closed his eyes and shook his head from side to side as if to shake off some memory. "It's bad," he said. "It's like being inside a big, dark box. All you know is what you need—food, water, drugs, sex. You don't know what's outside the box and you don't know how to find out. You're scared all the time."

I like to think about Calvin. His story is another example of a miracle, and there are so few of them in prison. Because he was a handsome, articulate, charming young black man, the Department of Corrections loaned him out to various local crime prevention agencies for their "crime fairs." These events, with their odd name, usually took place in shopping malls or schools and consisted of pep talks by

various members of state, county, or city crime prevention units urging young people to avoid drugs and illegal activities. They included
posters, films, and sometimes horrendous photographs designed to
scare the teenagers silly. Calvin was usually the main attraction. He
would tell his story with great earnestness and encourage the audience, often mostly black teenagers, to stay away from drugs, get an
education, and avoid the life sentence he was carrying. Calvin was
very good at this. So good that he came to the attention of the governor, who reviewed his record. Calvin was paroled in 1985. It was so
rare as to be shocking, but I guess miracles are often shocking.

When he got out of prison Calvin went to school and earned his
master's degree in counseling. He now runs a drug rehabilitation program in Phoenix. He came to see us in Tucson not long ago, bringing
his two beautiful daughters, and they stayed most of the day. After
they left I thought about something Calvin had said. "Going to prison
was the best thing that could have happened to me at the time," he
said. I understood what he meant, and that he was paying me a very
great compliment, but what a hideous gamble. And did he understand
the significance of "at the time"?

If he were to come into the system today, he would find the GED
program still there because it is mandated by law for U.S. citizens,
and he could probably learn to read and write on a basic level. But he
would not find the college courses that piqued his interest in philosophy and psychology and made it possible for him to get his AA degree.
And in all but four of the present state facilities, of which there are
now fifty-eight, he wouldn't find a writer's workshop where his ideas
would be listened to and discussed with respect, regardless of the fact
that he wasn't yet quite sure how to spell his name. Surely there must
be a better way for people like Calvin. To throw the dice, knowing
that if you lose, you will spend the rest of your life in prison, and the
chances of winning are one in a million. It's too hideous a gamble. But
he won. I call it a miracle. I call for more miracles, but we shouldn't
have to send our children to prison to teach them to read and write.

After Calvin and his daughters came to visit us, he applied to have
his civil rights restored so that he could vote, obtain certain clearances he needed in his work, and enjoy the other rights his fellow

citizens enjoyed. I wrote a letter to the Board of Pardons and Paroles in support of his request. He went to the hearing in Phoenix where several members of his family, and professional colleagues spoke on his behalf. He went full of hope. Not only was his petition denied, but he was insulted and humiliated in front of his colleagues and family, including his daughters. Black men who have been in prison and civil rights don't seem to go together in this country. Calvin called me after the hearing. He was crying and terribly angry. He had been a good and productive citizen for many years. He had obtained an education and entered the ranks of the professional class. His life was given over to helping others. "Why?" he kept asking me. "Why did they treat me this way? Is it because I'm black?"

I couldn't answer him. I didn't want to help channel all his positive energy into hatred. But I knew the answer. One has only to check the statistics. It was because he was black.

Then, in 2000, he tried again to have his civil rights restored, this time before a more liberal Board of Pardons and Paroles appointed by a more liberal governor. The board granted his request unanimously, and each member shook his hand and told him how pleased they were with his professional career and the positive effect he had had on the community. It was the same man, same accomplishments, same record, but a different board sitting in judgment. People in prison are constantly aware of this kind of disparity. They see it daily, and know that justice in America is capricious, often political, and almost always racial. So Calvin's civil rights have been restored, but he is still on parole. Since then he has repeatedly petitioned for absolute discharge from parole, and in 2005 that request was recommended by the Board of Executive Clemency but was denied by the governor.

Then in the workshop in 1974 there was Thetis. Oh my God! Thetis! I can't remember him without pain. He was a very young white man, and I assumed he was gay. How does a frail and probably bipolar, possibly gay young man whose name is Thetis survive in one of the toughest prisons in the West? Barely, if at all. During the first few weeks of the workshop, I could count on Thetis always being in the chair next to mine, but he almost never spoke. There was something terribly wrong. He didn't seem to be there all the time. He would drift in and out of awareness; his eyes would glaze and he would seem to be catatonic for a few minutes. Everyone was very tolerant of Thetis, and I followed their lead, even after I felt a hand stroking my sandaled foot under the table during the workshop. It was startling, but I merely moved my foot away and said nothing.

Then one day the men got into a discussion about solitary, the hole, or whatever it is called in various prisons, each of which has its own terms for torture. Somebody mentioned the "corner pocket" and then looked embarrassed and stopped. I asked what he meant by the "corner pocket." He explained, reluctantly, that at a corner of the main yard where the high stone walls met, the authorities had built a metal wall across with a metal door in it, making a tiny room in the shape of a triangle. No light entered it, and its only furnishing was a hole in the floor for a latrine. It was stifling in the summer and cold most of the winter. When the authorities found no other way to break an inmate's will, I was told, they would put him in the corner pocket for various periods of time and weld the door shut. There was a slot at the bottom where a tray of food could be passed through.

"Weld the door shut?" I said, not believing this part of it.

Suddenly Thetis began to speak, slowly and low, just above a whisper. Everyone else got very quiet. "They put me in there," he said. "They welded the door shut. Left me for fifteen days. When I came out I was crazy, like I am now. I guess I'll always be crazy." Tears were running down his face as he said this. He stared at his pale hands on the table in front of him.

Several of the other men were very near tears. The one sitting next to Thetis reached over and took hold of his shoulder. "You're okay, man," he said. "You're okay with us."

4

After the first six weeks the initial creative writing pilot program in 1974 was considered a success, and Nancy Pierce of the Arizona Commission on the Arts went back to her negotiations. This time she came up with a one-semester workshop under the auspices of Central Arizona College to begin in late September. I agreed to visit a group of the men once a week for the few weeks until the fall semester began, just to maintain the momentum.

One Saturday morning in mid-September I came in to find Charles Schmid and the others who met me in the outdoors visitation area in despair. They could hardly speak. Charles Schmid was striking a tree with his fist, again and again, until his knuckles were bleeding. They told me J. Charles Green was dead.

I had heard various bits and pieces of the story of this frail twenty-six-year-old. It was said that his mother had been a junkie prostitute and that he was born addicted. It was said that he had survived at Florence by allowing himself to become the property of a powerful black inmate who protected him from others while using him for his own sexual gratification. I knew J. Charles Green as a very talented, eager young poet and excellent student. But he was dead between one Saturday and the next, just like that. Gone.

Violent death was something I was going to have to get used to. He was so young, so frail, so talented. I want to say *innocent*, but that word doesn't mean very much to me anymore and I try not to use it. Can a young junkie who becomes a thief to support his habit be innocent? Can a weak young man in prison who must become a sex slave in order to stay alive be innocent? I would say yes and yes to these questions, but is there such a thing as innocence left in this world in the twenty-first century, or is it the product of Hollywood, like our view of the nineteenth-century West? I don't know the answer.

Charles Green died, presumably, of hepatitis acquired because of his drug addiction. I was told by the inmates who were in cells near his that he died of medical neglect. During the preceding week he had become jaundiced and weak. By Sunday evening he was having convulsions. According to the inmates, the officer on duty in Charles' cellblock had called the medical officer on duty. The medical officer asked the officer on duty what he thought the problem was, and the answer was "hepatitis," to which the medical officer on duty replied, "To hell with it. Most of the men in this joint have hepatitis. Tie him to his bunk and we'll deal with it in the morning." The officer on duty tied Charles Green to his bunk. By Monday morning, when someone finally got around to dealing with it, Charles was so far gone that even hospitalization could not save him. The inmates who were in nearby cells were witnesses to his agony. There is no way his life can be described in terms of guilt or innocence. Maybe horror. But not guilt or innocence.

There was nothing I could say to those grieving men. I could only grieve with them. I noticed that Charles Schmid was actually crying when he spoke of J. Charles Green, and he was trying to hide it from the rest of us. What had happened to the cocky little man who seemed to be concerned primarily with his image? The one who had probably killed three young girls just for the hell of it. He was devastated by this death. I had seen him fake concern for others before, and it wasn't always effective, not even when he was trying to express his appreciation for my help. There had been something a little too bright, a little too theatrical about his concern for others that had bothered me. But this was real. He was overcome with grief.

Since J. Charles Green had no family to claim his body, he was buried in the graveyard behind the prison, the potter's field called Comacho Hill, although it isn't really on a hill. I had not known of its existence before his death. There was a large irrigation canal that ran along the back of the prison with fairly high banks to prevent flooding. Between one of these banks and the prison wall was a rutted dirt road that led—I didn't know where until J. Charles Green was buried there—to a broad strip of sloping desert land. It was just an area of dirt covered with trash and debris. Evidently some of the Florence youths used this road as a lovers' lane, and it was strewn with beer cans and used condoms. The "tombstones," mostly in rows, some just scattered about at random, were low, unpainted concrete markers with no inscriptions. Most of them had license plates attached, each with a dead inmate's number on it—no names. There were a few very old wooden crosses, without any kind of identification at all.

This graveyard, I think, maybe even more than the condition of the men in prison, shocked me and made me aware of something. That we could take away a person's name and replace it with a number, that we had the power to do this, had never really penetrated by mind. But here it was. We could take away a person's name so thoroughly that even in death he or she was only a number. In regard to the prison I had felt fear, I had felt confusion and compassion and grief, but I don't think I had ever felt rage until I stood in front of that small concrete tombstone with a license plate with nothing but a number on it. *J. Charles Green,* I kept saying. *He wasn't that number. He was J. Charles Green. You took his name away in life and now you take it away in death. He was JOHN CHARLES GREEN.*

J. Charles Green wasn't the last of my friends to be buried in that potter's field, or the last that I wrote a poem to memorialize, but I did write a poem for him. It is blessedly short and has been reprinted many times in many places, so I'll let it be exposed one more time here where I have described the situation that produced it.

Certain Choices
for Charles Green

My friend, who was a heroin addict,
is dead and buried beneath trash
and broken bottles in a prison field.

He died, of course, because of the way
he lived. It wasn't a very good way,
but it kept him alive. When it couldn't
keep him alive any longer, it killed him.
Thoroughly and with great suffering.

After he had made certain choices,
there were no others available. That's
the way it is with certain choices,
and we are faced with them so young.

I have few friends, and none of them
are replaceable. That's the way it is
with friends. We make certain choices.

I tried to do something about that potter's field and those tomb-stones without names that haunted me. My efforts were ludicrous. I made phone call after phone call and wrote letters to various prison officials, some of whom referred me to the chaplain at Florence, a young Catholic priest. In response to my call, the chaplain suggested that we have lunch in a small Mexican restaurant in Florence to dis-cuss the problem and work out some strategy to correct it. It seemed as if I was finally getting somewhere. He had agreed with me over the phone about the deplorable condition of the graveyard and the prac-tice of burying inmates with no names on their tombstones. The men in the workshop had told me that behind his back everybody called the young priest the "Golden Butterfly," but even knowing this, I was not entirely prepared for what I met in the Mexican restaurant. He was gorgeous. Small and slight with eyes as blue as cornflowers and shoulder-length golden hair. His features were fine, and there was an expression of concern in his face that made one trust him immedi-ately. I had never met anyone like him. My first thought as we shook hands was that if he hadn't been a priest, he could have been a movie star. Why was he stuck in a prison in the middle of nowhere instead of ministering to a large congregation in some metropolitan area?

We talked for more than an hour at lunch. He totally agreed with my view of the situation and said he had already approached the war-den, Harold Cardwell, about the problem, but the warden had refused to discuss it with him. "Unfortunately," he said, blushing slightly, "I don't have much influence with Warden Cardwell." The idea of Cardwell and this priest in the same room together almost made me laugh. Cardwell, spouting obscenities, with his beer gut hanging over his belt, his little piggy eyes with a constant expression of distrust, and his hands like truncheons. He would probably have loathed this delicate, cultivated priest on sight. "However," the priest added, "there might be another way to go about accomplishing our goal."

He suggested that he go to the Catholic congregation in the town of Florence and ask for volunteers to clean up the graveyard. He thought Cardwell would permit it, although he would not permit a detail of inmates from the prison to do it. The other problem, involving the license plates, was more difficult. Since Cardwell refused to change the policy, any change would have to come from above him, from the office of the director of the Department of Corrections in Phoenix. A delicate situation. Cardwell had been known to fly into a rage at the hint that anyone might go over his head. However, the priest said, he had a meeting scheduled with the assistant to the director of the department in three weeks. He would present the problem to the assistant to the director and see what he suggested. I recognized and appreciated the risk this involved for the young priest, but he had the whole Catholic church behind him. All I had was the Arizona Commission on the Arts, and I wasn't too sure about them. I thanked him, and as I drove back to Tucson I felt very positive. Maybe I had finally got the ball rolling in the right direction.

I waited a month for the chaplain to contact me and then called his office and left a message. He didn't return my call. I left a second message with the same result. Later that week when I went into the prison, the men in the workshop had startling information about him. I don't know whether that information was true or not, but it explained the chaplain's absence. The inmates said the chaplain had been sexually involved with a male inmate. In fact, they said, he had "married" the inmate. They also said he had performed other homosexual "marriages" and participated in group sexual activities *in the chapel*. This information from the men could have been highly exaggerated of course, but whatever happened, it was sufficient for Cardwell to fire the chaplain and for the church officials to whisk him away quickly and quietly, and when the Golden Butterfly flew away, all my hopes for doing something about the cemetery went with him.

I could only imagine Cardwell's reaction to the knowledge of the priest's activities. He would probably have preferred a good whole-some stabbing or even an escape. At this point he was publicly deny-ing any gang activity in the prison, although the gangs were running the prison. I guess there was one more gang than he realized, and it was precisely the kind that would embarrass him most. The men in the workshop thought it was a wonderful joke on Cardwell, and from time to time one of them would put his open hands together, palms down, and make a motion like the wings of a butterfly. Then everyone would laugh. They weren't laughing at the young priest. They were laughing at the irony of the world. Two of the enormous systems that ran their world, and not always for the better, the Department of Corrections and the Catholic church, had both been demoralized by a golden butterfly with clay feet.

Oh, to fly over the prison walls like the Golden Butterfly!

Sometimes the past seems to be little more than a series of opportunities I never seized, or projects I never carried out, or a ball I fumbled and dropped. It was that way with the grave-yard behind the Florence prison. After I discontinued the Florence workshop in favor of several workshops in prisons closer to home and eventually in other parts of the state, I never went back. About twenty-five years passed while I worked in other Arizona prisons, but never again at Florence. Always in the back of my mind was that graveyard, down the long dirt road with the irrigation canal on the right and nothing much but creosote bushes and bare earth on the left. I dreamed about it sometimes. Something between a dream and a nightmare, where I would be shuffling around in trash and broken bottles beside an open grave and I would look up and see the prison, shimmering like a mirage in the distance. But I was occupied with other things. *I tried,* I told myself, *to do something about that terrible place. I did my best but fate was against me. Nobody cares about such a place. Nobody wants to see it. It's just the ultimate and final stage of being imprisoned. The final abandonment.* Recently, I went back to see Coma-cho Hill. It wasn't the most pleasant pilgrimage I've ever made, but

I had to see the graveyard again, to see if anything had been done about it, to see if all those inmates had been given their names back. I went with a friend I admire greatly, and it must have been difficult for him, too, since he is a former con who was nearly killed in one unit of the Florence prison. He is a biologist and was a member of the creative writing workshops in two of the Tucson prison units and is the author of *Wilderness and Razor Wire*, *Beyond Desert Walls*, and other books. His name is Ken Lamberton, and I have come to rely on him for companionship, help, advice, information, and support.

We found a metal bar stopping all vehicular traffic on the dirt road. So we parked just off the highway and hiked in, maybe less than two miles. I halfway expected someone to come along and try to stop us, but no one did. We could see Central and South Units, the old IER yard now much expanded, off to the north, and parts of the prison farm farther east. We could have driven in on the other side of the canal, but it would have meant crossing the canal on foot farther down, and while the canal was basically empty, there was about a foot of standing water in it from a recent monsoon rain. Lots of mud. So we hiked down the north side of the canal instead. It seemed farther than I remembered and I began to wonder if the graveyard had been moved somewhere else. Finally, when we saw it in the distance, I was astonished. It was a huge field of low white monuments glittering in the sunlight. Blindingly whitewashed. The ground around the monuments was bare and clean of all debris. There was a flagpole with a low stone wall around it, and a fenced-off area, evidently for funerals. I couldn't recognize anything and felt like I had stepped into another world by mistake.

While I remembered only perhaps forty-five or fifty markers scattered here and there in 1975, I now saw hundreds, all in neat rows. Except for the bare ground, it reminded me, in its symmetrical precision, of a military graveyard. The sheer number of graves indicated how the state prison system had expanded in the intervening years during which putting people in prison had become a frenzy. And these markers, I had to remind myself, represented only those inmates who had died or been executed while in prison and whose bodies were not claimed by relatives or friends. I wondered how many others had died in prison but whose bodies had been claimed by families or friends and buried elsewhere or cremated.

Some of the older concrete markers still had license plates attached to them, but these plates seemed to have the inmate's date of death instead of the inmate number or name. It was hard to tell for sure because they had been whitewashed over. Evidently at some point the prison policy had shifted from putting the inmate's prison number on the grave marker to putting the date of his or her death. Later, a tin metal plate had been added to all the graves with the inmate's name and date of death. Evidently the idea of license plates on a tombstone had struck somebody as a little too . . . what should I say? Bizarre? Flippant? Macabre? Some of the more recent markers had only the tin metal plate with the name and death date. Several of the graves were caving in, probably a result of the recent rains. We found the graves we were looking for. The metal plate on J. Charles Green's marker said,

John Green
9–17–74.

But the marker troubled me. I remembered the grave as being oriented north and south. Now it was oriented east and west, as were all the other graves in the cemetery. Most of the graves were now arranged chronologically by the date of each inmate's death.

As I remembered it, the graveyard had been casually organized, if at all. Several short rows of graves and other markers here and there in no particular order or pattern. Some of the graves were oriented east and west, and some north and south. *So,* I thought, *the graves that were here when I was last in this place, in 1975, have been moved to conform to the neat military rows of graves I am seeing. It must have been a huge job to move so many graves.* I wondered when this project of realigning the graveyard and placing the names on the markers had taken place. Evidently, judging by the license plates on the markers with death dates whitewashed over, it must have taken place in two stages, and in the later stage the names were added. *Well, it was about time,* I thought. Ken and I noticed two markers with women's names on them. There were probably several others we didn't see. We walked carefully around those graves that were caving in.

While I appreciated the fact that the Department of Corrections had finally seen fit to put the names of the inmates rather than their prison numbers on their tombstones and had cleaned up the grave-yard, something was bothering me still, something I couldn't quite put my finger on. It had to do with chronology. I had never been in a graveyard where the graves were so neatly chronological.

From the graveyard, we drove into Florence and to the Pinal County Historical Society Museum, an impressive museum and archive that had become the recipient of the Della Meadows Collection of prison materials. Della Meadows was the first female employee of the state prison system, and one of the many prison units at Florence is now named after her. She was a gentle, spinsterish woman, although she was married, whose appearance completely masked both her intel-lectual ability and the power she ultimately enjoyed, although, of course, always behind the scenes. She was hired originally as the warden's secretary and became an administrative assistant without which several wardens could probably not have functioned. She was the warden's handmaiden, even Harold Cardwell's, but she also oper-ated quietly in a subversive mode.

I went to see Della Meadows once in her home, at her invitation. It was in the midseventies while I was trying to do something about the graveyard. I imagine that she invited me to her home because she didn't want our conversation overheard by the warden or anyone else in his office. We discussed the appalling condition of the grave-yard behind the prison. She suggested that I get in touch with the chaplain and also made other suggestions I don't remember, but I do remember how surprised I was that she was truly subversive. Without exactly criticizing the warden or his policies, she left the impression that she disapproved of both. But there was really little she could do. I came away feeling that she would support me, sub rosa, in any way she could, but that she would not place her position in jeopardy. She lived in the dictatorship and served at the pleasure of the dictator.

Della retired in December of 1983. She was an avid member of the Pinal County Historical Society. At Christmastime 2003, she and her husband were killed in a fire in their house stuffed with the files, clippings, lists, memorabilia, and records she had gathered over many decades at the prison. The Della Meadows Collection, now housed at the Pinal County Historical Society Museum, is of enormous value to people like me. When Ken and I went there, most of the collection was housed in manila folders, and many of these were singed around the edges from the fire. The workers at the historical society had been sorting through it and collating what it contained. Ken and I found some clippings about several members of the workshop in the folders, and some information about riots that helped us date some events in the past, but the surprising information came from the workers at the historical society and from an expert on prison matters they brought in. He was Martin Hall, a teacher who had been doing research on the prison cemetery for years.

What Martin Hall told us was astonishing, and it was something that the employees at the museum and any others who had researched the prison in depth already seemed to know. He said that when the graveyard at Comacho Hill was being redesigned, the prison authorities paid little attention to which body was under which marker. In some cases they moved only the markers and left the bodies where they had been. There was no dependable correlation between the name on a grave marker and the body beneath it. The prison had no complete and accurate record of exactly who was buried in the graveyard or exactly where they were buried. The markers had been lined up with military precision and whitewashed. The names and death dates had been added chronologically, as if the whole thing were a giant filing cabinet. This meant that no reliable DNA could be obtained from the bodies at Comacho Hill, no matter how important it might be. It also meant that if the family or descendants of an inmate buried there decided they wanted the body exhumed and buried in some more pleasant and respectable place, they wouldn't know for sure whose remains they were exhuming. As the truth sank in, Ken and I looked at each other, not in disbelief but with a kind of horror. What this said about the attitude of the prison administration toward the inmates, dead or alive, would have been beyond belief if I had not spent those years at Florence. I had thought of the Florence prison as a dictatorship when I was working there. Now it had expanded to many times its original size. Again I was reminded of T. S. Eliot's words, "Death's other kingdom."

In a later phone call, Martin Hall gave me one more grisly detail. He said that two of the men buried in that graveyard had been accidentally beheaded when they were hanged. Those two bodies would be the only two that could be identified for sure, and in those cases there was only a fifty-fifty chance of accuracy.

5

When the new semester began in the fall of 1974, the workshop met at seven in the evening in the same classroom in the IER yard. Tom Cobb was living and teaching in Safford, so I was on my own. Under the auspices of the Arizona Commission on the Arts, Tom would soon be directing workshops in two prison facilities near Safford. My workshop was smaller than the pilot program had been, about seventeen men and made up mostly of the core group from that program plus a few new members.

During the summer, while I was noticing changes in Charles Schmid, I had undergone certain changes too, although I was aware my changes were superficial. Like the great majority of American boys, I had been entranced with Western movies and grew up wanting to be a cowboy. I could even ride passably well because, as I was growing up, I had a horse on my grandparents' farm. One thing I had learned from Hollywood was that you could be anything you wanted to be if you had the right costume. So in 1974, when I was forty-one, a university professor and published poet, I found a good excuse to get the right costume, and as soon as I put it on I knew it suited me. I could be the cowboy I had always wanted to be.

Actually, it started more as camouflage than costume. At least it was "protective coloring." When I began to direct the creative writing workshop at the Florence prison, I had to cross the main yard and part of a smaller yard twice each time the workshop met. The main yard was often filled with men milling about, exercising, talking, or just hanging out. I often had to shoulder my way through this crowd, which didn't bother me. What bothered me was what was above me. Above all of us on the catwalk that ran along the top of the twenty-one-foot wall were the guards, each armed with a high-powered rifle. Many of them, as far as I could tell, appeared to be very old, probably retired deputy sheriffs. I mean really old for a man to be carrying a high-powered rifle in a crowd—like at least seventy. Not as old as I am now, but almost. They scared the hell out of me.

What if some little scuffle or even a major melee broke out while I was crossing the yard, and what if one of those guards, who probably couldn't see very well, started shooting? What chance did I have of not being mistaken for an inmate? I figured it at about zero percent. But all those guards wore western shirts as part of their uniform, cowboy boots, and cowboy hats—felt in winter and straw in summer. And when one of them was crossing the yard, he was easily distinguishable by his cowboy hat. Voila! I became a cowboy. One might think of it as cowardice, but I called it prudence. There's a fine line between them, I guess. After all, I said to myself, I wasn't getting paid to go into the prison, so I sure as hell didn't want to get shot while I was in there. There was also a certain amount of vanity involved. I had a small waist, flat belly, no hips to speak of, and I looked damned good in boots, tight jeans, and a cowboy hat. At least I thought I did, and that's what counts for a forty-one-year-old man.

My first adventure in prison with my new costume should have been enough to cure me of cowboy hats forever, but it didn't, although it made me understand the meaning of terror, the kind of fear I don't think I had ever yet experienced except when I was crawling under live machine-gun fire in basic training when I was an army draftee. I don't remember for sure which night of the week the workshop met, but in keeping with the Central Arizona College schedule, it was a weeknight, possibly Monday. As the fall progressed, darkness came earlier each week. One night I entered the prison just at dusk wearing my cowboy hat and full regalia. The light, as it often is in the desert at that time of day, was magical—an amber green haze that suffused everything, probably caused by something as unromantic as dust in the air. The sky was still glowing with a golden light while the prison yard beneath its high walls was in shadow, almost darkness.

The process for getting into the education yard, where my group met, was byzantine beyond belief. After crossing the main yard, one came to a small iron door in the peripheral stone wall. At that door, one stopped and shouted as loud as possible "Guard!" Eventually, one of the guards on the catwalk above would lower a small basket on a piece of twine. In the basket was a huge key. It was at least nine inches long and looked like something out of a gothic novel. One placed the key in the huge keyhole of the door and, by using considerable strength, was able to unlock the iron door and, using still more strength, push it open. Then, carrying the key, one went through the door, closed it, and locked it from the other side. At about eye level there was a small opening in the iron door, and once the door was locked, one reached back through this opening and placed the key in the basket, which was raised by the guard on the catwalk. To anyone acquainted with contemporary prisons with their electronic sally ports, the process would seem medieval, which, of course it was, even in 1974.

When I crossed the main yard that night, it was deserted. Chow was long since over, and the men were either in their cells or in classrooms in the education yard. I got to the iron door and yelled "Guard!" as I always did. The little basket came down as it always did, and I reached into it to get the key. But there was no key. Instead there were many little transparent plastic bags filled with white powder. I froze, but my mind was racing. From above, all they could see was my cowboy hat. They couldn't see my face. Somebody had made a terrible mistake. I had been told by men in the workshop that the mainstream drug trade was carried on by guards to supplement their extremely low salaries, but I hadn't believed it. Now I had seen too much, far too much for an outsider.

As I stared as if hypnotized at the little packets of white powder for what seemed like a very long time, possibilities were racing through my head. Would they shoot me now and make up a story to account for it later? Should I try to run back across the main yard? I'd never make it if they wanted to shoot me and say they thought it was an escaping inmate. I couldn't get through the iron door because I didn't have the key. Ultimately there seemed to be nothing to do but stand there. I could actually feel a bullet entering my body just between my shoulder blades.

Then, suddenly, the little basket was pulled up to heaven with its precious contents, and just as suddenly it came down again with the key in it. *So this is it,* I thought. *They're going to let me go into the education yard at least.* By this time I was on automatic pilot, but I noticed as I put the key in the lock that my hand was shaking badly. As I went through the door, I decided my only hope was to play dumb, positively stupid, and that shouldn't be too hard for me. It was a long shot, but it seemed like the only shot I had. I must tell no one. That would be suicide. I must act as if I had no idea what was in the basket

I tried to appear totally relaxed as I went back through the iron door that night after the workshop, like a naive idiot. I walked with a group of inmates from the workshop most of the way across the main yard, talking and laughing, until they turned off to the right and I went left to the main gate. The worst part was after I exited the main gate and was walking to my car in the deserted parking lot under the bright perimeter lights. I was thinking what a good target I would make from up on the catwalk. But I put my faith in my cowboy hat. No inmate in the entire prison wore a cowboy hat. If they shot me "by mistake," they would have to explain away the cowboy hat.

Maybe it was something as simple as that. Maybe they thought I was really stupid and naive. Maybe I was. Maybe the guards sensed that I was too scared to tell anybody what I had seen. And if I did, how could I prove it? So the result of all my terror was that nothing happened. The drug trade continued. Hard drugs have always been cheaper and more readily available in prison than in the free world. I continued to go into the prison once a week, and after a few months got over being afraid, although my heart always raced a little each time I approached that particular door and yelled "Guard!" hoping to find nothing but the key in the basket.

Thinking about it now, the irony is so heavy it almost makes me laugh. I see myself in danger from a well-organized and heavily armed drug-smuggling ring in the employ of the state while I am crossing a shadowy prison yard and depending for my protection on the presence of several murderers and other convicted felons. How's that for irony? It also seems curious to me that in thirty years as a volunteer in the state prisons, I have never been threatened, either physically or verbally, by a prison inmate, but I have experienced terror from my contact with some of the guards. This has been true in spite of the fact that I have been constantly critical of the inmates' writing and have offended and hurt hundreds of them with my critiques.

It is also true that I am much safer in the prison classroom than I am in the university classroom. In recent years three professors in the College of Nursing at the University of Arizona were murdered by an irate student. I have never heard of a teacher, any teacher, being physically harmed by an inmate in the Arizona state prison system.

We have a tendency to accept the stereotype, amounting to a myth, that all prison inmates are violent and potentially dangerous. On the other hand, to suggest that the people who run or staff our state prisons are often habitual lawbreakers seems almost taboo, as if it violates our American sense of fair play. Considering what the CEOs of some of our largest and, until recently, most successful corporations have done to their workers, perhaps the American sense of fair play should be considered an outmoded concept.

It would be unrealistic to expect a higher level of morality from people who work in prisons than we expect from people in any other workforce. And the guards who smuggled cocaine into the Florence prison in a basket, while scaring the hell out of me, never shot me when they had both cause and opportunity. I was aware of how desperately underpaid they were, and what a huge temptation it must have been to triple or quadruple their income every week.

And when the female correctional officer whose responsibility was classification at the Santa Rita facility where I was directing a workshop years later, the person who decides if a particular inmate will or will not be sent to a facility that has a drug rehabilitation program, or will be sent to a facility far from his family and children, the person who makes these decisions each day, was arrested with a sizable stash of illegal drugs in her car, I was dismayed but willing to consider this an individual instance of someone who indulged in the same practices for which many of the inmates whose lives she controlled were incarcerated.

And when, last month, a female correctional officer in a juvenile facility pleaded guilty to "solicitation of unlawful sexual conduct" with a boy in the facility, I felt that the entire situation was merely a sad comment on human frailty. But reading further in the *Arizona Daily*

Star, I found that the civil suit the boy, now a man, is filing against the state of Arizona "alleges Arizona Department of Juvenile Corrections officials knew about the allegations and failed to report them to the police for at least a year." This suggests, although it does not prove, that at least some prison officials feel they can ignore the law.

On the other hand, anyone who works or lives in a prison has got to realize the power of prison folklore and to suspect that some of the activities or incidents so firmly believed by the inmates might never have happened. When I was told by the inmates at Santa Rita that all the booths provided for the lawyers to talk to their inmate clients were bugged, I was ready to believe it, but since I have been unable to find any evidence of this, I assume the entire thing must have been prison folklore.

A few years earlier I had arrived in the classroom at the Cimarron Unit to find the entire group of inmates acting in strange ways, pointing at the corners of the ceiling, mouthing voiceless words I couldn't understand, gesturing rather than speaking. I was baffled until one of them whispered to me that the room was bugged. It is possible that this was true, but why would the Department of Corrections go to the trouble of bugging the classroom where the creative writing workshop met? I can think of reasons, but they sound paranoid. Could they have believed that our discussion would have revealed something about gang activity, drug smuggling, an escape plot, an imminent strike or riot? If they believed this, they had no idea what kind of discussions we had in the group. I didn't examine the room for bugs, but I have come to believe they didn't exist. At that time the Cimarron Unit was getting increasingly bizarre and surreal, but I can't imagine that the administrators of even that ill-fated unit were so far gone as to bug the classrooms.

Even taking into consideration the prevalence of prison folklore, which has little if any relationship to fact (although it often portrays very real attitudes), I have come to the conclusion, after thirty years of observation, that there is something about the nature of the job of confining people against their will that either attracts or creates (possibly both) people who have a very casual attitude about their relationship to the law. This is the conservative view. The other view, probably more realistic, is that many of the people who seek this kind of work have a deficient moral sense, although there are major exceptions.

I remember one Christmas at what was then the Arizona Correctional Training Facility, the first unit built in the Tucson complex, a prison for young offenders under twenty-five where I established a creative writing workshop to run simultaneously with the Florence workshop. Some charitable group—I can't remember which—donated enough Christmas trees so that each living unit, or "pod" as they were called, could have its own tree. Two weeks before Christmas I watched those Christmas trees leaving the complex on the tops of the guards' cars or in the backs of their pickups. It was one of their Christmas perks. "Merry Christmas," I called to one of them with bitter irony as he was pulling out, and he responded with great good cheer, "Merry Christmas to you." And on Christmas Eve, when my wife and son and I gathered around our Christmas tree to open our presents, as was traditional in our family, I thought about the many young men in prison for whom just the smell of a Christmas tree would have been enough of a blessing for Christmas.

6

I don't believe in prisons. After working as a volunteer in the state prisons for more than thirty years, I don't believe the American prison system as we know it should exist. The American prison system is not only a corrupt system, but a corrupting one. It corrupts those who are employed by it and those who are incarcerated in it. It corrupts the contractors who build the prisons and the businesses that supply the prisons with food and materials. It corrupts the legislators who are coerced by threats from the prison administration to allocate larger and larger amounts of money to build more and more prisons. It corrupts the community that clamors for a new prison in order to grow and thrive financially off the misery of others. It corrupts the taxpayers who support it out of fear and on whose backs the entire rotten system rests. It even corrupts the do-gooders like me who try to cut down the recidivism rate and make prison a little less of a hellhole for the people who are forced to live in it. In order to continue our work, we must become subversive and devious.

As for the inmates, they get brutalized or they get butchered or they get out, but precious few of them, like Calvin, now running a successful drug rehabilitation program in Phoenix and with his civil rights restored, get out in a better condition than when they went in. Those few are the miracles. For the majority, it is true that prison is a breeding ground for crime, a crime factory, a crime school with highly accomplished teachers.

As long ago as 1973, the year before I began my first prison workshop, Jessica Mitford, in her brilliantly researched book *Kind and Usual Punishment*, called for the abolition of all prisons in America, citing studies indicating that if American prisons were abolished, the crime rate would actually go down. Since she made that recommendation and since I began teaching as a volunteer in prison, the total prison population in this country has ballooned, partly because of the "war on drugs" and mandatory sentencing laws. As the journalist Scott Shane of the *Baltimore Sun* said in 2003, "With a record-setting two million people now locked up in American jails and prisons, the United States has overtaken Russia and has a higher percentage of its citizens behind bars than any other country."

Shane goes on to say that most foreign governments view the American prison policy as "a blot on society." I view it from a somewhat different angle, partly from the inside out, and its significance terrifies me. About three years ago a young inmate said to me, "You know, prison isn't really too bad for me. For the first time in my life I have a bed to sleep in and three meals a day and *we all sit down to eat together*." It was the last clause that got to me, and I suddenly realized what he was saying, what he intended to say: *For a sizable portion of the population, prison has become a substitute for the American family, the American home. As the American family ceases to exist, the American prison takes over its functions.* This is the most frightening condemnation of our culture I can think of. It cuts across racial and economic lines and levels. It means dehumanizing on a massive scale.

But it is not entirely true, as the young inmate said, that prisoners all sit down together at meals, and that isn't exactly what he meant. He meant that many of them sit down at the same time, depending on the feeding schedule and the capacity of the chow hall. The blacks, however, do not sit with the whites. The Hispanics sit with the Hispanics, and the Native Americans, unless they are partly black or Hispanic, sit in their separate place. Those who insist on violating these arbitrary seating patterns will eventually be the victims of violence, often deadly violence.

This incredible emphasis on race and ethnicity in prison is merely a reflection of our culture. In fact, the prison system itself is a kind of microcosm of our culture, deny it however much we will. It reflects what we are with amazing accuracy. Not what we would like to be or what we pretend to be, but what we are. Our prison system is the dark mirror of our contemporary culture, what the garbologist finds out about us by going through our trash, what the psychiatrist finds out about us by digging into our psyches.

While our political attitudes ebb and flow between liberal and conservative points of view, between the religious right and the skeptical left, one thing remains a constant in our culture: we are a violent people. We have always been a violent people. It is easy for us to see the violence in other cultures, but difficult for us to see the violence in our own, since we often mask our violence behind any one of a hundred euphemisms, rationalizations, or principles such as "rugged individualism" or "constitutional rights" or "religion" or "protecting and expanding democracy" or "capitalism."

We created the geographical outlines of our nation largely through violence and a belief in "manifest destiny," which meant that we believed we had the divine right to acquire anything in our path by violent means. It began when we dealt with the natives of this land by means of violence, and that violence escalated until we attempted to solve the greatest social issue our nation ever faced, slavery, by means of insane, fratricidal violence. We have been involved in one war after another during the last sixty years, and yet we fancy ourselves a peaceful, nonviolent people. When our leaders identify their major endeavors in terms of violence (the War on Poverty, the War on Drugs), it seems perfectly natural to most of us.

At the same time, we are a fearful people. Fear rules many aspects of our lives, probably because we recognize, deep down, that we live in such a violent culture. We react with fear to the violence we see in the media, and all too many of our leaders play on that fear for their own purposes. Consequently, our prison policy, and even our judicial system in most cases, is driven by these two forces: violence and fear. Now there, as my father used to say, "is a pair to draw to." And unless our society can change in basic ways, our prison policy will continue to be driven by these two forces. Since I don't foresee basic changes in our society in the near future, I can only call for the excision of what has become a major societal cancer—the American prison system. Such excision could be accomplished, I feel, in the next fifteen years if it were done in coordinated stages and supported by the political will of the people. It would involve a massive rethinking of where we put our resources for the best results.

Everywhere I go I encounter people who are greatly troubled and confused by this issue as they see us moving toward the point where half of our society will be spending most of its money to keep the other half in prison. Eventually, I believe, if we continue on our present path, the system will collapse because of the impossible economic burden it will eventually place upon us, but that collapse will involve dreadful suffering for many of us. By functioning out of fear *now*, we place ourselves, or possibly our children, in much greater danger *then*.

People realize this and are asking the right questions. How can we control a prison industry that is spinning further and further out of control and expanding daily like a virus? How can we compensate or convert the economy of those communities whose income is dependent on the prison industry? How can we rescue the American family that often creates attitudes and patterns of behavior almost guaranteeing that its children will wind up in prison? What can we do about a judicial system that is widely perceived to be unjust, where the poor and people of color are punished disproportionately while those with sufficient assets can literally buy "justice"? How can we achieve rehabilitation for those who need it? How can we educate ourselves to consider the time a person spends in prison as a window of opportunity rather than merely a period of punishment? How can we lower recidivism rates of between 60 and 75 percent, recidivism rates that indicate our prisons have become revolving doors punishing the same people again and again, and often for the same offenses, without ever addressing the reasons why they commit those offenses?

These are the questions I am being asked by people in churches and schools and discussion groups and social gatherings. They are questions being asked by people of all political persuasions who feel they can no longer bear the burden imposed by our present prison system—not only the financial burden but, perhaps more pressing, the burden of guilt we feel. It is immoral to do what we are doing to thousands and thousands of people. I am encouraged to see, recently, my deep concerns, the result of thirty years of observation, reflected in the faces of the people I meet from day to day, people who have had no direct experience with prisons and who might not agree with my political views. But they are good people and they recognize a real problem when they see one. They are also beginning to realize that the solution to this problem must come from them, since our government, whether county, state, or national, has made little attempt to solve the problem and has, instead, simply made it steadily worse.

The American prison is, of course, only the final destination for those who have entered into a process beginning with the local or federal police system and passing through the county, state, or federal judicial system. These systems have often proven themselves to be not only faulty, vindictive, and sometimes controlled by fanatical local pressures, but racially prejudiced to an appalling degree. This last feature of our judicial system, racial bigotry, has just begun to receive much public attention, although Jessica Mitford described it in *Kind and Usual Punishment* in great detail in 1973, and members of several minority groups have spoken out about it for decades.

Marc Mauer, in *Race to Incarcerate*, provides more recent and even more chilling statistics regarding race and prison. "A black boy born in 1991 stood a twenty-nine percent chance of being imprisoned at some point in his life, compared to a sixteen percent chance for a Hispanic boy and a four percent chance for a white boy." This phenomenon obviously permeates our judicial system, resulting in the disproportionate racial demographics in our prisons, both state and federal. There the racial tension comes to the surface in a thousand ways, some of them violent. It is unrealistic for anyone to expect the prison to correct this problem that has been thrust upon it by a prejudiced judicial system reflecting the prejudices of a largely bigoted society. To correct the situation in its final manifestation in prison is impossible. Some prison administrators use this racial situation to create riots and squeeze more money out of state legislatures, a few try to correct it, and the wiser ones just live with it as best they can, as one lives with the fact that water is wet.

But it is curious and interesting to compare our present system of prisons with another system that most Americans either countenanced or encouraged for many years until it became impossible for many of them to countenance it any longer. I am referring, of course, to the system of slavery.

Both slavery and our contemporary prisons are self-perpetuating economic systems depending for their continued existence on the abject misery of an entire population. It is, to a large extent, even the same racial population.

Both systems depend on a population with no civil rights, a population from whom the ability to make choices has been removed, and those in that population who do not do as they are told are often subjected to hideous punishment.

The adults in both populations are often thought of and treated as children. The male adults in both populations are generally considered dangerous, especially sexually. The female members of both populations have often been sexually exploited by their male "keepers."

Both systems have produced a population that is largely unable to function satisfactorily *outside the system*.

Both systems have been the economic support of many communities. Any attempt to remove the system from the community it supports has been met with a firestorm of resistance and in the case of slavery a civil war.

The policy of manumission of slaves before the Civil War and our current parole and release policies for prisoners are, in practice, the same kind of policies.

Each system has produced its own subculture, which has had a profound effect on the mainstream culture. Each subculture has produced its own distinctive language, music, art, folklore, and moral and religious beliefs.

Both systems are based upon withholding freedom, civil rights, and basic dignity from an entire population. Because they are built on the debasement of humans and human values, both systems are corrupt. Both systems corrupt anyone who is involved with them.

All the racial issues that exist on the outside exist inside the prison, but they exist there in a pressure cooker, and they are much more obvious and potentially dangerous. At some point during the roughly eight years in the 1990s that I directed the workshop at the Santa Rita facility near Tucson, the Arizona Department of Corrections tried to force a degree of racial integration generally not attempted in most prisons. Since two inmates were housed in each cell at Santa Rita, it was decided that whenever a prisoner was transferred out of the prison or got out on parole or completed his sentence and was released, he would be replaced in that particular cell by a man of a different race than the man remaining in the cell. It was believed that after a few years of this policy, nearly all the cells would be "integrated." I first became aware of the policy one day in the Santa Rita workshop.

"Where's Mark?" I asked, expecting that he had a visit that day.

"He's in the hole."

"What did he do?"

"He didn't do anything. It's what he wouldn't do."

Then they explained the policy to me. In order for the system to work, the administration had to obtain from the inmate currently in the cell his agreement that he would not offer resistance if a man of another race was moved into his cell. Mark was white. After his celly left, the administration tried to move a black man into the cell with Mark. Mark objected loudly and was sent to solitary until he changed his attitude. But Mark, who had little race prejudice and would, under different circumstances, have had no objection to a black cell mate, never changed his attitude because if he had agreed to cell with a black man, members of the Aryan Brotherhood would have attacked and possibly killed him. He had decided that spending the rest of his prison sentence in solitary was a viable alternative to death. Ultimately the prison administration realized that the cross-racial policy wouldn't work and dropped it.

The administration of the Florence prison that Tom Cobb and I entered in 1974 used racial tension, as embodied in gangs, for its purposes. The warden, Harold Cardwell, one of the last (I hope) of the old-school "bull" wardens, believed in allowing the prison gangs to handle their own differences and problems among themselves. He said that he would rather have the inmates killing one another than killing his guards. The major gangs developing in the prison at that time were the Black Brotherhood, the Mexican Mafia, and the beginnings of what would ultimately become the Aryan Brotherhood, the most feared and fearsome of the three. As detailed in attorney Thornton Price's book *Murder Unpunished*, the warden had placed a house trailer in the middle of the main prison yard and installed in it a very smart, very clever inmate named Larry who controlled the nerve center of the prison. I met Larry shortly after I began to teach the first workshop at Florence, and saw him often. By means of runners and telephones, this inmate clerk could stay in touch with every part of the prison; and since he was, presumably, loyal to the warden, so could the warden. But Larry, one of the kingpins of a corrupt system, was also corrupt and more than capable of playing all ends against the middle. The result was extortion, slaughter, and butchery for a long period.

To give Cardwell some credit, things had been even worse before he arrived. In June 1973, exactly a year before Tom Cobb and I walked into the Florence prison, after Warden Frank Eyman retired and was replaced by his business manager, "Bud" Gomes, the prison had become a zoo according to Price's *Murder Unpunished* and according to accounts I received from several inmates who were at Florence during Gomes' tenure as warden. The hobby shop had been converted into a factory to manufacture zip guns, and many of the inmates were armed. Drugs and homemade booze were always available. On June 22 a glue-sniffing inmate went berserk, knifed two inmates, beat up on several others, and took over one of the cell blocks. He murdered guards Dale Morey and Theodore Buckley.

One result of this carnage was that Cardwell was brought in as the new warden in 1973. He was a man who made deals, a gambler, a pragmatist. I think he was cunning rather than intelligent. Unfortunately, some of the inmates were more cunning, and probably more intelligent, than he was. Whether or not Cardwell ran the prison as he did in order to get the results he got is debatable. I know of a later case within the Arizona prison system when I felt strongly that there was a deliberate attempt to focus pressure on a specific unit in such a way as to create a riot, but I think the impetus for that action came from above, from somewhere in the office of the director of the Department of Corrections in an attempt to extort appropriations from the state legislature, a body that always seems to respond best to fear. Whether or not the Florence warden's methods were designed to produce riots and violence or were, merely, the misguided policy of a not-too-intelligent man, they certainly did produce riots and violence.

But during that first six-week pilot program in the summer of 1974, Tom Cobb and I were so busy we were pretty much oblivious to the tension around us on the yard, especially the racial tension. The members of the workshop, although they included men from all racial groups in the prison, were compatible, and the spirit of cooperation was so high that Tom and I didn't really understand what the situation was on the yard in general.

7

As 1974 became 1975, I was becoming more aware of the racial tensions on the yard at Florence, and I watched what was happening in the workshop with a kind of amazement. It is a phenomenon I have noticed over the years in other writing workshops in the various state prison units.

At first the black inmates sit on one side of the room, and the Chicanos sit somewhere else in a bloc, both groups looking at the Anglos and at one another with veiled contempt or hostility. Then, as the workshop progresses over the next few months, interesting things begin to happen. I have seen this happen dozens of times, but it never ceases to surprise me to the point of awe. I suppose it is caused by the fact that you can't discuss and criticize someone's most cherished ideas and creations without coming to feel some empathy with that person. Or it might be that having everybody's writing criticized is an act of shared pain that bonds the sharers. Perhaps it is influenced by the fact that the workshop director treats every member of the workshop with the same degree of respect and the same degree of critical severity. These are only possibilities. Actually I don't know what causes it, but I know it happens and it violates the established norm of any prison.

The people in the workshop come to think of the group as transcending racial and ethnic boundaries. Soon a black member isn't afraid to praise something a white member wrote. Then the seating arrangement gradually changes. Then one day a man says, "I'm sorry I couldn't type my work up this week. They took my typewriter away." And a man of a different race says, "Give it to me. I'll type it for you for next week." Such a thing would be unthinkable in the general population, and seasoned members of the prison staff marvel at it when they become aware of it, although few have ever been in a position to become aware of it. After it happens, everybody is helping everybody else in the workshop. On the yard and especially in the chow hall the inmates must observe the protocol of strict separation of the races, but in the workshop a man's racial or ethnic background simply helps give him a unique voice and a respected individuality.

During that fall semester of 1974, under the auspices of Central Arizona College, the workshop had gone well in the estimation of the prison administration. I hadn't got into any major trouble, and the program was popular with the inmates. (Of course the administration didn't know about my stumbling onto the little packets of white powder in the basket let down from on high by the guards, and I certainly wasn't about to tell them.) The workshop's major hitch was that somebody stole, out of a locked closet, all the books the Arizona Commission on the Arts had bought for us. No one except prison staff members had keys to the closet. Duane Vild, the director of education who had been very helpful in getting the workshop started, was greatly embarrassed. I had been circulating the books to the inmates and always getting them back.

At the end of that semester, at the beginning of 1975, I finally got what I had wanted all along—an ongoing workshop that met once a week on Saturdays under the auspices of the Arizona Commission on the Arts. The makeup of the group at Florence changed somewhat as the months passed, but the core of dedicated writers remained. The death of Charles Green in 1974 was staggering, but we recovered. Stephen Dugan, the Irish jailhouse lawyer, emerged as one of the leaders. He had the best education of the group and became the best critic of the work submitted. He also began to publish at an astonishing rate. Cash, the lanky Kentuckian with a scar on his face who was working in the prison law library, sometimes had access to duplication facilities. He also became a kind of ground wire for the group. Whenever we got too far afield or too crazy, we could count on Cash to ask a question that would bring us down to earth and ground us.

Each meeting was exciting. New talent was emerging every week. Michael, Jimmy, Roman, "Big John," Robert, Greg, Tony, the other Jimmy, and others. The energy level was so high that I felt I was riding some kind of wild, unbroken horse. I couldn't really direct it. All I could do was grab for the saddle horn and hang on while we careened in all directions.

The energy in the workshop increased when the first poem was accepted for publication by a journal. Suddenly they got the idea. One after the other they realized that publishing their work was not a hopeless dream. It was a possibility, distant and elusive maybe, but a possibility. The critical feedback they got from the workshop became pure gold to many of them. Nearly every week someone had an announcement: a reputable magazine had accepted another poem or prose piece. We cheered. And when the magazine came out and the workshop member could see his work in print with his name on it, it was a life-changing experience. Now they dared to hope, to look toward a future that might be remarkably different from what they had come to expect. Watching this happen was exciting. I left the prison each week wildly exhilarated.

Most of them knew they were plugged into something important, and it was fascinating to see how they reacted. Michael Martin, a tall, lanky redhead who had been attending Arizona State University on a baseball scholarship when he became hooked on heroin, wrote quiet, imagistic poems filled with pain. He had been sixteen when he came home from school one afternoon and found his father's body hanging in the basement. Every Saturday morning Michael got up earlier than the others who were housed in the education yard so he could sweep and clean up the room the workshop met in. He was not assigned to do this, nor did anybody ask him to. When I thanked him, he blushed furiously—even his ears turned red—and stammered something incoherent. Being the self-appointed janitor was his way of show-ing he appreciated the workshop. His lyric poems were haunted and haunting.

Several of the men who had jobs as clerks typed for the others and made enough copies of each piece of work for everybody, and that usually meant typing the same piece over and over with as many sheets of carbon paper as the typewriter would accommodate. We hadn't been able to wangle the use of a ditto machine on a regular basis, but sometimes one of the clerks could use one surreptitiously while somebody else stood outside the door to whistle if he saw anybody coming. I was finding out that nearly everything worthwhile that got done in the prison had to be done sub rosa.

         Of the members of that original group, the two who have become the most successful as writers and the most famous are Stephen Dugan and Jimmy Santiago Baca. Jimmy's appearance in the workshop was very brief because he spent so much time in lockup. He talks about this at length in his second memoir. He fought hard to get into the workshop, although I knew nothing about it. I remember looking up one morning and there he was, dark, brooding, intense, and with a hair-trigger sensitivity. In a month or so he was gone again, back to lockup because, I was told, he had taken on the Mexican Mafia. Then the letters started coming, letters filled with his long, discursive poems. I recognized the talent and the energy in his language, a reflection of his own burning energy, but the work was also undisciplined, indulgent, and wildly out of control. In my letters I told him so, again and again. Slowly the work began to improve. I have found out from him in recent years just how painful for him that process was. It was also painful for me.

Years later, when Jimmy had won a National Book Award and become a famous writer, he came to visit us and stayed at our house. One afternoon, when Lois and Jimmy and I were sitting on the terrace, he said he wanted to show us something. He took out his wallet and extracted a piece of paper that was so thin from wear it was almost transparent. He unfolded it with great care to prevent it from falling apart.

"I've carried this all these years," he said. "I've memorized it and it's helped to keep me from going back to prison."

I recognized it as a letter from me, and I even remembered writing it because it was a response to a letter from Jimmy that had made me angry. I realize now that it wasn't really Jimmy's letter as such that had made me lose my cool; it was the accumulated effect of getting many letters each month from men in prison, most of whom were complaining about their treatment, which I could do nothing about.

Jimmy's letter, complaining about his treatment and his problems, was simply the straw that broke the proverbial camel's back. Part of my reply was, "I don't see how anybody as smart as you could be so stupid as to do something that would get you sent to prison where you knew you would be completely under the control of those who are less intelligent than you are. You brought this situation on yourself and I'm tired of hearing you complain about it." It was the harshest letter I had ever written to anyone in prison, although I have written some that are even harsher since then. I probably should have waited until I cooled off to answer Jimmy's letter, or perhaps I should not have answered it at all, but it turned out for the best.

I have also had to be harsh, terribly harsh and critical, of the creative work of hundreds and hundreds of inmates. As hard as it has been for them and for me, it may be the one thing, perhaps the only thing, I have done right all these years. Some can't handle it and drift away. Some fight and argue with me and usually lose the argument because they don't have the support of the rest of the group. Others bite the bullet, settle down, read and write furiously. They have a hope and a belief in themselves they must have in order to survive what they will face in the future. I drive them on with the whip of criticism, trying not to notice the scars their shoulders already bear. I can teach them to write well and honestly. It is the only gift I have for them, but it is a powerful gift.

The letter Jimmy Santiago Baca showed us reminded me of the thousands of letters I have received from people in prison over the years. Of them all, a couple stand out for me, and in neither case had I met the writer. One was from a man I assumed to be middle-aged with an Hispanic name. He was submitting a poem for consideration to the magazine *Walking Rain Review* that my wife Lois and I have edited and published since 1989. His tone was sweet and very respectful. He said his wife was also in prison, and that his mother had recently died but he was not allowed to go to her funeral. He said that if his poem could be of any help to anyone, it would please him, and I could use it in any way I wanted to. Then, in a postscript, he apologized for his handwriting. He was learning to write with his left hand because he had recently lost his right. How do you answer a letter like that? I don't think I'll ever know.

The other letter that stands out in my mind began, "I don't think of myself as just your average murderer . . ." I didn't answer that one. He didn't seem to need any encouragement.

In 1975 tensions on the Florence yard increased. Warden Cardwell seemed to be oblivious to the increasing gang activity. The men in the workshop grew more and more jittery and nervous, although they tried to hide it from me. It was the macho quality exacerbated in men's prisons. Their attitude was that no matter how bad it got, they could live with it—or possibly die with it—but they would not show fear or weakness.

In spite of the turmoil in the main yard, Charles Schmid, beyond the walls in the outside trustee dormitory, was on a roll. He was attending the workshop and also writing to me every week. His letters crackled with excitement. He was polishing and working on the poems the Phoenix editor Ramona Weeks had agreed to publish in a chapbook of his work. The incredible energy that had survived death row, solitary confinement, repeated beatings, and everything the prison could dish out was finally focused. He was a new man.

Shortly after the death of J. Charles Green at the end of the previous summer, Charles Schmid had approached me with his latest idea. He wanted to change his name legally. He didn't feel like "Smitty" anymore, and he wanted a new name to signify that he was a different person. He wanted me to help him come up with a suitable name. Looking back on it now, I am ashamed that I was willing to do it, willing to influence a person, any person, in a matter as important and personal as the choice of his or her name. At the time it didn't seem to bother me at all. Subconsciously I must have felt that I had created this man and now I had the right to name him. I knew no shame. I was playing God, but I would soon realize I was closer to Dr. Frankenstein.

Charles said he liked the name David and possibly the last name Lamb. Both too Biblical, I said. I shudder now to think of the sacrificial significance of "Lamb." David might be okay, but I thought of him as a "Paul." That was Biblical too, but he looked like a "Paul" to me. Perhaps subconsciously I remembered that the apostle Paul had changed his name from Saul at the time of his conversion. We talked about the possibility of Paul Davidson. I said I thought he should have a last name that was somber, suggesting mourning or something like that. Maybe something with "ash" in it. Somehow, almost in unison we came up with "Ashley," and we both knew it was right. Two weeks later he changed his name legally to Paul David Ashley. Paul David Ashley was born at the age of thirty-one. He would live eight months. I would watch him die, cursing myself for a fool.

During those eight months the workshop had a visit from the poet W. S. Merwin, who was in Tucson to do a reading for the University of Arizona Poetry Center in early February of 1975. When I asked him if he wanted to go into the prison with me on Saturday, Bill Merwin said, "No, I don't want to go into the prison. I hate prisons. I can't stand prisons. I will go."

I have heard Bill read his poetry many times and know he can mesmerize an audience in about three minutes, but I have never seen him do it as thoroughly and effectively as he did with that audience of seventeen men, all convicted felons, some of them murderers. It might have had to do with the fact that when Bill was a very young man he had been incarcerated while in the navy. He told me about that scarring experience after we left the prison. It might have been simply that he is one of the most sensitive and compassionate people alive. Whatever it was, it was beyond anything I or the men could have expected, although they had read much of his work and we had talked about it in the workshop.

As we discussed several pieces of the men's writing that day, Bill seemed to be most impressed with the poetry of Paul David Ashley. I'm pretty sure I had not yet told him anything about Paul's background or crimes. I try not to discuss these things with visitors. Bill knew it was a maximum-security prison and that some of the men in it were murderers. Beyond that, I don't think he knew anything about what any individuals were serving time for. In spite of that, toward the end of the workshop Bill seemed to single out the work of Paul Ashley for attention, and the energy moving back and forth between them flashed like lightning. I could feel it and almost smell it. Here were two men who lived at incredibly intense levels and took enormous risks, and they recognized one another. One was probably a mass murderer and one was a famous poet. One was infamous and the other was considered a literary saint. What was the quality they had in common? Passion? A realization that every moment they lived was precious? Had Paul's close approach to execution given him some kind of value system, some appreciation of life that Bill had intuitively? I puzzled over it then, and I puzzle over it now.

At the conclusion of the workshop I was too busy getting Bill out of the prison to give it much thought, but I thought about it later. Bill's conversation with Paul was so intense that he wanted to stay and continue it. I kept telling Bill we had to go. "Count" was coming up immediately, and no one left the prison during "count." If we didn't get across the yard quickly, we would be trapped for an indefinite period. If the number they came up with at count was the wrong number, it could be a very long period. Finally I took hold of Bill's arm and quite literally dragged him the first part of the way out, until his intense contact with the members of the workshop was broken.

W. S. Merwin went back into the workshop with me in 1977, on his next visit to the Poetry Center at the university. Again it was a shattering, exhilarating experience, and it came in the midst of the most violent and frightening period we had experienced. Even a partial list of writers who have visited the workshop over the years is impressive. In addition to W. S. Merwin it would include Jon Anderson, Barbara Anderson, Terry McMillan, Carolyn Kizer, Benjamin Saenz, Steve Orlen, Jim Paul, Alberto Rios, William Wilkins, Jimmy Santiago Baca, Terry Tempest Williams, and many more. We have also been visited by those who have written about the experience of prison from various points of view, such as Patricia McConnel, author of *Sing Soft, Sing Loud*, and Lewis "Bud" Merklin, the psychiatrist who wrote *They Chose Honor*. In recent years, several members of the staff of the foundation that now funds the workshop, the Lannan Foundation, including Patrick Lannan, have visited the workshop.

I have been careful not to bring into the workshop anyone who did not have legitimate business there—no voyeurs—and I have had to be very firm with some who wanted to go in. It won't come as news, I suppose, but it is true that there are some women, blessedly few, who will do almost anything to get to meet a man in prison, especially if he is young and handsome. It took me a while to catch onto this, but over the years I have developed the ability to spot those women at about forty yards, and while I try always to be polite to them, I can be adamant. As for the female guards, also blessedly few, who have their pants tailored to the point that they seem to be painted on, who flirt with, tease, and torment the sex-starved men, I have no control over them, but I have no respect for them either. Theirs is one of the more insidious forms of torture inflicted on the incarcerated, one more indication of how corrupt the system can be.

Michael Mulcahy, a University of Arizona professor, produced the documentary film *Correction* in 2003. It deals with the current training of the corrections officers for the Arizona Department of Corrections and shows that 50 percent of the new officers trained leave the department within eighteen months. After a showing of his film, he told the audience that he had interviewed the head of the Department of Corrections and asked, "What is the state prison system's biggest problem?" The answer was "sexual relationships between the Department of Corrections staff and the inmates." I had generally believed that most of this went on in the women's prison, where some of the women were willing to offer sexual favors to their male guards in return for favors and benefits. Recently, with the great increase in female guards in male prisons, I have heard of several instances of relationships between male prisoners and female guards. Considering that many of the females who become guards in Arizona state prisons are very young, not well educated, and sometimes not very bright, such situations are inevitable.

There is a crude old saying: "A hard man is good to find." Being "sex starved" is one of the few attractions a man in prison has to offer any available female, and many are the females attracted by it. One of the men who had been in the workshop confessed to me later that for the first year after he was released, he told all the women he met that he had just got out of prison that morning. His record of sexual conquests made Don Juan's pale in comparison.

‖ *The Horror*

Whether the pitcher hits the stone
or the stone hits the pitcher,
it's bad for the pitcher.
—Spanish proverb

8

On March 20, 1975, less than two months after Bill Merwin's first visit to the workshop, the telephone rang just as Lois and Brad and I were sitting down to dinner. It was Katharine, the mother of Charles Schmid, who was now, legally, Paul David Ashley. Using every ounce of control she could in order to be coherent, she told me that Paul had been attacked in the trustee dormitory and stabbed repeatedly. They had taken him by ambulance to the little county hospital in Florence where the doctors determined that he had to be transported to Maricopa County Hospital in Phoenix. His condition was critical. She and her husband Maurice were leaving for Phoenix immediately.

I told her I was on my way, but I had twice as far to go as she did, so I would call Ramona Weeks in Phoenix. Ramona, one of the editors of Baleen Press, had agreed to publish Paul's first book, and had published several of his poems in her magazine already. Maybe she could be there when the ambulance arrived.

I called Ramona and she said, yes, yes, she would go to the hospital and try to be there when they brought him in. She had never met Paul, but she had corresponded with him extensively and she knew and admired his poetry. In minutes she cranked up her old diesel Mercedes and was on her way to the hospital. I started out from Tucson in my faithful pickup without even the forethought to take a toothbrush.

I don't remember how I got into the hospital, but I was directed into some kind of large emergency area. It was an extensive open space, and as I rushed in I slipped and nearly fell. Struggling to regain my balance, I realized that the floor was covered with blood, Paul's blood. I could see him lying on a gurney, apparently unconscious. Ramona Weeks was beside him, holding his hand and talking to him. Her hands and arms were covered with blood and there was a smear of blood on her forehead. Katharine and Maurice were huddled together a little to the side. I think Katharine had fainted and was being revived. All the color had drained from her face.

They were just about to wheel him upstairs to surgery. "I'm here, Charles," I said, using the name I thought he would recognize best. "Hang in there." He opened his eyes and there was some slight movement of one of his hands, and then they took him away.

I remember many things about the next ten days, but I don't remember which day they happened. I seemed to be sleepwalking, and was, undoubtedly suffering from lack of sleep. Some of the time I was in Phoenix, some of the time in Tucson, and I remember nothing about getting back and forth the 70 miles between.

About a year before that dreadful March night, Katharine had requested that I take over Paul's power of attorney because she felt inadequate to handle his affairs if he should become incapacitated. She was not in good health, she said, and did not trust her judgment or her knowledge of legal matters. Paul was strongly in favor of this move. I very reluctantly agreed to accept, although my knowledge of legal matters was far from good. At least I had access to good legal advice. I remember these conversations, but I do not remember ever signing any papers. Perhaps I did and forgot it, but I have no copy of a paper I might have signed. I'm not sure the power of attorney was ever transferred, but Katharine evidently thought it had been, and I wasn't about to argue with her while we were standing in a pool of her son's blood. She must have spoken to somebody at the hospital or filled out papers to that effect before I ever arrived at the hospital, leaving me responsible for all medical decisions that required permission.

We were told that Paul would be in surgery for hours. Katharine's face had become a strange, pasty color. She was very ill. I was afraid she might go into shock. Ramona and I urged Maurice to take her home. We said the two of us would stay until Paul got out of surgery and call her about the results. In the meantime she should rest at home. Finally, Katharine agreed, and Maurice led her away. Ramona went to the ladies' room to clean herself up as best she could, and then the two of us went to the surgical waiting room. We sat there the rest of the night. It must have been during that night, but it could have been during a later surgery on a different day or night, that a nurse rushed in with a clipboard, calling my name. "We need your permission to remove Mr. Schmid's right kidney," she said. "Would you please sign here?" I asked if it was necessary to save his life. She said it was. I signed.

And it may have been that night or another night when a young doctor came into the waiting room, calling my name. "We need your permission," he said, "to remove Mr. Schmid's right eye." I signed. I signed him away, little by little, piece by piece. My creation, my new man risen from the ashes of a monster.

He lived for ten days. I remember some things that happened during that time very clearly, but the order of events is jumbled. In my memory it is a period in which time stops, as if I were functioning out of time. At some point a member of the hospital staff came to me and said, "Blood is running out of him as fast as we can pump it in. We are depleting the hospital's blood supply." She explained to me that if blood of any type were donated at the Red Cross in Paul's name, more blood units would be released to the hospital.

"Even in Tucson?" I asked.

"Anywhere."

Back in Tucson, I spent the morning on the telephone. When Lois and I arrived at the Red Cross blood clinic there was a line of friends and former students waiting to give blood, but before we could donate our blood, there was an ugly scene. A volunteer working in the blood center had grown irate when she was told that a young woman was giving blood to be credited to Maricopa County Hospital in the name of Charles Schmid. "That monster!" she said. "If you had any idea what that monster did you wouldn't give your blood for him."

The woman attempting to donate blood, a young friend, came to me in tears, and I went to the woman who ran the clinic. She chastised the volunteer and sent her home for the day. It seemed the only thing to do since more than fifty of the people giving blood that day were donating in the name of Charles Schmid/Paul Ashley. All the blood the hospital had given him was replaced.

He asked for me during all his periods of consciousness, but prison regulations would not permit me to visit him in the hospital because I was not related to him. Finally, Katharine was able to get permission for me to see him on the eighth day. After I saw him I knew he would die, and I hoped it would be soon. He lay unconscious and hideously mutilated in a nest of tubes and hissing, gurgling machines. I talked to him for a long time, but saw no sign that he could hear me.

In the basement of the Maricopa County Hospital there is a long, long hallway that was, in 1975, painted that bilious shade of light green so common in state or county institutions. With its fluorescent lights and echoing emptiness at three o'clock in the morning, that hallway was a thing nightmares are made of. There was one place where, if you opened a door on the left you would find vending machines, including a coffee machine, and if you opened a door on the right you would find yourself in the morgue. That's where I wound up late one night during my death vigil, exhausted and confused, when I was in search of a cup of coffee. After ten days that's where Charles Schmid/Paul David Ashley wound up too.

At some point during those ten days, while I was in Tucson, I received a call from Warden Cardwell's secretary, Della Meadows. She said the warden wanted to see me and it was urgent. Could I come to Florence? I arranged to stop on my way to the hospital in Phoenix on the following morning. When I walked into the warden's small outer office, Katharine was sitting in a chair against the wall, looking as if she were carved from stone. Evidently she, too, had been summoned. Or else she was there to beg the warden to permit me to see Paul. I sat down beside her and held her hand. I felt that we were lost children in a hostile, alien world. The door to the warden's inner office was open, and we could hear him talking on the phone but we couldn't tell what he was saying. The tone was angry. Suddenly he slammed down the receiver and said in a very loud voice audible throughout the outer office and beyond, "God damn Charles Schmid! I wish I'd never heard of Charles Schmid!" Katharine's grip on my hand tightened slightly, but her facial expression never changed. Soon Della Meadows, obviously embarrassed by the warden's outburst, told me he would see me now.

Warden Cardwell looked as if he were suffering from indigestion. His coloring was bad and his eyes were almost lost in the swollen flesh around them. I don't know why, but for some reason during the few minutes I was in his office, I focused on his hands. I don't think I had ever seen hands like that before. They were packed to the limit with flesh or muscle or fat, I couldn't tell which. Each finger was like a sausage that had been filled too full and was about to explode.

As soon as I sat down, Cardwell handed me a manila folder of papers. "This is the poetry of Charles Schmid," he said. "We want you to read it and let us know if there is anything in there that might suggest who attacked him or who hired somebody to attack him. Does he mention enemies or who he was afraid of? Anything like that."

I had already read these poems, and I knew they were mostly love poems and poems of regret for his past actions, but I didn't tell the warden that. Instead I stared at him in amazement. For this he had asked me to make a 140-mile round-trip?

"I don't understand," I said. "Wouldn't it be better if you or one of your staff read the poems? They're in English."

"We don't read poetry!" he said. And that was that. I have often pondered exactly what he meant by that statement. Did he mean that he and his staff did not read poetry because it might somehow taint them, possibly turn them into wimps or homosexuals? Or did he mean that they *couldn't* read poetry—didn't know how to, as if poetry were a foreign language? Perhaps it was both. I'll never know.

I have before me a "Reporter's Transcript of Proceedings" of the inquest, or as it says "In the Matter of the Inquisition held upon the Body of CHARLES HOWARD SCHMID Jr., Deceased." The inquest took place in the Justice Court of East Phoenix before "Hon. Ben Arnold, Acting Justice of the Peace, Ex-Officio Coroner" and a coroner's jury on April 4, 1975. Deputy County Attorney James Minter conducted the inquest. The transcript is a horrifying document.

Six witnesses are called to testify. Four of them are employees of the Department of Corrections, all working at Florence. One is a detective with the Phoenix Police Department, who has almost nothing pertinent to add, and one is the Maricopa County medical examiner, who provides a report of his autopsy on the body.

Sergeant George Goswick, a guard at the prison says:

Schmid was laying on the floor real close to the door. In fact, we had to move him a little bit in order to get the door open. And he was in a big pool of blood and had stab wounds all over him. One eye was stabbed out and about the only place there weren't blood on him was his lips. I guess he had licked them or something like that. But other than that, he was covered with blood and the dorm was pretty well smeared with blood, the front area of it. And the door you could see where it looked like hand marks, where he had tried to get out but apparently didn't have enough strength to get the door open. . . . All he said was very faint and weak at the time. He looked at me and he said help me.

Sergeant Goswick then testifies that after Paul was taken away in the ambulance, he and other guards searched the area and found in a nearby dumpster a box whose contents included "two pair of shoes containing bloodstains, one sweatshirt containing bloodstains, two pairs of pants containing bloodstains, two homemade knives that appeared to be recently washed." Numbers on the clothing were those of two inmates, Ferra and Eversole, who also lived in the outside trustee area two dormitories away. In addition to the shanks, the homemade knives, one of which was fashioned from a can opener, another knife was found hidden in a broom in Dormitory 3, where Ferra and Eversole were housed. At one point a juror questions Sergeant Goswick about this knife. The others seem homemade, but this one seems to be manufactured. Goswick's answer is: "Yes, ma'am. That's a boughten knife. Right. It's a factory made knife. It's not homemade." This means, of course, that the knife was provided by somebody on the outside and smuggled into the prison. When asked if there could have been more than two people involved in the attack, Goswick answers, "Anything is possible in the prison."

The next witness, John Vance, is a paramedic at the prison. He helped load Paul into the ambulance and was with him during the ride to the Pinal County Hospital in Florence, along with Deputy Warden Dwight Carey. He is asked to describe the victim. "Inmate Schmid was laying on the floor. He had several stab wounds in him. He had a sucking chest wound, which means his lung was punctured. He had three stab wounds in his abdomen where his abdomen was protruding out of his stomach. His right eye had been stabbed and several other lacerations."

When asked if Paul said anything while the paramedic was administering first aid, he answered, "On the way to the hospital Mr. Carey asked him who had done it. And Mr. Schmid, he didn't say who did it. And then he asked him again. When he asked him, Schmid asked me what his chances were to make it. And I told him they weren't very good, that more than likely he wouldn't make it. . . . He said Sneaky Pete and Dirty Dan. And when asked, then he stated that their last names were Ferra and Eversole."

Deputy Warden Dwight M. Carey then testifies. He spends a good deal of time explaining the housing arrangements and prison procedures in such a way as to absolve the prison from any charge of negligence. Then he verifies his conversation with Paul in the ambulance and repeats the names Ferra and Eversole. "Arriving at the hospital," Carey says, "I immediately called back and notified the warden and they picked the two inmates up."

One section of the transcript of the inquest is the report of Dr. Heinz Karnitschnig, the Maricopa County medical examiner, who performed an autopsy on Paul's body. His external examination determined that Paul was "a normally developed and well-nourished white male, five feet, three inches tall, and he weighed 145 pounds." He states that he found forty-seven stab wounds in Paul's body. The description of these wounds requires two pages in the transcript. "The wounds that did the most damage were two wounds, one that went into the right lung to the approximate depth or penetration of three inches and the other one that went into the right flank and punctured the right kidney and the approximate depth of penetration was also three inches."

I also have before me a copy of the verdict of the inquest jury, a separate document listing the names of the jurors whose charge was "to inquire into the cause of death of Paul David Ashley aka Charles Howard Schmid Jr." Their conclusion is that "said death was the result of multiple stab wounds to body, apparently inflicted by inmates Ferra and Eversole, also known as 'Sneaky Pete' and 'Dirty Dan.'"

Paul's funeral was pathetic and surreptitious. Katharine had prevailed upon the elderly priest at the Catholic church in Florence to perform a mass for Paul. The priest had agreed only on condition that it not be announced in any way, since it was somehow a violation of church policy. I don't know if this was because Paul was a notorious murderer or because he wasn't a practicing Catholic, but I suspect that both reasons weighed with equal heaviness in the mind of the elderly priest. We met in the church in the late afternoon: the priest, Katharine and Maurice, Lois and me, and, as I recall, two other elderly people. I never knew if they were friends of Katharine or just members of the congregation who went to all church services because there was very little to do in Florence. I think they must have been friends of Katharine. Otherwise, I don't know how they would have found out about the mass because it was so secretly performed.

Katharine had also determined that Paul should be buried in the prison burial ground, Comacho Hill, where J. Charles Green was buried less than a year before. She said she feared that if he were buried in a cemetery to which the public had access in Tucson or Florence or Coolidge, his grave might be defaced and desecrated. It was far less likely that such a thing would happen on prison property, especially since his prison number, but not his name, would be on the grave marker. She had a point I could understand, although I dreaded that hideous potter's field as if it were the gateway to Hell. Beneath Katharine's decision, I think, was the fact that she couldn't afford to pay for a plot and gravestone in a regular cemetery. As long as Paul had been alive, she would put her soul in hock to save him, but once he was dead, she had to save her body. She and Maurice were barely making enough money to survive. Lois and I discussed the possibility of offering to help with the expenses of a burial plot elsewhere and a marker, but decided that the risk of offending her fierce pride was too great.

And so, following the hearse and a car full of "security officers" from the prison, we drove down that narrow, dusty lane between the prison and an irrigation canal, the four of us, and stood beside the grave site, knowing it would eventually be covered with a small concrete marker identified by a license plate with an inmate number on it. I wondered if the security officers were there to make sure the body of Paul Ashley, even after his hideous mutilation and an autopsy, didn't rise up from the coffin and escape. Certainly they were not there to show their respect. They had none.

I said to myself that I represented all those men inside who would be at the graveside if they could. The next week, when I went into the workshop, one of the men said, "Your wife had on a yellow hat." He was right. They must have had someone stationed either very high in the prison to see over the perimeter wall, or someone outside the wall. So at least one of them witnessed and reported to the others on the sad interment of the man who had been Charles Schmid but had become Paul David Ashley.

There was never much doubt about who murdered Paul David Ashley. The question was "why?" Different people have given different answers, and the puzzle has really never been solved, although some hold one theory or another with great certainty. All of the theories involve his past in one way or another.

I have a copy of the prison newspaper, La Roca, dated June 1974, a couple of weeks before Tom Cobb and I began the creative writing workshop at Florence. In it is a photograph of eighteen inmates posed for the camera, members of a "club" called the High Wall Jammers whose purpose, the accompanying article says, is "to set up and organize a custom bike club and repair course inside the prison." They are working with the administration to do this. "Their main interest is motorcycle mechanics and 'custom' motorcycle (Chopper) building." Prominent on the front row with his shirt off is "Smitty." At the end of that row, sitting cross-legged and wearing a hat and dark glasses so that very little of his face is showing, is "Sneaky Pete." The caption under the photo lists "Dirty Dan" among "Brothers not shown here." All the brothers are white. Four of them—Big John, Mouse, Spider, and Smitty—would become members of the creative writing workshop. Looking back from this vantage point, one can see in this photo the beginnings of the Aryan Brotherhood in the Florence prison, although the legitimate aims of this group will be co-opted and diverted by later leadership. It was an unstable brotherhood as it morphed its way toward becoming one faction of a full-fledged and powerful gang. Some of its original members stayed with it as it grew and found brutal leaders in such men as "Stretch" and "Red Dog," resulting in many of the fourteen murders committed inside the prison between 1976 and 1977. Some of its original members removed themselves from it early on or were murdered or got out of prison and didn't look back.

One theory of the death of Paul David Ashley is that he was in the process of trying to extricate himself from this group but that he knew too much about their plans and activities. One theory is that he had been involved in a drug deal with other members of the group and had ripped them off. One theory is that the members of this group believed he had become a snitch in order to get outside-trustee status. One theory is that "Sneaky Pete" and "Dirty Dan" were hired by someone on the outside, someone related to one or more of the girls Charles had been convicted of killing. For a time, for a rather long time, I believed that, whoever killed him, I was responsible for his death.

Several members of the press evidently accepted the "snitch" theory, assuming that he had traded information on some of the High Wall Jammers for his relocation to the trustee area and his job working with the dogs. It is true that Warden Cardwell made such deals with inmates. I don't believe Paul was a snitch, but the question is whether or not members of the High Wall Jammers thought he was.

On the other hand, most of the inmates who were at Florence at the time believed that the attack was an outside, paid-for job, and they even said that "Sneaky Pete" and "Dirty Dan" were paid $20,000 to do it. Today, if one asks the inmates or former inmates who were in Florence at the time, this is what they believe. To them, the presence of the manufactured knife is convincing proof that somebody on the outside wanted to have Paul murdered, and that person provided one of the weapons.

I did not remember ever having met either "Sneaky Pete" or "Dirty Dan," although I might have passed them on the yard without knowing who they were. But I was not quite finished with "Sneaky Pete" yet. Months later, after the two of them were convicted of the murder of Paul Ashley and their life sentences were extended (on paper), they were returned to the main yard of the prison. One Saturday morning, while members of the workshop were sitting around the long table in the classroom discussing somebody's work, the door at the end of the room toward which I was facing opened and a small, dark-haired young man entered. He moved without making a sound, catlike. As he came slowly forward toward the table at the end of which I was sitting, someone near me whispered "Sneaky Pete." My adrenaline went crazy, but I managed to keep talking, although I doubt that what I said made much sense. The newcomer walked silently the length of the table and circled behind me. I was terrified but determined not to turn around. By watching the faces of the men in front of me, I could gauge his progress. He stood behind me for a couple of minutes that seemed like hours, and then slowly made a complete circuit of the table and left the room, never making a sound.

"What was that about," I asked, visibly shaken.

"He was just checking you out," one of the men said. "He wouldn't do anything in front of all of us. It's not his style."

"But why would he want to check me out?"

"He knows you were a friend of Paul's. He wants to see how you react to him. If you're a threat to him. If you're going to put out a contract on him."

"How did I do?"

"You did good. He thought he would throw you into a panic, but you simply ignored him. It was great to watch."

"Well, it sure as hell wasn't great for me."

I never saw "Sneaky Pete" again.

Long before that chilling little incident, on the Saturday after Paul's death, I had decided what I had to do. I reasoned that the Charles Schmid I had first encountered on death row was a self-preservation machine. He had well-developed antennae for danger. Later he became more trusting, less suspicious, more open to real affection and friendship. He learned to love and trust. He claimed that I was responsible for the changes he had gone through. He let down his guard. He lost his antennae for danger. The result was butchery. I was to blame, and I wasn't fit to go on working with people in prison. My feelings were strengthened by the fact that, when Katharine gave me Paul's books, I discovered his copy of my first chapbook, *Journal of Return*, had bloodstains on one of the inside pages. He must have been reading it when he was attacked. In a letter he had said, "Just finished re-reading 'Journal' . . . god, it's so damn breathtaking. My heart thumps wildly when I read it. So damn good. Polished and elegant . . . makes me proud and envious at the same time . . . if I just had one good poem." I could imagine him sitting with his guard down, reading my book, when he should have been alert to danger.

I met with the men in the workshop that Saturday after Paul's funeral and told them it was the last meeting we would have. If they still had some of the books I had brought in, they could keep them. I told them I was probably responsible for Paul's death. I had played God, and a man who was dear to me was dead because of it. I didn't deserve their respect or attention and I wouldn't trouble them any further. I would stop meddling in the affairs of others. I wished them well. I hoped for each of them the greatest success in the future. When I rose to go, someone took hold of my arm, gently, and sat me back down.

They had something to say to me. They too were suffering from Paul's death. They too had seen the transition and had come to have great affection for a man they once did not trust and considered a monster. Yes, it was true that he had suffered horribly and died, but he had died as a whole, caring, feeling human being, something he had not been earlier. He had had at least one year, probably more, during which he was a whole man, not a psychological cripple. That year was, for him, worth all the years he might have lived as "Smitty."

I bowed my head and listened to them as they told me, one by one, that I could not afford guilt because it was a luxury I did not deserve. And who knew better than they did about guilt? I must go on with the workshop. Paul would have been outraged to think that he had caused me to give up the workshop for which he and J. Charles Green had given so much energy to get started. The men spoke for almost a half hour. I listened. I think I cried a little. I think some of them did too, but we had learned to mourn our losses together and without shame. I was mourning for the loss of my own innocence as well as for the loss of Paul. They, who had in most cases blown their innocence at a younger age, knew it.

Then one of them came up with my line, the way I often started the workshop: "We have work to go over. Let's do it." And we did. Since then, although I suffer from self-doubt and the knowledge that I often fail with inmates when I should succeed, I have never played God. I have come to realize, however, that the changes I had seen in Charles/Paul were caused by inner rather than outer forces, possibly hormones or some changes in the body. I have read that most young "sociopaths," if they survive, undergo such changes when they reach a certain age. Sometimes this change occurs in their thirties, sometimes in their forties. The fact that I happened to appear on the scene about the time Charles reached the right age was simply a coincidence. I had nothing to do with the basic changes that took place in him, although I had helped direct the new impulses and sensitivities he felt. I had watched the birth of a new person, a person who was whole rather than severely damaged; and I had foolishly believed, in my vanity, that I was responsible for his birth.

He was born Charles Schmid, but when he died he was Paul Ashley. Because Charles Schmid was a monster and Paul Ashley was not, his journey was long and hard. Few have come such a distance. Paul Ashley died for the sins of Charles Schmid, although we don't know for which sins. We know who killed him, but we don't know why. Charles Schmid was a child vigorously rejected by his birth mother and loved fiercely by his adoptive mother, but he suffered from the inability to love. Paul Ashley was born into the realm of poetry, into the beauty and power of language, and he flourished there all his short life.

Things were happening fast at the Florence prison between 1975 and 1977. The riot must have happened in the spring of 1976. I wish I had kept a better record of the dates, but I was very busy and the idea of writing about what I was living never occurred to me. It's hard to describe the time I was having in the prison, but it was something most of us university professor types don't get to experience. It was painful, it was wild, it made no sense, it was exhausting, it was depressing, it was exciting, it was beautiful, it was horrifying, it was more than I could handle. I stumbled through it as if I knew what I was doing, and I didn't. It changed my view of prison, of people, and of myself. It shaped my life and bent it, the way the wind on the coast shapes and bends trees. I just tried to hang on.

The workshop had become a group of inmates bonded into a unit, writing like mad and, in many cases, getting published. I think they were pretty sure the riot was going to happen, but they didn't know exactly when. They also knew, I suspect, that the riot would begin as a quarrel between the Black Brotherhood and the Mexican Mafia, but that it would probably be co-opted by the emerging Aryans who would bend it to their own purposes, which usually involved extortion and paying off old scores.

One afternoon we were all sitting around the long table in the bare classroom with no windows and only one metal door. We were discussing somebody's poem. Looking back, I can see all the signs I was unaware of then. The group that met me and walked across the yard with me had been a little larger than usual, but I thought nothing of it. There was some kind of tension, some kind of excitement in the air, but the men were often excited over their work. We went to work as usual, discussing the poems and prose pieces on the worksheets for that week. After a while I heard something like a car backfiring in the distance. It didn't register as anything unusual. But the men in the workshop knew exactly what it was—a zip gun. In those facilities that have certain kinds of industries, such as the license plate factory at Florence, inmates have access to everything they need to produce a gun that has sufficient power to be lethal, although such a gun usually lacks the precision of a factory-made gun. They work best at close range.

What happened next was almost like a ballet, and it happened so fast I didn't have time to get up out of my chair before it was accomplished. The men must have discussed this possibility among themselves earlier and arrived at a plan. I was the only one they hadn't let in on the plan. Everyone in the room knew exactly what to do—everyone except me—and I just sat there like an idiot with my mouth open. The only sound in the room was the scraping of chair legs on the concrete floor as the men pushed their chairs back from the table. Four of them went quickly to the door, a metal door with a brass bar on the inside, a bar that needed to be pushed down to open the door. Two held the bar up so the door could not be opened. The other two stood ready to help them if needed. The rest of the men simply gathered closer to where I was sitting, almost surrounding me and assuring me that I was safe. It all happened in seconds, before I was aware of what I was safe from.

The noise outside increased. We could hear several more zip guns and shouting in the distance. The shouting grew louder. Evidently the rioters were moving in our direction. Somebody tried the door. All four men held the bar. Somebody pounded on the door, hard and fast. The muffled sounds of shouting and talking increased. Then we heard the louder retorts of regular guns and the sounds of men running in all directions. Confused shouting. More pounding on the door. Something being said over a bullhorn at a distance, but we couldn't understand the words. Then an unnerving loud crash on the door. Everyone jumped. "Tear gas canister," somebody said. We could smell tear gas very faintly. After about twenty minutes the noise faded somewhat, as if most of the rioters were moving on somewhere. Again somebody tried to open the door, cursing and pounding on it, then evidently went away.

The man whose poem we had been discussing when the noise began said, "Let's get back to work," and we did. For the next two hours we sat around the table and, at first, discussed the men's work. Four men stayed on the door at all times, taking turns. It was obvious to me that I was in very good hands. When we ran out of work to discuss, we talked literary theory, and when we ran out of literary theory, we told jokes, some of which, I have to admit, were scurrilous.

After more than an hour, when I asked, "How long do you think this is going to last?" the answer was, "Can't tell. Depends on the cops. I'll bet the sonsabitches forgot you're in here. But they sure as hell haven't forgot we're in here. Shouldn't be too much longer. At the first sign of trouble the cowboys cut and run. They don't come back until things have quieted down and they can get on all their bullet-proof gear and masks and assault weapons. But it's pretty quiet out there now, so they should be coming around before long. Then we'll all be in lockdown for a long time. No chow tonight. I hope everybody ate a big breakfast. In here, you gotta eat it when you can get it. Even SOS is better than nothing."

One of men picked up a gallon butt can from the table, carried it to the far corner of the room, turned his back, and urinated into it noisily. When he returned to the table he said, "We may be here a long time, but at least we've got a pisser in the back. Don't be shy, girls."

It turned out to be a short riot, a mini-riot, and really only a rehearsal for the real thing that was to come the following year. After about two hours a guard pounded on the door and identified himself. Very cautiously the men opened the door a crack to make sure who it was. Then three guards in full riot gear ordered everybody out. I was quickly escorted to the left through the little gate into the main yard. The men in the workshop were herded to the right around the corner of the building. I didn't have a chance to say "thank you."

I found out later what happened to them that night. Some of the dormitories had been damaged in the riot, so the men who lived in the "education yard" spent the night outside on the ground. This also gave the prison authorities an opportunity to make a thorough search of the dormitories, looking for hidden weapons or drugs. The entire prison was locked down for several days. No guards had been hurt in the riot. I was told later that about twenty inmates were injured, two seriously. The fact that the riot occurred while I was on the yard was coincidental. The men in the workshop had not wanted to be involved, and they had not wanted any of the rioters to see me and get any ideas about hostages. I had never been in any real danger, thanks to the members of the workshop, and as far as I know none of them were ever rewarded or commended in any way for what they did that day. However, it was extremely hard for me to be critical of their work afterward.

The riot was only one indication that the prison was growing increasingly violent as the gangs fought one another for power, influence, and booty. Three months after the murder of Paul Ashley, Larry, the inmate Warden Cardwell had installed in an office-trailer in the main yard, was shot six times in front of hundreds of witnesses. According to the book *Murder Unpunished* by Thornton Price, Larry had been the prison's unofficial banker. He had a sweet racket going with a partner on the outside. Friends or family members of an inmate would deposit money with Larry's partner, or those inmates who were veterans and were getting GI money when they took college classes would have these GI checks deposited with Larry's partner. Larry would then arrange for the cash to be smuggled in by a guard or a visitor. Inmates were not allowed to have cash, and cash, on the prison yard, was worth at least twice its value on the street. For this service, Larry charged 20 percent. His rate was considered exorbitant, and many of the inmates were bitter about it, but one of them, a tall, gangly man called "Stretch," took it upon himself to do something about it. Stretch was ambitious, and as the Aryan Brotherhood was forming, he wanted to be its headman and effectively run the prison. His daring attack on the much-disliked Larry earned him that spot, and although his sentence was extended, it didn't matter to him because he was already serving a life sentence without the possibility of parole. Such additional sentences, like the ones given to "Sneaky Pete" and "Dirty Dan" for the killing of Paul Ashley, are called "paper" sentences, since they exist only on paper and do not affect the actual length of time a "lifer" is serving.

By late 1975, if Warden Cardwell didn't know, as he claimed, that the prison was being run by the gangs, he was blind. Even volunteers like me could see it. From the outside, it appeared that the administration was running the prison. From the inside it was obvious that a few inmate despots, the generals who commanded the various gangs, were running the prison while constantly shifting allegiances and targets. To be targeted by such a gang leader was, in most cases, to be a dead man, although Larry survived in spite of six bullet wounds.

Somehow, surrounded by fear and the constant threat that any one of its members might run afoul of one of the gangs, the workshop continued to roll and even gain momentum. Before his death, J. Charles Green had submitted a manuscript of poems to Joe Bruchac, editor of Greenfield Review Press, and Bruchac had agreed to publish it as a chapbook. When that book came out in 1975, after the agonizing death of J. Charles Green and the murder of Paul Ashley, it was a sad victory for us. Its title was *First Words*—Charles Green's last words and the first book to come out of the workshop, which now had two empty seats at the long table. We were functioning in a world of bitter loss and irony, but we were functioning.

This atmosphere was supplanted by something more cheerful when, to my astonishment, Stephen Dugan, who first arrived in the workshop with a tennis racket, began to publish like an old pro. Underneath the Irish blarney was solid talent and strong ambition. His first book of poetry, *Letters for My Son*, was published in both paper and cloth editions in 1975 by one of the most prestigious small presses in the country, Unicorn Press in North Carolina. We were still celebrating that in November when he won first prize for poetry in the PEN's annual writing contest for prison inmates. The winning poem displays the remarkable restraint and understated dignity in his poetry that critics have commented on ever since.

I feel that Stephen Dugan's early poetry is of real significance in the history of poetry coming out of modern American prisons, and primarily because it isn't "prison poetry." He avoided the mawkish, the sentimental, the self-pitying, and the highly subjective lyric that has traditionally been written by most prison inmates. (There have been noted exceptions to this in the work of a handful of political and minority prisoners.) As a writer in prison, Stephen also seemed to do everything first. He adopted a quiet, contemplative tone from models like William Stafford and James Wright. He learned absolute control of diction and tone. He learned to discipline his emotion and marshal it as needed. Several other members of the workshop learned from him and followed his lead.

The same year Stephen won first prize in the PEN contest, the entire Arizona creative writing workshop won a special award from PEN for the quality and quantity of their entries in the contest. We had been noticed by an international organization, and noticed big. In spite of the killings, in spite of the fear, morale in the workshop was high.

Then Stephen achieved another first, and for the National Endowment for the Arts in Washington DC the roof fell in. Stephen was awarded a National Endowment for the Arts Writer's Fellowship, the first such award ever given to a prison inmate. The amount was $6000, worth much more in 1977 than that amount would be today. These awards are given to writers on the basis of work already done, and there are no strings.

I was on a reading tour, and as I checked into a downtown hotel in Pittsburgh, the desk clerk handed me a message that was waiting for me. "Call Leonard Randolph, N.E.A. Urgent," and a phone number. I didn't know Leonard Randolph, but I knew he was the director of the Literature Program of the National Endowment for the Arts. I'm not sure how he tracked me down at that hotel. Perhaps he had talked to my wife, Lois, who was then the director of the University of Arizona Poetry Center in Tucson. When I got him on the phone, he sounded a little cranky, but there was a playful undertone.

"What in the hell are you doing in Pittsburgh? You're supposed to be in Arizona. Who's minding the store? I hope you aren't just letting that gang of yours run amok." Leonard had a great sense of humor, and since it was almost 10:00 p.m. in Washington, he might have had a drink or two.

"I'm on a short reading tour," I said. "Only for a week and the

prison is locked down anyway. I can't get in. We had another stabbing."

"We had a little bloodletting around here, too," he said dryly.
"Mostly mine. A kind of firestorm. Somebody complained to a conservative congressman that we gave a Writer's Fellowship, a large
amount of the taxpayers' money, to some felon in Arizona who is
serving time for robbery and forgery of Supreme Court documents.
Seems he altered prison files and almost got a number of men out
before they had served their full sentences. You wouldn't happen to
know who that was, would you?"

"I guess I do. Is there something I can do to help?"

"No. I just wanted to let you know that we are holding the line. The
press or some political types may try to contact you. We are depending on the fact that Stephen's work was chosen on its own merit. The
panel judged blind. They didn't know whose work they were reading,
and they chose his work for a fellowship because it was very good. We
stand behind that."

"And he'll get the money?"

"Absolutely. I wanted you to assure him of that."

"Yes, I will. Thanks for letting me know. It'll mean a lot to the
guys."

"And what in the hell are you doing in Pittsburgh? Doesn't W. C.
Fields have a line like 'all in all, I'd rather be in Philadelphia'?"

"But nobody in Philadelphia invited me."

"Tough! Maybe they found out what you do in Arizona. And tell
that gang of cutthroats you work with that I said, off the record, they
are producing great stuff."

The National Endowment held firm and Stephen got his check,
although I would not permit the money to fall into the hands of the
prison administration. The check was mailed to a friend of his in Tucson, and she put it in the bank to be available for him when he got
out. But Stephen wasn't through astonishing us and the world yet. He
published a chapbook in 1976 and two more books in 1977. He had
become an associate editor of a small press in Austin, Texas, and his
poems were being accepted into some of the best literary journals in

the country. His momentum was contagious to the rest of the men in the workshop. The prison administration permitted journalists into the prison to interview him. His handsome, smiling face began to appear in newspapers and literary journals. He rode the crest, affable as always, charming as always. The dark years of Stephen's domination by drugs and alcohol had not yet come. They would be waiting for him when he was released from prison. His fellowship money would not last very long.

By 1977, J. Charles Green and Paul Ashley were dead, Jimmy Santiago Baca was struggling alone in lockup, sending his poems to me, suffering from my relentless criticism and not yet publishing, and Stephen Dugan was already famous. The book by Paul Ashley that Baleen Press had planned to publish, *The Unfinished Man*, was never to be published. It must have been late in 1975 or early 1976 that Ramona Weeks, one of the editors of Baleen Press contacted me. She was distraught. She had received a threat or threats—I don't know whether they were phone calls or came through a third party—that if she published Paul's book, she would be killed. Ramona was a single mother raising her teenage son. She had decided that the threat was too real. I understood. I filed the manuscript of *The Unfinished Man*, trying to remember which of us had decided on that now dreadfully ironic title, Paul or me. I felt that the same person (or persons) responsible for Paul's butchery was now threatening Ramona. She had made the right decision.

Before Ramona decided not to publish Paul's book of poetry, I had asked W. S. Merwin if he would write an introduction to it, fully aware of how difficult that task would be. After I had given him a copy of the manuscript, Merwin did write a two-page introduction. It is a remarkable document. As one would expect, since it comes from one of the greatest contemporary American poets, it is beautifully written and sensitive to all the peculiar and tragic circumstances out of which the poems were produced: a murdered poet who was himself a murderer. Merwin asks that the reader come to the poems first as poems, and warns that "the particular circumstances behind Paul Ashley's writings might cloud judgment of them as poems." The poems, he says, judge us "concerning our view of the nature and value of humanity, its capacities for regeneration." The introduction is one more brave and generous gesture from the pen of a brave and generous man.

In addition to the many poems and prose pieces by men in the workshop published in magazines in 1977, there was one other chapbook whose title contained still more irony, at least from my point of view, a point of view which I realized was becoming increasingly twisted. Greg Barker was one of the outstanding writers in the group. I don't remember how he made contact with Desert First Works press in Tucson. That press had been established by two wonderful Tucson women, Ann Haralambie and Sonia Young, to publish chapbooks by Arizona poets of marked ability. They had decided to publish the poetry of Greg Barker in a chapbook titled *Deliverance*.

The Saturday morning after *Deliverance* was published, I came into the prison with a large box containing many copies of Greg's book. When I got to the workshop, lugging the box of books for Greg, he wasn't there and nobody seemed to know where he was, although there was a kind of awkwardness I couldn't account for. The men seemed to be pleased that Greg had published but somehow embarrassed about my attempt to deliver the books to him. I couldn't make heads or tails of it. All I could do was carry the books back out.

Later that week I learned that I had probably passed Greg on my way in. At about the time I was coming in, he was going out, hidden in the garbage truck. I was delivering copies of his book to him while he was seeking a different kind of deliverance buried under the garbage in a truck leaving the prison. I can't remember how long it was before he was recaptured. Several months, I think. There was a reason for that escape beyond the desire to get out of prison. Sometimes, during those years at Florence, escaping was the only way to stay alive.

11

In 1977, in the Florence prison, seven inmates were murdered and twenty-four were stabbed. It appeared to me that the warden's refusal to acknowledge that gang leaders were running the prison resulted in more and more attacks. The image that the men in the workshop came up with most often was a tin can, getting hotter and hotter, and they were in it. Racial and gang problems were out of control. The warden seemed to play one gang against the other while pretending to the outside world that none of them existed.

Recently I was talking to an old friend who was an inmate at Florence in those days. He said, "Sometimes people tell me about their trouble and I say, 'Trouble? Don't bother me with your trouble. You don't know what trouble is. Trouble is when they rack [open] your cell door and you go to chow and you don't know if you'll be coming back.'" That pretty much describes what life was like in the Arizona State Prison at Florence in 1977 under Warden Harold Cardwell. Those who have recorded this out-of-control era usually concentrate on 1977, but for us it had begun in 1975 with the murder of Paul Ashley. It seemed as if it would never let up.

At some point in 1976, the head of the Mexican Mafia issued an order. Any Chicano who remained in the creative writing workshop, where they would be working closely with men of other races and ethnic backgrounds, would be subject to severe, possibly deadly reprisal. I didn't know about this order, but one Saturday I arrived to find all but one of the Chicanos in the workshop missing. Even then I thought it might be a coincidence, since Ray Arvizu remained. "Little Ray," we called him, sweet, shy, mostly a pair of large, scared eyes in a round, juvenile face. He was Greg Barker's brother-in-law, the younger brother of Greg's Hispanic wife. Greg, who was later to escape in the garbage truck, was a leader in the workshop. He was small and wiry but quick and prison-wise and a very talented poet. Ray and Greg were as close as brothers could be, although Ray was Mexican and Greg was Anglo. Ray stayed in the workshop because Greg was in it. Perhaps he thought Greg could protect him.

Had I known about the Mexican Mafia's policy, I would have insisted that Ray leave the workshop for his own safety. I didn't find out about that policy until it was too late. They caught little Ray Arvizu in a stairwell and stabbed him to death. He struggled, but he was small and they were many.

Somehow, I cannot believe Ray was killed simply because he was the only Chicano who refused to leave the workshop. It is possible that the main reasons for Ray's murder lay elsewhere and that the real target was Greg. Because of their closeness, it might have been felt that if one were killed, both would have to be. I want to believe this because I can't bear to believe that little Ray was murdered because he insisted on staying in the workshop. I am sure, however, that as soon as Ray was murdered, Greg knew his life was in immediate danger. His escape, just as his chapbook was published, was an act of desperation to save his own life, and it was successful. It was, as his book was titled, "deliverance." The dedication of that book reads: "For Ray, Cuñado, un deseo cariñoso Dell fondo de mi corazón: y que en donde estes horita tengas, dicha y felizidad que no encontrastes en esta bida terrestre . . ."

The spelling and general construction suggests that Greg spoke Spanish but didn't read it much. As far as I can translate it, it reads: "For Ray, brother-in-law, a loving wish from the bottom of my heart: that wherever you are doing your time you have the happiness and good luck that you never found in this earthly life."

Ray's murder rocked us, and we hoped against hope that Greg could stay out long enough to survive. The grapevine had it that he was a dead man if he came back. If he had attempted vengeance for the murder of Ray, I didn't know about it, but it was certainly possible, considering how he felt about Ray. By now, however, violent death had become so much a part of our lives that we did not react with the intensity we once had. I recognized this in myself. *My God,* I thought. *What's happening to me? Each time it's easier. Each death is less shocking. I come in each week and take the roll as casually as I would in a university classroom, fully aware that if someone is missing, the chances are he was butchered during the preceding week. This place, this mad horror of a place, is destroying something precious in all of us.*

Our next loss in the workshop came on January 4, 1977, the year that set a record in the history of the Florence prison for violence and murder. It was undoubtedly a hired killing paid for from the outside, but several members of the prison administration, including Warden Cardwell, were suspected of collusion. In his book *Murder Unpunished*, the lawyer Thornton Price, who represented a gang member accused of another murder at Florence in 1977, describes the "threads and tentacles spreading in all directions into the corrupt culture of Arizona State Prison, with the criminals and crimes intertwined. One crime cannot be understood without understanding another; one feud cannot be understood without understanding another. One gang's actions cause another's reaction. One hit leads to the next until each act of violence seems to propagate its successor in a cycle without end."

It's easy, in hindsight, to show Cardwell's pathetic egocentrism that permitted him to become the dupe of the most clever and most dangerous con men in the prison, like Gary Tison, who was known to be Cardwell's "pet." The warden seemed to react to the flattery of these men by giving them what they wanted, and he sometimes denied even protection to those who would not fawn on him, no matter how severely they were threatened, like Tony Serra. Looking back, I could understand this. Cardwell was playing God, and I doubt that he was ever able to realize it. I was able to see what he was doing since I, too, had been guilty of it. That pathetic need to be flattered, to be needed, even to be loved was motivating the hard-nosed, hard-swearing, tough, former marine prison warden just as it had motivated the do-gooder poet. We were both guilty. There were also the external pressures on him. I don't know how severely some of the more corrupt pressures, political and private, influenced him, but there are indications they did, especially in the case of Tony Serra.

Tony was a charming, good-looking Italian who could have lived next door to anybody in an affluent suburb, and his neighbors would have been pleased to have him. Before Tony joined us, there had been no white-collar criminals in the workshop that I was aware of, although I didn't know what everybody was in for. It was a standard joke in the workshop that nobody needed to protest his innocence since I knew they were all totally innocent and pure as the driven snow. In fact, nobody in the whole damned joint had ever committed a crime, I said, with mock seriousness. Most of the members were in for murder or drug-related crimes of burglary or robbery, and they made no attempt to hide it, especially after I gave them the "pure as the driven snow" speech, which they found wildly amusing. No one appreciates irony as much as writers in prison, who live with it constantly.

Tony was sophisticated, sharp, smooth, and intelligent. He was also very quiet. I can't remember much about his writing except that it was prose and indicated that he was literate and educated. He was serving an eight-to-ten-year sentence for land fraud. Tony had been the sales manager for the Great Southwest Land and Cattle Company, a company that, among other crooked dealings, would sell the same lot to different unsuspecting easterners again and again, and then sell the mortgages to different banks. It was part of the empire of Ned Warren, who was called "the godfather of land swindlers" by the Arizona Republic on January 4, 1977, the day Tony was killed. Warren was said to be connected with the Mafia, and the tentacles of his organization reached into the office of the Maricopa County attorney's office, and possibly included Harold Cardwell in some way. The Phoenix investigative reporter, Don Bolles, who was investigating the activities of organized crime in Arizona, and particularly the activities of Ned Warren, was murdered by means of a car bomb.

In August of 1976, while serving his time in the Arizona State Prison at Florence, Tony had been interviewed by two members of right-wing Republican congressman John Conlan's political campaign organization, who later broke their promise and allowed the interview to be published in the Arizona Republic because it implicated Conlan's chief political rival, Congressman Sam Steiger, verifying rumors that had linked Steiger to Ned Warren's activities. Tony had also said he knew where incriminating documents that had disappeared from the district attorney's office were buried in the desert.

Once the interview was published, Tony was as good as dead unless he could get transferred or placed in protective custody. Warden Cardwell and the director of the Department of Corrections, John Moran, came to see him and threatened him, according to a letter by Serra, that he had better keep his mouth shut. Tony obviously felt that both Moran and Cardwell were affiliated politically with Senator Steiger. As it turned out, Steiger and Cardwell were friends. Tony pleaded with Cardwell to be transferred or placed in protective custody because he feared he would be killed. Cardwell refused.

At a meeting of the workshop in December, Tony asked me if I could deliver a letter to his wife. He said it was urgent. At that time, I did not know what was going on in his life, although I had some vague idea. I told him I could not deliver a letter. Volunteers were expressly forbidden to carry letters out of the prison or into the prison. It would jeopardize the entire program if I carried a letter to his wife. "All the letter is," he said, "is asking her to come visit me this coming weekend. She had planned to skip this weekend because of other commitments. It's important that she come and bring the children. I may be . . . going away."

"You mean you're expecting to be transferred?"

"Something like that. Well, if you can't carry a letter, can you simply go by and tell her to come visit me next weekend, that it's important. And ask her to bring the children."

I couldn't see how this would break any rules. He wrote down the Tucson address for me, and I promised I would stop on my way home that afternoon and deliver the message. I remember that quick stop, although I don't remember the house except that it was in an upper-middle-class neighborhood in Tucson. I rang the bell. A handsome woman, willowy and well groomed, opened the door, soon to be joined by two small children who peered at me as children do at a stranger on their doorstep.

"My name is Richard Shelton. I teach in the prison at Florence. I'm sorry to intrude but I have a message from Tony."

Her eyes grew wider, and there was an intake of breath. "You've seen him?"

"Yes. This morning. He's in my workshop."

She was obviously frightened by this strange redhead in cowboy hat and boots who appeared at her door. She was trying to decide whether to trust me. She stood on one foot and then the other, the door not even half open.

"I teach the creative writing workshop."

"Oh," she said, "creative writing. Yes. He's told me about it."

"He asked me to tell you that it's important for you and the children to come visit him next weekend in spite of your other plans. He says he thinks he might be transferred if you wait till the following weekend. I just wanted to tell you. He says it's important."

"Yes," she said, looking like an animal caught in a trap. Her thin hand was a claw around the edge of the half-opened door. I didn't understand why then, but she looked at me as if I had just shot her and she was going to slide down the door and die at the feet of her children. "We will go. Thank you."

I fled to the safety of my pickup and got out of there, shaken, not knowing why.

Later in December Tony was attacked while he sat on the toilet by a man with a lead pipe, but he was able to fight off the assailant, whom Tony refused to identify. He was treated at the prison infirmary and released into the general prison population. Again he requested protective custody or transfer, and his requests were refused by Warden Cardwell. On January 3 Tony was attacked in the license plate factory by at least four men. He was stabbed fifteen times and beaten with a length of pipe. He put up a tremendous battle, pulling out whole handfuls of his assailants' hair. Finally, when he was subdued, they drilled through his forehead with an electric drill.

No one was ever punished for this murder. At the investigation that followed, it was felt by many that Cardwell was to blame. Gary Tison, who would become a national terror in 1978 when he escaped and rampaged through the West with his sons and another inmate, killing as he went, was a prime suspect. Tison was the favored and favorite inmate of Warden Cardwell, whom Tison flattered constantly.

At some point in 1976 Gary Tison had interviewed me in front of a television camera for the prison's closed-circuit TV. I remember him as being urbane and charming, and having his fingers in many pies, but even then he had a grisly reputation. He had visited the workshop once, and I was relieved when he said he was too busy to join it.

After Cardwell was moved to the Department of Transportation and after the governor fired him from that position, he returned to his native Ohio and accepted a position with the Ohio prison system. People like Cardwell, once they get into corrections, usually find a way to stay. It is their natural element. They swim through its murky waters like sharks at play. I don't know what such people would do if there were no prison industry to absorb them, but on the other hand, perhaps most of them would not exist if there were no prison industry to produce them.

In 1976 and 1977 there were often weeks when I couldn't go in because the prison was under lockdown because of strikes or violence. I would drive to Florence only to be turned away. No one would call me in Tucson to tell me the prison was locked down, and when I tried to call early in the morning before setting out, I couldn't seem to reach anybody who could answer my question. One winter morning I waited in the rain for almost an hour before someone bothered to tell me that the prison was locked down.

As I cursed and stamped outside the prison gate while the cold rain ran down the back of my neck, I was cursing myself for a fool as much as anything else. *How could anyone with an ounce of self-respect allow himself to be treated so badly by a prison staff made up largely of cretins?* I asked myself again and again, and each time I came up with the same answer: nineteen men who had names and faces and personalities, no two alike, who were in an insane place and trying desperately to maintain their sanity by means of writing. Men who were funny, sad, sometimes obscene, sensitive to criticism, sometimes courageous, often scared, eager to improve their writing, generally intelligent, often badly educated, trying to stay alive in a very dangerous place. Men who had told me that for two to three hours each week they could be free. For those hours, if the workshop met, they could treat one another with respect and affection, regardless of their color or background. For those hours they could discuss things that were very dear to them without fear of being ridiculed or ignored. And if I couldn't get in, the workshop couldn't meet. It was as simple as that. They would have no freedom that week.

In spite of the terror I saw in those men's eyes each week, something good happened in 1977 that helped to solidify the workshop and define it. It also gave us hope for the future. A graduate student in the Master of Fine Arts program in creative writing at the university, the program I taught in and had helped to found almost a decade earlier, had started up his own press. His name was James Hepworth, and he named the press Blue Moon Press. One of the first books Jim wanted to publish was an anthology of poetry of the men in the workshop. He asked Stephen Dugan to edit it, and I guess it was Stephen who gave it the title *Do Not Go Gentle* from the title and opening line of a poem by Dylan Thomas, "Do not go gentle into that good night, . . . Rage, rage against the dying of the light." Maybe it's just me, but I see the titles of all the books that came out of the workshop during those years as eerily ironic or prophetic, much more than any of us realized at the time.

Certainly Greg Barker's *Deliverance* couldn't have been more on target; Greg was literally delivered out of the prison in the garbage truck long enough to survive. Charles Schmid/Paul Ashley's *Unfinished Man* is enough to make anybody think about prophecy; he couldn't have known how short his life would be, although I'm sure he recognized that it might not be very long. The title of Stephen Dugan's *Rust* suggests the relentless wearing down of the spirit as the years go by for someone in prison. In it there is a passage in which he looks under his bunk and finds mushrooms growing. Stephen's *Soon It Will Be Morning* suggests an inmate's restless, chafing spirit and his waiting for an awakening into a real life in the free world, which Stephen eventually achieved. Then, as the murders were increasing all around them, and the empty chairs in the workshop were ever more apparent, somebody come up with a title from a Welsh poet most of them had never heard of until they became members of the workshop. *Do Not Go Gentle.* As far as I could tell, none of those who had gone had gone gentle. They fought for life against a corrupt system that would not permit them to live. Paul Ashley's and Tony Serra's struggles against their attackers had been monumental. According to those nearby, J. Charles Green's struggles against his restraints as he was dying were fierce. I don't know how hard Ray Arvizu struggled. The information I got suggested that he didn't have much of a chance to struggle.

So the anthology of poetry by men who had been in the Florence workshop between 1974 and 1977 was published under the title *Do Not Go Gentle.* It included the work of sixteen men, two of whom were dead, while several others, at the time of publication, were out of prison. As an editor, Stephen Dugan was generous. The work is uneven but filled with energy and often rising to brilliance. It includes three very early poems by Jimmy Santiago Baca that clearly indicate the energy of his language and his brilliance with images: "crystal rafters of sunrise / float as they do in your eyes." It includes, as most anthologies do, the work of several poets who have never been heard of since, not a bad thing in this case since they stayed out of prison and led productive, nonliterary lives.

It includes a whole batch of beautiful, dark, and troubling lyrics by Michael Martin, our self-appointed janitor. Michael did not go on to publish in spite of his talent, which I feel was prodigious. After his release from prison he married Maria, who became one of my favorite students at the university, and I was "a member of the wedding." Michael and his wife lived in Tucson for a while, and he was sometimes mistaken for my son because he too was a red head with freckles. I was always proud when that mistake occurred. Maria died of cancer, and Michael Martin is . . . I don't know where Michael is. I hear rumors that he is lost, drifting through a half-life of drug addiction, jails, and self-torture. His haunted spirit is apparent in those early poems. They are truly prophetic of what his life would become. He might have been one of America's leading poets. I think he had the ability. I failed him. It's one of my greatest failures in all thirty years of work with inmates. In a poem called "Looking for Someone," he wrote:

> now my shadow sits on the corner
> and i stand across the street
> without even a shadow
> looking for someone
> anyone
> to fill the emptiness
> despair has breathed deep into me

The anthology *Do Not Go Gentle* was, for a poetry anthology, very successful. It was cited as one of the ten best books of the year by the National Library Association. It was a handsome volume with a photograph on the cover of a lightning strike above the desert. Within the workshop, the anthology did wonderful things for us when we needed them most. It gave us something tangible, something we could touch to prove to ourselves that we were accomplishing things. It was a symbol of our unity, our togetherness. It identified us, and we needed all the identity we could get in a mad world that seemed to be picking off members of the workshop one by one, a world where we had precious little protection from the prison administration and were either ignored or derided by the prison staff.

12

We couldn't have known that we had hit bottom at the end of 1977, and that there was nowhere to go but up. I didn't know there was a bottom to that spiraling nightmare I had blundered into, and the men in the workshop were too busy trying to stay alive to think very far into the future. There was still to be much violence in the prison and, in 1978, the murderous rampage across the southwestern United States of Gary Tison, his sons, and his fellow escapee. But the workshop was spared any more violent losses, and Cardwell got the boot in October of 1978. In June of that year, the governor had appointed Ellis Mac-Dougall, a professor at the University of South Carolina, as director of the Department of Corrections. It took MacDougall almost four months to get rid of Cardwell. The mills grind slowly.

I think of the years 1978 to 1982, the years during which Ellis MacDougall headed the Department of Corrections, as the years when one man, with a small group of supporters, was trying to drag an enormous coach up a hill on a muddy road, with most of the other members of the Department of Corrections as well as a majority of the members of the Arizona State Legislature, hanging on to the rear of the coach, trying to hold it back. Inside the coach, of course, powerless to do anything but shout encouragement to MacDougall and his few supporters, were all the people incarcerated in the Arizona state prison system. Members of the workshop knew they were moving very slowly, but for the first time they knew they were moving in the right direction. Up. Up toward the light and the hope of something besides being demoralized, tortured in one way or another, and often butchered. Up toward the humanity that most of the inmates sensed they had a right to, in spite of their crimes.

Positive things were happening outside the Department of Corrections as well. At least one very positive thing. A woman named

Shelley Cohn became literature director of the Arizona Commission on the Arts in August of 1976. She believed in what the workshop was doing, and she enthusiastically supported my hope that it might be expanded. With Shelley aboard, everything went into high gear. I had never worked with anyone quite like her. She had a combination of charm, energy, and doggedness in the face of opposition that made her the perfect advocate for the workshop, both with the members of the Arizona Commission on the Arts and with a semiliterate prison administration. She had a way of breezing into an antagonistic warden's office, explaining how the commission would foot the bill and the prison would get all the credit, charming the warden's socks off, and breezing out with exactly what we wanted, an expansion of the workshop program. She was a wonder. Again and again she left me in slack-jawed amazement.

Shelley suggested that I apply to the commission for a grant on a much larger scale than I had previously been awarded. This would permit us to expand the program and would provide mileage expenses so that workshop directors could drive to some of the more remote prisons that were springing up in the state. She felt that, given my track record, the commission might approve the grant. She also suggested that I come to the arts commission meeting in Phoenix when the grant request was presented and sit on the sidelines with the observers. I would not be permitted to speak at the meeting unless some member of the commission asked me questions, but if that happened, I might have the chance to make a real pitch. Some of the commission members were conservative, and she thought it would be a good idea for me to be there in case I was given the chance to overcome resistance. Prison was not a very popular issue with the arts commission, especially in light of the news that had been coming out of Florence during the past several years. Why would an arts organization want to pour money into a murder factory? Perhaps, Shelley thought, between the two of us we could give them some valid reasons.

The meeting of the Arizona Commission on the Arts took place in the fall of 1976 and was Shelley's first meeting as a newly appointed staff member. Somebody did ask me a question—I think Shelley saw to that—giving me a chance to speak, and I described the workshop and how important it was to the men in it. Several of the commission members were enthusiastically in favor of the grant. Among them, the lawyer Marvin Cohen was particularly eloquent. There was also strong resistance. One member of the commission was the wife of a judge who had been the recipient of threatening letters from an inmate he had sent to prison. Several of her friends on the board were wavering, not wanting to side against her on this matter, and others were simply undecided. Public funding for arts outreach in prisons, unlike arts outreach in the public schools or communities, was controversial. The commission seemed to be polarized, with Marvin Cohen on one side strongly urging approval and the judge's wife on the other in adamant opposition.

During the discussion I watched Shelley. She was young, vibrant, alive, and absolutely in her element. I could tell that this was what she loved—the struggle, the give and take of heated debate about funding for the arts. None of us knew then that eight years later she would be appointed director of the Arizona Commission on the Arts, a position she was to hold with distinction until her retirement in 2005.

Then, as the verbal tug-of-war at the meeting dragged on, something quite incredible happened. One member of the commission had not spoken throughout the discussion. He sat in silence and with a dignity no one else in the room could begin to match, a formidable presence in his tall black felt hat with a feather, his beautiful jewelry, and his unshakable reserve in the midst of all these chattering white men and woman. He was Charles Loloma, the internationally known Hopi silversmith who had single-handedly revolutionized the art of contemporary Native American jewelry design. He made a fist and began to pound, softly and rhythmically, on the table, while he chanted: "Give him the money! Give him the money! Give him the money!" It was a two-beat chant, with stresses on "give" and the first syllable of "money." "GIVE him the MONey, GIVE him the MONey." Soon several others had joined in the chant, as if it were part of a sacred ceremony. It was one of the most remarkable exhibitions of one man's charisma and power I have ever witnessed. We got the money.

As a result of support from the arts commission, Tom Cobb, who had been my partner in the original Florence workshop and had become a faculty member at Eastern Arizona College, could start a creative writing workshop at the prison conservation camp in Safford and another workshop at the correctional facility at nearby Fort Grant. The Swift Trails Conservation Camp, a small minimum-security prison, provided firefighters for the heavily timbered Pinaleno Mountains, where Mount Graham reaches 10,717 feet. The inmates at Swift Trails were also available for hire in the surrounding communities, especially Safford and Wilcox, where they were employed to help build or renovate buildings, do landscaping and yard maintenance, and act as janitors. I visited this workshop often and later took it over.

While I was directing it we had a funny incident. At least I thought it was funny. One of the young men didn't show up for the workshop, and the others said he was being confined to his quarters as punishment. He had been working as a janitor in the grade school down the road. Seems he was caught *en flagrant* in a broom closet at the school with a very willing young female teacher. The following week he was back in the workshop, strutting a little and enjoying the envious glances of the other men.

The first time I went to Swift Trails Camp I was shocked when the inmates, looking tanned and healthy, walked into the classroom each wearing a long hunting knife on a scabbard hanging from his belt. All my previous prison experience had been in an out-of-control maximum-security prison where knives were the homemade kind called "shanks" and were always concealed unless they were being used on somebody. When the men at Swift Trails explained to me that their knives were part of the equipment they needed to fight fires, I suddenly realized that there was a vast difference between this kind of minimum-security prison, where the men had an important job to do and did it, and what I was used to at Florence, where knives were used only for murder or self-protection.

At Florence, where there was no real security for the individual inmate, many of them carried shanks in order to defend themselves, and having a shank did not necessarily mean a man was a member of a gang or that he was violent. In fact, during those dark years, I think everyone who could obtain or make a shank kept one hidden in his cell or on his body as a means of self-protection. They often wore them strapped to their inner thighs so as to avoid detection when they were being "patted down." Guards who were doing the patting down avoided a man's genital area, and if the shank were strapped high enough on the inner thigh, it would usually go undetected unless the inmate was subjected to a strip search.

Later, when I was working with the men at the Safford Conservation Center with their long knives, it occurred to me that they had a distinct advantage over the men I had been working with for years at Florence. By carrying their knives openly in scabbards on their belts, they didn't have to worry about cutting their testicles off every time they sat down.

I have not been inside the Arizona State Prison at Florence since I met for the last time with the workshop I directed there from 1974 to 1980, although I have stayed in touch with several of the men from that workshop who call, write, or visit me often. We were friends at Florence in the dark days of the seventies. Now we are simply older friends. We share the knowledge of those who didn't make it out of Florence alive. We honor their memories and the memories of our other friends from Florence, now scattered all over the country, in or out of prison. The Florence prison has grown exponentially and become many prisons. I have established writing workshops in thirteen other prison facilities at one time or another, as prisons proliferated in Arizona, but none of them at Florence.

When I try to remember what it was like at Florence, what comes back to me, other than the faces of the men in the workshop, are the sounds and the silences. Florence was a place defined by the almost unbearable noise of confined life, and the prophetic silence of death. I remember both its noise and its silence.

Sometimes at night when I was crossing the deserted main yard, it was so still I could hear coyotes howling in the desert outside the prison, howling as if in pain. Then a guard's laughter would flare like a match flame from the parapet on the wall above, and the silence would return—a listening, waiting kind of silence, expecting to be shattered by a gunshot, a cry, a siren, or the clang of the huge metal gate behind me as I left for the night.

Once I was taken into Cell Block 2. I don't remember why I was taken there or who took me. Perhaps it was a little private tour some member of the administration was giving me. Such things were not unusual in those days, although it does seem that I had a particular destination in mind and that I stopped at a specific cell and talked to a specific inmate, but I have no recollection of which inmate. All I remember is the noise. It was as if I were inside some huge drum being pounded on mercilessly. I was in shock because of the noise that struck me in the face as soon as I walked in, like the 110-degree heat strikes me in the face in August as it bounces off the Tucson sidewalks. I felt assaulted, as if by some huge animal who was pressing against me, sucking all the air out of my lungs and squeezing my head between its terrible paws. I had never before experienced noise like that.

CB 2, as it is called, is a tall, austere building with considerable dignity when seen from the outside. It could house a London bank. The prison folklore says that it was a monastery before the rest of the prison was built around it in 1908–9, but the official history says it was built in 1932. It has good lines and good proportions, with tall windows. I had passed it many times and thought that it looked out of place, neoclassical, surrounded by other nondescript structures. From the outside I could hear a kind of low roar coming from it, but I was completely unprepared for the noise level inside. It is actually a large concrete cage divided into many smaller metal cages. It has three tiers of cells with metal bars across the front of each cell and catwalks running around the upper three levels. Hundreds of televisions and radios were blaring on dozens of different channels and stations. The clang of metal on metal was deafening. Men were shouting to each other in several languages, having to shout to be heard over the din. Several men were trying to play guitars, no two the same song. Toilets were flushing. Men were cursing, laughing, singing. Everything in CB

2 that isn't concrete is metal, except the inmates and their bedding. The sounds ricochet off nearly every surface. There was a metal railing around the catwalks, but not high enough to prevent depressed or despairing inmates from diving off the upper tiers to their deaths on the concrete floor below.

One of the men in the workshop told me about a time when that happened. He said they were marching along the catwalks and down the stairs to go to chow when everything went silent after somebody shouted, "Look! Up there. It's Joey." Then the only sound was the sound of a guard's boots on the metal floor of the catwalk, running toward Joey, who was balanced on the railing along the top tier, his feet dangling in space. Then one clear voice screamed from the other side of the cell block, high and hysterical. It could have been the voice of a woman, but there were no women in the old monastery that day. "Go for it, Joey!" And without a word, he did. Some of the men looked away from the body and the pool of blood spreading out from it on the concrete floor. Others couldn't, and stared as if hypnotized as they were herded past on their way to chow.

III *Moving On*

Today many states are having trouble paying for the incarceration binge they indulged in during the "tough on crime" 1990s. As a result, prisons compete with other social programs, such as the improvement of public schools, for decreasing funds. Prisons, unfortunately, are winning.

—Laura Magnani and Harmon L. Wray, *Beyond Prisons*

13

When I was hired as an instructor in the English department of the University of Arizona in 1960, I was assigned to share an office with an older, experienced professor, probably because they thought I would need oversight and direction, and I did. He left the next year, and I'm sorry I can't remember his name after all these years. He was kindly and avuncular and answered all my questions with great patience. Just as I was about to go teach my first class of freshman English, he patted me on the back and said with the kind of irony so typical of English professors, "Just remember, Dick, you're dealing with the criminal element." I have often wondered if it was irony or prophecy. But I have learned from my experience with inmates that such terms as "the criminal element" are misleading. They suggest the monolithic view of those in prison—that they are all alike. The percentage of minority members and those from backgrounds of poverty is higher than in the free world, but there is as much diversity among those in prison as there is among those on the outside. A program or system that attempts to deal with inmates on anything but an individual basis will fail most of the time.

My work in prison has made it possible for me to get to know, and often know well, hundreds of people I would not have met otherwise, and it has enriched my life beyond my ability to say. Sometimes maybe my life has become a little too rich, but I'm not complaining. If I had it to do over again, I would, and I'd try to do it better. The inmates I have worked with range from an elderly man my wife refers to, quite seriously, as "the most boring man in the world" in spite of the fact that he murdered and chopped into small pieces two members of his family, to a man who murdered thirteen women in a few minutes when he was eighteen years old, a man who later gave his chapbook of poetry the title *You Ain't the Man Your Mama Was*. They include a man who has won the most prestigious award for nature writing offered in this country, the Burroughs Medal, a man of such humility and nobility of spirit that I admire and respect him as I do few others. And a woman who killed two of her abusive husbands, and a man who has won a National Book Award, and a man who died in agony while tied to his bunk, and so many men who were murdered I can't bear to think about it.

Between these extremes are those I feel great pity for, those I respect, those who give me the creeps, those I am in awe of, those who baffle me, those who are repellent to me, those with enormous talent, and those who have touched me so deeply I will never be the same. Some of these men, after their release from prison, have become something like sons to Lois and me. Others have simply disappeared, or remained good friends.

On the other hand, some of the people I have worked with have been singularly unpleasant, like "the Drooler" at the Manzanita Unit (I don't think he could help it) or the "Mad Whacker" at Santa Rita. One of the men in the workshop described the Whacker's penchant for public masturbation as "in the laundry, on the stairwell or behind the trash cans, and always staring at you while he was doing it, his eyes blazing with lust." He probably couldn't help it either. The one who bothered me perhaps the most was a young Chicano drug dealer who insisted on telling me about his past, although I didn't want to hear about it. He and his associates had been ripped off by another group, made up of two men and a young woman. In retaliation, they kidnapped all three of them and, he said, "beat them up."

"Even the woman?" I asked, hoping against hope.

"I drop-kicked that bitch like a wet paper bag," he said as if he were proud of it.

I guess we all have our limits, and I had reached mine. I left his name off the list of those who were authorized to come to the workshop. Somehow I can deal with people who have committed hideous crimes, but not with those who brag about them.

Looking back, it feels as if I have been living in a huge ongoing novel by Charles Dickens with hundreds of characters as varied and vivid as those Dickens created. Sometimes more vivid. I think Charles

Dickens would have approved of what I've been doing all these years. In *American Notes* Dickens describes his 1842 visit to the Eastern Penitentiary on the outskirts of Philadelphia, a prison on the Quaker model relying heavily on solitary confinement, a model that drastically influenced the development of later American prisons. Dickens was appalled at the psychological suffering of the inmates. "There is a depth of terrible endurance in it," he said, "which no man has a right to inflict upon his fellow creature." Later he adds, "It is my fixed opinion that those who have undergone this punishment MUST pass into society again morally unhealthy and diseased."

Many people who ask me why I have continued with this kind of work, and without pay, do not understand when I tell them that I do it because I'm selfish, because it has provided me with good and loyal friends on a scale few can hope for. It has improved the quality of my life far more than my work has helped any of the inmates I've dealt with.

I have been asked to give statistics on recidivism among the hundreds and hundreds of inmates who have been in the creative writing program, but I can't. I'm a teacher, not a statistician. I feel sure, from those former inmates who have kept in touch with me over the years, that the recidivism rate for those who have been in the workshop for at least a year is much, much lower than the rate for the general population. This might, of course, be accounted for by the fact that the creative writing program attracts those inmates with the best educations, possibly those who are most sensitive and intellectually ambitious, most likely to "make it." Either way, it doesn't matter to me. I think this program does appeal to the more intelligent and sensitive inmates, but it appeals to them in a powerful way nothing else offered in the prison does. The program has proven that it can change their lives. I sometimes think that the more sensitive and intelligent inmates have it the hardest. They often see through the system, and they recognize that they are being directed by those who are their intellectual inferiors. It's a dreadful position to be in, especially when they recognize that they are there because of their own weaknesses or illegal actions, in spite of their intelligence.

The people in the various prison creative writing programs can be very bright, but they often have dreadful academic backgrounds. Again and again I am reminded that one can be taught to think, and one can be taught not to think. I spend much of my time awakening sleepers, but once they get awake, the sky's the limit because it was there all the time, buried. We think in language. I teach language. I understand the mechanics of language, and I understand its enormous power.

14

In 1979, when I and Will Clipman, the poet and former student whom I had chosen to direct one of the two workshops at Florence, first entered Arizona Correctional Training Facility on Wilmot Road about twenty miles east and south of downtown Tucson, the paint was hardly dry on the walls. We were still directing two workshops at Florence, but unlike at Florence, everything at Arizona Correctional was new and clean and functional. Even the guards were younger and more professional, and some of them were women. This was something it would take awhile to get used to. And, unlike at Florence, I had actually been called and invited by one of the counselors, with the approval of the deputy warden, to come and establish a workshop in that facility. It felt strange. I hadn't had to fight my way in or rely on Shelley Cohn of the Arizona arts commission to do it for me.

I remember the moment Will and I approached the front door of the facility for the first time, and I remember it clearly. I had actually opened the door when I saw a stricken look on Will's face from which all the color had drained. He turned and ran back to the car in the parking lot. I thought he must be suffering from a sudden bout of nausea or some kind of illness I didn't know anything about, although he had always appeared to be in excellent health. In a moment he was back, looking better.

"What in the hell?" I said. "What was that all about?"

"I just remembered I had two joints in my shirt pocket," he said, looking sheepish.

I was irritated and amused and frightened. There was nothing I could do but laugh, cross my fingers, and pray. I knew that most of my graduate students of Will's age smoked grass. I also knew that we were entering a prison where the inmates were about the same age he was, and nearly all of them were in prison because of some involvement with drugs, sometimes grass. The irony hit me again, and we weren't even into the facility yet. The irony. The damned irony. Why had we begun to send so many of our children to prison? Why had marijuana been criminalized at all? I thought about the era of prohibition when my father was about the same age as Will. All his friends drank illegal alcohol, and he ultimately became a bootlegger and lived outside the law. Now alcohol was legal and we had decided to criminalize another popular substance. Why? Could it be that the gods enjoy irony?

The idea of segregating the young inmates at Arizona Correctional from the older repeat offenders was basic good sense, and it came out of Ellis MacDougall's directorship. Unfortunately, it was not continued after he left. Prisons are crime schools where younger inmates learn criminal attitudes and activities from older, more experienced inmates. It has to do in part with the OGs and the attitude of the younger inmates toward them. OG stands for "old gangster" and refers to those inmates who have a real criminal history, often including multiple violent crimes, either a life sentence or a very long sentence, and a great deal of experience in prison. These men, or at least those who have leadership qualities, often become the inmate government of any prison they find themselves in, and they are looked upon by most of the other inmates as a kind of royalty. Some of them become the leaders of gangs. Others go it alone. Either way, they are respected and often feared. They not only establish the prison code, they enforce it. They see that snitches and those who steal from other inmates are punished. They decide whether individual homosexuals will be tormented, tolerated, ignored, or used as sex objects. They often orchestrate the murder of sex offenders who have victimized children. They enforce the seating by race in the chow hall, the pecking order on the recreation field, and control certain guards who can be used as mules to bring in drugs. They control the availability of drugs and sometimes become rich.

The great majority of the young men at Arizona Correctional were in prison for drug-related crimes. Many of them were bipolar and had attempted to treat their problem with drugs. Most were first-time adult offenders, although many had juvenile records. I was becoming aware that more and more people were being incarcerated at younger and younger ages. The courts were cracking down on the possession and sale of marijuana and illegal drugs and giving stiffer sentences for drug-related crimes. The public had become convinced, largely by the state's demagogues and ambitious politicians who found the issue of drugs a sure way to get elected, that because the state shared a border with Mexico, it would soon be overrun by drug-crazed maniacs unless something drastic were done. The state legislature led the battle.

Even people outside Arizona are aware of how wacky some of our past governors have been, but what they might not realize is that at any given time there are members of the Arizona State Legislature who make our craziest past governors seem quite sane. This was illustrated at Arizona Correctional Training Facility just before it opened when a group of state legislators were invited to tour the new facility. Instead of institutional white or that dreadful shade of light green so common in state hospitals and prisons, the planners of the buildings at Arizona Correctional had decided to paint each of the cells in one or the other of three pastel colors thought to be soothing. I can't remember exactly what all the three colors were, but I remember one of them was light blue, and I think one of them was pale yellow. At any rate, one of the female legislators in the touring group noticed that the cells were painted in different colors, and she registered an immediate objection. It was, she said, a waste of the taxpayers' money to use more than one color of paint on the prisoners' cells. The corrections employee who was guiding the tour assured her that the paint cost the same, regardless of what color it was, but she could never understand his explanation and insisted that painting the cells different colors was a waste of the taxpayers' money.

Both Will Clipman and I were delighted at the talent we found in that lively bunch of men at Arizona Correctional, probably the wildest and most energy-filled group I had worked with since I taught in the seventh and eighth grades in Bisbee. They were alive with youthful vitality, and the workshop exuded an atmosphere of zany playfulness and hope. The men knew they were lucky to be there rather than at Florence, and although the educational program was slow getting started, they took advantage of everything they could. The workshop met in the library, which was, for a long time, merely a term to identify a room. There were no books.

The young inmates at Arizona Correctional also made a great deal of noise, only some of which was music. The prison provided musical instruments, and members of the workshop formed their own hard rock group, complete with electric guitars, drums, and amplifiers. They often composed their own songs, which they insisted I listen to. The room they practiced and performed in had concrete floors and concrete-block walls and no furniture except a few metal folding chairs. The music ricocheted off the walls with a volume I felt sure could knock a person down. Fortunately, on Sunday nights we were the only occupants in the building, and even the guards retreated quickly when the music began.

We developed a standard operating procedure for their monthly "concerts." They would take their places in front of the microphones, tune up, and be all ready. I would run to a room down the hall whose door I could leave open or closed depending on the volume of the music. At the end of each number I would dash back down the hall and applaud wildly, then run for cover as they prepared to start the next piece. This arrangement worked out well for all of us. They got to play their music for an audience and I got my exercise. Their ears were obviously damaged beyond repair, but I hoped to save mine for a few more years.

I have a copy of an old *COSMEP Prison Project Newsletter* dated Spring/Summer 1981. COSMEP stands for "Committee of Small Magazine Editors and Publishers," and the newsletter was published by Carol and Joe Bruchac in upstate New York. This issue features "Arizona's Incarcerated Writers," and on its cover is a photograph of Will Clipman and four of the men in the Arizona Correctional workshop. I think I took the photograph, but it doesn't say anywhere in the magazine. What's interesting and unusual is that three of the four inmates have almost shoulder-length hair and three of them have moustaches. It's also interesting that they aren't wearing any kind of uniform. One has on a plaid flannel shirt, one a T-shirt, one a blue work shirt, and one some kind of tunic with fancy embroidery.

This picture has Ellis MacDougall written all over it. Before he came to the Department of Corrections, all male inmates had short hair, no facial hair, and wore the uniform: blue chambray shirts and Levi's, with Levi jackets and black stocking caps in winter. By 1981, fighting intense pressure from the department, MacDougall had been able to relax the code to the point that men in all facilities were permitted to wear their hair at least collar-length and have some facial hair. Even beards were permitted for a while. At Florence the inmates still wore the uniform. After MacDougall left, everything reverted back to the way it had been and then, in later years, became increasingly restrictive. Now all inmates in the state, male and female, wear only bright orange. Orange sweat pants and sweat shirts or T-shirts and orange shorts for sports and recreation. Even their caps are orange. Joe Curry, a large, barrel-chested man who was in a later workshop, always referred to himself as the "orange pumpkin."

Inside this 1981 issue of the *COSMEP Prison Project Newsletter* is another photograph of the same group at Arizona Correctional Training Facility sitting around a table in the library with noticeably empty bookshelves behind them. As writers, they were a talented group. William Aberg—Dear Billy, as we have come to know him over the years—was as talented a poet as I have ever encountered among my students anywhere. He calls us now from Maryland each week. I recently presented a series of Billy's poems in three prison workshops, poems written between 1979 and the midnineties, and all having to do with drug addiction. Most of the inmates were stunned by the poems. Some gasped and were unable to articulate their strong response. I told them that this was their challenge. If they wanted to write about drugs and addiction, try to do it as well as Billy Aberg did. I hoped that none of them would have to pay the price he has paid and is paying for his years of addiction. Here is one of the poems he wrote while incarcerated at Arizona Correctional. His mother is a devout Catholic.

Devotions

It's too easy
to describe, the match flame
charring the spoon, the blown veins,
the ravenous ghost who throws stolen
gold and gems into a lake
of pain that ripples
out in circles to everything

it loves. I remember
now, in April, the old chapel
on a hill of mountain laurel, windy
maple and oak, grass
speckled white with dogwood blossom—
there, in the flickering red

scent of the votive cups,
my mother genuflects and turns to kneel
under the feet of the Virgin, slips
some coins in a box and prays,
lighting a wick in my name, that I find
healing, keep healthy, have enough
to eat. That I know how much

she loves me. But that I never come home again.

Billy is profoundly bipolar. His wild mood swings have led him to drug and alcohol addiction and to repeated suicide attempts. Once he took drugs and lay down on a railroad track, where he lost consciousness. The next train was a freight, and the engineer managed to get it stopped a few feet from where Billy lay, unconscious.

Lois and I have discussed how Billy's life has become entangled with ours as a curious ironic phenomenon. He is about the same age, height, and coloring as our own son, Brad. Like Brad he is bright and creative. But while Brad, even as a teenager, was drug-free and psychologically sound, and as an adult has been enormously successful,

Billy's life, almost since childhood, has been an endless cycle of bipolarity and alcohol and drug addiction. Very few teenagers, we realize,
have been as little trouble to their parents as Brad was to us. Did Billy
come into our lives, we wondered, like a debt we owed because we had
gotten off so easy with Brad?

In the fall of 1981, I drove east on a poetry-reading tour that
included a reading at the Library of Congress in Washington DC. Billy
was still in Arizona Correctional, where Will Clipman was running
things in my absence. I spent the night with Billy's family in their
gracious home just outside Washington, in suburban Maryland. It
was a wonderful visit, and they treated me like royalty. Billy's father,
a quiet, thoughtful man with a twinkle in his eye, worked for the
federal government in some high-level, hush-hush capacity. Billy's
mother, Cathy, was cheerful, kindly, and full of fun. She too has a history of bipolarity, but her symptoms are controlled with medication.
I met Billy's sisters, his brother, and even his grandfather, the patri-
arch of the charming, typical upper-middle-class family. Then there
was Billy, in prison back in Arizona, Billy who had dragged all of them
through one hell after another, and yet they loved him, it was obvious, and would do anything they could for him. They also felt guilt
they should not have felt.

They honored me because they believed I had been kind to him
and he had told them I was very important in his life. And yet . . .
they couldn't deal with him, and I could deal with him only because
of the controlled situation in which I found him, and because I was
not related to him and could maintain some distance. Also, perhaps,
because I recognized his truly enormous talent. I wonder how many
good, mainstream American families live as this one was forced to—
going about their daily routines cheerfully and successfully while
their hearts are broken because of a son or daughter hidden away in a
prison or a mental institution, a son or daughter whom they love and
whose disaster they consider their personal failure and blame themselves for.

The following year Billy's parents came to Arizona to visit him.
They planned to stay only three days, but Cathy fell and broke her leg.
It was a nasty compound fracture requiring that she stay in a Tucson

hospital for almost two weeks. We insisted that Billy's father move into our guest house until they were able to return to Maryland, so we got to know both of them pretty well. In the evening, after he left the hospital, Billy's father would come into the house and usually we would talk about Billy. I doubt that Billy ever really realized how much his father loved him in spite of everything.

Our own struggles with Billy were to come after he was released from prison two years later, when he remained in Tucson, enrolling as an undergraduate student with a creative writing major at the university. My office became his refuge, and I advised him about what courses to take in order to graduate, since he already had a couple of years of college work. Regardless of what courses I advised him to take, he often enrolled in courses that would not count toward his degree, courses like photography and Russian, and then dropped them early in the semester, although he always completed the creative writing courses, whose teachers considered him brilliant.

At first he shared an apartment with his best friend, Michael Keyes, who had also been a member of the Arizona Correctional workshop and had also gone directly from the prison to the university, majoring in English. Both of these students were able to enter and remain at the university because of Pell Grants. One of the most demanding and intellectually rigorous professors in the English department at the time, Dr. Douglas Canfield, came to me to say that Michael Keyes was the most intelligent student he had encountered in twenty years of university teaching. I wasn't surprised.

Michael had been at Florence before Arizona Correctional was opened. Now a successful university professor in an East Coast state, he recently e-mailed me the following: "When I hear about Az on the news it usually involves crime or something related to the prison. I see Florence on the news and in my dreams and, like everyone else, I want at times to go back, admit that it really is my home, not this other house-like place where I merely sleep and pay the mortgage and care for the cats. I guess that you know the syndrome." Yes, Michael, we are all haunted by Florence, trying to find and reclaim what we lost there. Only monsters get out of Hell intact.

After Michael moved east to go to school, Billy tried to live alone.

It was a mistake. He had several girlfriends, but romances didn't seem to last very long for him. His emotional need was so great that he frightened most girls away. He played electric guitar in a rock group that included two others from the prison workshop, but the group had problems getting along and disbanded. The one constant in his life was his writing. I didn't know it, but he was on maintenance doses of methadone all this time. Each time the doctor changed his other medications or he didn't take his medications, he had terrible episodes of depression or manic phases in which he couldn't remember what he had done. But others did. Once he wound up in the psych ward of the county hospital. Finally, when he was living alone, he went back onto hard drugs.

The upshot was a terrible night that started in the student union cafeteria and ended with Billy's arrest, charged with attempted armed robbery and everything else the authorities could think of to charge him with. When it hit the fan with Billy, it really hit the fan. He had dinner with my wife, Lois, and me in the cafeteria of the student union. Then I went off to teach a class and Lois drove home. Lois tried to get Billy to accept a ride home, but Billy insisted that he ride his bicycle to his little apartment upstairs over a garage on Ash Alley. Only he never made it home. Instead he went to a pharmacy, pulled out a small pocket knife, and demanded drugs with which to commit suicide. The cops were there before he could get out of the pharmacy. When they searched his apartment, they discovered other problems like a large stolen IBM electric typewriter he had somehow carried home on his bicycle. Like several antique guns, one of which he had threatened somebody with during one of his manic phases, and one of which might have been stolen. The conditions of his parole had specifically stated that he was to have no contact with firearms. They also found a fruit jar full of pills of all colors and descriptions, uppers, downers, and every direction in between. Billy went to the county jail to await trial.

Somehow, he wound up with a smart lawyer who contacted us and explained that Billy was facing the probability of fifteen years in the state prison and then another year or two in federal prison on the gun rap. He said he was inclined, depending on our testimony about Billy's behavior the night of the robbery, to go for an insanity defense, which would more than likely put Billy in the state mental hospital for a year only, and then possibly a short stint in the federal prison on the other charge. But it was a gamble, and if he lost, Billy would surely do the time. Lois and I said "Go for it."

At the trial, we were not allowed to hear one another's testimony, but our testimonies agreed. We described how, that night at dinner, Billy made a big mess on the table with his food, how he crammed food in his mouth as if he were starving, how his speech was slurred and incoherent and his motions were speeded up and uncoordinated. At one point a pretty girl and an older man walked past our table with trays of food and sat down on the other side of the room. Billy jumped up, took out a little notebook, and ran over to them. When he came back he told us he had asked for the girl's phone number and her father had nearly knocked him down. Then I saw the pair hurrying out of the cafeteria with their meal unfinished.

From the moment I was introduced on the witness stand, I saw trust and support on the faces of several members of the jury. I wondered how many people on the jury had family members with severe psychological problems. Evidently enough of them did. The verdict was unanimous: innocent by reason of insanity. Billy spent one year in the state hospital, and another year divided between two federal prisons. When he got out he lived in a halfway house in Tucson for a time and then returned to Maryland, where he has lived in various structured situations and finally, as his health continued to deteriorate, back home with his widowed mother.

During Billy's stay in the state mental hospital in Phoenix, he organized two poetry readings for the patients, in which we both participated. Both readings were well attended, although I had the feeling some members of the audience were too heavily drugged to be very critical. When I had just begun to read my first poem, I noticed that a man in the front row, probably in his sixties, had his left eye closed. I assumed this meant that the eye had been injured or lost and the eyelid was permanently closed. Later I looked in his direction again and it was the right eye that was closed. I began to look up often, and discovered that he was alternating, closing one eye for about five minutes, and then the other. I was fascinated. After the reading, I couldn't help but ask him about it.

"I'm saving them," he replied. "I use only one at a time so they will last longer."

Remembering my attempts to save my ears at the heavy metal concerts given by the men in Arizona Correctional, I said, "Of course! That sounds like a very smart plan to me."

15

There is an anthology called *The Promise of Morning: Writings from Arizona Prisons* published by Blue Moon Press in 1982. It was edited—that is, the selections were made—by "W. M. Aberg," actually Billy Aberg before he settled on a name to publish under. It is an astonishing collection of work from the inmates in the various workshops, including the women's workshop in Phoenix. It represents the flowering of the Arizona prison creative writing workshops as they flourished with the support and encouragement of the Arizona Commission on the Arts, with Shelley Cohn as the director of its literary program. Jay Barwell, who had been running the two prison writing workshops in the Safford area, is credited as the "Project Director" for the anthology, and in his afterword he outlines the scope of the creative writing program in Arizona prisons. "Workshops now exist in each of the state facilities—Arizona State Prison in Florence, Arizona Correctional Training Facility in Tucson, Safford Conservation Center, Fort Grant Training Center, and the Arizona Training Center for Women." (With the exception of the Florence prison, all of these facilities were fairly small. Today the state prison system includes ten huge prison complexes, each made up of multiple prisons.)

The anthology is a tribute to the men and women who published in it, but also, I think, to the teachers who worked with them and to the Arizona Commission on the Arts, and particularly Shelley Cohn, who believed in the artistic and rehabilitative potential of the prison writing workshops enough to support them for years.

Jay Barwell's afterword is worth quoting at more length. He says:

The chemistry of a writer's workshop in prison is no different than that in a university. Granted, more limitations exist . . . but the momentum of discussion and debate, the process of communication, is no different than what I've experienced in any setting. Maybe stronger. When the workshop is succeeding, we are for those two or three hours, it seems, outside. . . .

Above everything else, the Workshops create a sense of community, of comraderie [sic]. It is one of the few places on the prison grounds where a Black, a Hispanic, a Native American, and an Anglo can meet comfortably, offering criticism and being criticized, asking for opinions, sharing ideas and collaborating on small projects. As one inmate put it, "The Writer's Workshop is a buffer zone. It's the only place I feel comfortable with just about anyone."

The anthology contains the work of two dozen writers, six of whom were from the original Florence workshop. The high quality and professional polish of their work is not surprising, since three of them had already published books. What is astonishing is the work of the youngsters from Arizona Correctional, particularly Aberg, Michael Keyes, and a Native American called Walking Eagle. Michael Keyes, who was to become an undergraduate English major at the university when he was paroled and would go on to teach literature in college, contributes both prose and poetry to the anthology. His short fiction, "Menage," is one of the best pieces on drug addiction I have ever read. His poetry is dark, intense, and has great impact.

All told, *The Promise of Morning* probably marks the high point of the first decade of creative writing workshops in the state prison system of Arizona. By the time it was published, all of the original members of the Florence workshop were either transferred to some other unit, released from prison, or dead. Even before the anthology was published, the Arizona Commission on the Arts announced that it would be unable to sponsor the prison creative writing workshops any longer. It was partly the political climate and partly the fact that somebody on the commission noticed that Shelley Cohn was spending a large share of her total literature budget on prison writing workshops, mostly to reimburse the people involved with the workshops for their mileage. I understood. I had always suspected that the bubble would burst and I would someday be on my own again. My major worry was not about funding, but about authority. Without the Arizona Commission on the Arts behind me, would I be allowed to go into the prisons at all?

I'm the guy who does what's in front of him, the daily routine. I'm generally dependable but I have never been good at planning ahead. When the Arizona Commission on the Arts bailed out—and I didn't blame them—I knew I was going to have to plan ahead and I was going to have to plan ahead for the long haul. By then I suspected it would be a very long haul. I had chosen to spend increasingly large amounts of my time working with people who were or had been in prison, people who were not high on other people's lists. I could give a rational explanation for why I had done this, but it seemed much too late for explanations. I did it because it was what I did, and I wasn't about to stop because I could see hard times ahead. I sensed that the only hope for the program was for it to contract and expand like an accordion, but never to let the music stop entirely. It was an instinctive strategy for survival.

Giving up the two Florence workshops was wrenching, although none of the original members were still in them. When I said good-bye to the members of the workshops and looked into their eyes, I felt like a traitor, but I didn't lie to them, much as I wanted to. I didn't tell them I would be back. I told them good-bye. They were used to people telling them good-bye—their parents, their wives, their children—and it was something they understood.

I felt ashamed about it, but I was relieved not to have to face that 140-mile drive every Saturday. Several times, on the way home on hot afternoons in my un-air-conditioned pickup, I had gone to sleep at the wheel for brief periods. Once I found myself completely off the road, bouncing through the desert. Once a kind motorist behind me had seen me begin to drift toward the edge of the road and had followed me all the way, honking each time he sensed that I was nodding off. I will never know who sends such angels, but over the years I have been surrounded by them. Probably because I need so much help.

I reduced the program to the workshop at Arizona Correctional Training Facility, the first unit in what was to become the enormous Arizona State Prison Complex at Tucson, although I didn't yet know about that future expansion. There Will Clipman and I worked with our lively crew. We no longer had the energy-draining drive to Florence or the expense of it. I had contracted the program. Then I waited. Without the Arizona Commission behind me I was a free-floating entity, flying by the seat of my pants. Nobody at Arizona Correctional challenged my status. I began to be aware that it didn't matter to them whether or not I was sponsored by the Arizona Commission on the Arts. What mattered to them was that I didn't give them any trouble and my program was popular with the inmates. Evidently I had established a slight track record. To what extent my university credentials affected all this I couldn't tell. Perhaps the prison authorities didn't know that I was in no way sponsored by the university. I never suggested that I was.

In the meantime, I had received a call from the director of education at the Pima County Jail. He said he had heard good things about the prison writing workshops and would like me to start one on a volunteer basis for adult male detainees at the jail. He said the jail had almost no programs and the men had much time on their hands. I had been curious to know what it was like to be incarcerated in a county jail, since all the inmates in the prison workshops had previously been in a county jail for varying lengths of time while they were awaiting sentencing. What, I wondered, had that experience been like, and wouldn't it be advantageous if interested inmates in the county jail could have workshop experience before they were sentenced so that they could step into the prison workshop and hit the ground running? I went to the jail, which wasn't far from where I live, met the young education director, and agreed to start up a workshop that would meet one afternoon each week.

I promised to run the workshop for one year as a volunteer, and I did, but it was not a successful year, and I found that running a program in a county jail could be very frustrating. Some of the disadvantages I encountered, like the rapid turnover of inmates, are indigenous to county jails, and I had anticipated them. But other problems were peculiar to that particular jail. For me, one of the worst of them was the architecture. The men's unit at the Pima County Jail is a modern high-rise building with six floors. There must be some stairways somewhere, although as far as I could tell, they were never used.

There are two large elevators. The first time I got on one of the elevators to go to my workshop on the third floor, I realized, with a shock, that there were no buttons to press for the various floors. Nothing. By watching what the staff members did, I figured out that the moment anyone got on the elevator, he or she was on camera. If we wanted to go to the third floor, we held up three fingers. For the fourth floor, four fingers, and so on. And nobody wanted to go to the fifth floor if it could be helped. The elevator stopped on that floor by mistake at one point, and I stepped out, thinking I was on third. What I saw and heard, even in that brief minute before the elevator came back to rescue me, was enough to put the fear of the Lord into me. Screaming, howling creatures were hurtling past the elevator, bouncing off the walls, and some were spinning like dervishes. After that, nobody had to warn me that the fifth floor was where they kept the crazies.

I was standing at the front desk in the lobby one day, waiting to pick up my badge, when the locksmith came in. He was the man they called whenever they were having trouble with any of the many electronic locks in the building.

"Where's the problem?" he said to the guard on duty.

"Fifth floor," she answered with a malevolent smile.

The locksmith grew immediately pale. "No!" he said. "Not the fifth floor. Anywhere but there."

"Fifth floor," the guard repeated, obviously enjoying his reaction.

The last I saw of him he was standing on the elevator holding up five fingers and his entire hand was trembling.

In addition to the elevators, I found the attitude of much of the staff at the county jail disconcerting. After Cardwell left the Florence prison, the staff there and later at the Safford and Fort Grant facilities and Arizona Correctional, although sometimes arbitrary, had generally been polite, and if they resented my presence in the prison, they seldom showed it. They had been either friendly, businesslike, or gruff, but never threatening or rude. Things were different in the county jail. Several of the staff members and even the counselors were rude and surly. There were a couple of tough female guards, each between 200 and 250 pounds of solid muscle, who were truly frightening and even threatening. They had mannish haircuts and a good deal of facial hair that suggested steroids, testosterone, and an unlimited potential for violence. I felt, like most men do, that it would be shameful to be beaten unconscious by a woman, but I knew, although I was in pretty good shape, that if I had a physical altercation with either of these women, I would lose, and I would be lucky to survive.

The men in the county jail workshop were not permitted to have pens, but I was allowed to bring in pencils for them to write with. Suddenly a directive came down that I could pass the pencils out at the beginning of the workshop, but that I must retrieve them at its conclusion. This meant that most of the men would have nothing to write with between workshop sessions. I asked an administrator what had brought about this change, and he told me somebody had written something about one of the large female guards (I can only imagine what) on the wall of the elevator in pencil. I objected vigorously to the new policy concerning pencils, but it was not changed, so each week I had to collect the pencils and take them out with me. I felt like a kindergarten teacher collecting the crayons.

Only one of the men from the workshop in the county jail wound up later in one of my state prison workshops, but he proved to be extremely talented as well as gentle and sad. We all became very fond of him. By the time, many years later, when he was paroled out of the prison, he was legally blind. He was a very young man who had, I was told, while under the influence of drugs, including psychedelics and alcohol, killed two of his friends. According to what I was told, no motive was determined. His sentence, which came down while he was in the county jail, was forty years to life. Upon being given that sentence, he went to his cell and went to sleep. He slept for the next three days. When I arrived and they told me he had been asleep for three days, I went to his cell and tried to wake him. By shaking him, I could get him awake enough to mumble apologies for not being able to go to the workshop, but he would immediately go back to sleep. I had heard of narcolepsy but had never really seen it. Here it was, protecting him from the shock of reality that he would eventually have to face. But later, maybe when he was more prepared to face it.

Although a few people stay in the county jail as long as two years or even longer if their court procedures are pending and drawn out, most of them are there for only a few weeks to a few months. None of the men in the workshop lasted the entire year, and although they seemed to enjoy the workshop and the books I brought in, I saw little improvement in their work. At one point I arrived at the workshop with my little box of pencils to discover that not a single member of that day's group spoke English. We got through it somehow, with my wretched Spanish, but mostly it turned out to be a language lesson for me. They loved to help me increase my Spanish vocabulary, often with expressions I might have been better off not to know unless I wanted to get stabbed in a bar in South Tucson.

16

The next call came from a counselor in the Cimarron Unit, a medium-security facility of the rapidly growing Tucson complex. As a volunteer, would I be willing to start a creative writing workshop there? They had had a riot that destroyed one of the cell blocks, and they had become aware of the need for more programming. I had no funding and nothing to recommend me but my track record, but I agreed to it. It was only about twenty miles from my home, as opposed to seventy miles to Florence, so I wouldn't need mileage, and I could circulate my own library, which was fairly extensive, to members of the workshop. My major concern was a backup, in case I had to be out of town. Will Clipman's career as a musician had taken off like a rocket, and he was no longer available to help me. Now, evidently, I didn't need any kind of sponsor. I laughed about this when I realized I had become an institution all by myself.

I drove out to the Cimarron facility and met the counselor at the staff entrance. I think we were both a little surprised. She had, I imagine, expected someone a little more professorial or academic looking. Her first comment was, "Cool running shoes." I had expected someone a little more institutional. She was young and beautiful, a petite redhead with that magnificent, glowing, and almost translucent skin some redheaded women are blessed with. She took me into the facility and showed me around. I would have to come out the next Saturday and go through orientation, which included being fingerprinted and photographed for a badge with my picture on it. I would have to get a TB test. All of this was new since my days at Florence.

As we moved through the facility, I became aware that she had something in her mouth, and soon she let loose with a well-aimed plume of brown spittle that could mean only one thing. She was chewing tobacco. I found it hard to believe that this gorgeous creature was chewing tobacco. I knew it was sexist, but I couldn't help associating chewing tobacco with the bristle on a male chin, or a discolored beard. Later, after we got to know each other better, she talked about it. She had taken up chewing in an attempt to quit smoking, but then she couldn't give up chewing. She was getting married soon, she told me, and leaving the Department of Corrections, and she was determined to quit chewing tobacco before she walked down the aisle. I never found out whether or not she did. Thousands and thousands of women have gone on their honeymoons with men who chewed tobacco, so I guess her husband-to-be could go on his honeymoon with a wife who chewed tobacco, but I didn't envy him that part of it.

I found out later why the riot that they had just gone through at Cimarron, a riot that basically destroyed one large cell block, was called the "orange riot." An inmate was eating an orange, and for some reason a guard decided to take it away from him. Such a petty act can cost the state thousands of dollars and result in the loss of lives when it is the culmination of months or years of harassment and inhumane treatment. When one inmate breaks and goes berserk, he can sometimes be followed by many others who identify with him, especially if they are all members of the same racial minority. This riot was obviously aimed at the prison rather than any other group of inmates, since no lives were lost but a great amount of physical damage was done to the facility. One entire cell block had been almost totally gutted. I was told the damage amounted to over one million dollars, but that figure was prison scuttlebutt.

The next Saturday morning after I met the beautiful tobacco-chewing bride-to-be, I showed up for "orientation" at what had been the old Arizona Correctional Training Facility but had now become the Rincon Unit for male adults of all ages. The transformation and the philosophy behind it corresponded with the fact that Ellis MacDougall was gone as director of the Department of Corrections. I wasn't totally aware of it yet, but the Arizona state prison system had entered a vortex that would lead it steadily downward. The vortex included longer and longer sentences, more and more overcrowding, increasingly punitive policies, and disastrous leadership. The policy of keeping the younger inmates segregated from the OGs had been discontinued as soon as MacDougall resigned.

At this point I had been directing creative writing workshops in the state prison system for about thirteen years, and in that time the number of inmates had increased from between 2,000 and 3,000 to almost 11,500. Full-time staff members had increased from about 1,000 to over 5,000. I had managed to survive a riot and the most bloody year in the history of the Florence prison, the most dangerous prison in the state, but I had never been properly "oriented." I had no idea that these orientations for volunteers were to become annual nightmares beyond my wildest imaginings.

Since the majority of the prison volunteers are religious volunteers who conduct various kinds of church services in the prison, the entire volunteer program at the huge Tucson complex is administered by a division called Programs Administration, under the direction of the head chaplain at the Tucson complex. Nonreligious volunteers, such as those who conduct Alcoholics Anonymous and Narcotics Anonymous meetings, and a very few educational volunteers like me, are simply lumped in with the religious volunteers and given over to the mercy of the head chaplain. (Currently I and my associate, Mac Hudson, are the only educational volunteers in the huge Tucson complex.) When I first began at Cimarron and for many years thereafter, including my years at Santa Rita, probably fifteen years in all, I suffered from annual orientations that I believe are best described by a line from Dante: "Abandon all hope, ye who enter here."

Only a few things I have experienced in thirty years of prison work have been as bad as the orientation sessions conducted by that particular head chaplain, and I and the people who worked with me were forced to endure them each year until that particular head chaplain retired and a younger man, intelligent and reasonable, took his place. It wasn't orientation; it was brainwashing—bald, unadulterated, and so offensive as to be comical at times. After a few years I knew most of the chaplain's lines by heart, so they didn't bother me too much anymore, although his attempts at humor still made me wince.

The chaplain held what I have come to think of as the "monolithic" view of prison inmates.

They are all alike.
All are attempting to take advantage of volunteers.
None can be trusted.
All are conniving to cheat, rape, or kill a volunteer at any
    moment.
All are con artists and drug addicts who will attempt to use you
    to bring in drugs.
All are plotting to escape.
All are violent.
There are no exceptions.

He began his sessions by cautioning the male volunteers about their neckwear. If we wore a necktie, he said, the danger that an inmate would use it to strangle us was very great. Consequently, only clip-on ties should be worn. All of this he demonstrated by attempting to strangle himself with his own tie, only to have it come off harmlessly in his hand, a clip-on tie. This melodramatic demonstration got very old over the years after I had seen it many times. Finally I asked him how many volunteers he knew of who had been strangled with their own neckties. Since none had, he didn't answer, but merely glared at me.

The chaplain's patter was either silly or offensive, sometimes both. He would say such things as, "Of course I realize that none of you vote," or "I know you all exceed the speed limit on Wilmot Road getting out here." He showed a Department of Corrections film in which a prison visitor was caught smuggling drugs into the prison. Then the chaplain nattered on again. None of the information he gave was of any practical value, the kind of information the volunteers needed to know, like whether they were supposed to use the staff or inmate toilets, and where those toilets were, or what to do if an inmate had a seizure or became ill, or what to do when an alarm sounded, or what materials—books, pens, pencils, religious tracts, and so on—could be brought in. None of this practical kind of information was covered because the chaplain was too busy, for six hours, convincing us that we were all potential drug smugglers or, at best, the intended victims of mad killers. At Florence, I had given up trying to find a bathroom and simply used the open-air facilities provided for the inmates. Later, at Safford, I did the same thing, in spite of the female guards wandering about. Even this unsatisfactory arrangement would not be an option for a female volunteer in a men's prison. Such mundane and undramatic matters were not considered important by the chaplain. His dire warnings managed to scare off many of the potential volunteers, which I can't help but believe was his purpose all along. The fewer volunteers he had, the fewer problems he would have to be bothered with.

One of the chaplain's main rules, which he uttered as if it were one of the Ten Commandments, was that no volunteer was ever, under any circumstance, to have any contact with an inmate after that inmate was paroled or released. What kind of rehabilitation system is this, I wondered, when the time of reentry into society is precisely the time when the former inmate needs the most support and encouragement? The rule was too illogical and stupid to be treated seriously, although it was seriously troublesome to many of the religious volunteers who wanted to welcome the paroled or released inmates into their congregations, where the men would have spiritual guidance and a ready-made support group.

Years later, after I had been to many of the chaplain's orientations, when I and three former students were conducting workshops in the Tucson complex and all three of them threatened mutiny if something wasn't done about the orientation sessions, I wrote a two-page letter to the complex warden complaining, in detail, about the sessions we were all required to attend once a year. By that time I had been working in the state prison system about twenty years and felt that I was sufficiently oriented to continue on without undergoing the chaplain's annual torture. The warden wrote back that he appreciated my concern and that he would look into the matter. The way he looked into the matter was to give my letter to the head chaplain, the cause of the problem. Nothing about the orientation sessions changed except that the chaplain would stop in the middle of his patter from time to time to glare at me. I would look up from the crossword puzzle I was working and glare back.

Antagonizing the head chaplain would not have been such a problem except that he controlled all clearances into the workshop. When I wanted to bring in a visiting writer, as I often did, I would send a letter giving the date of the proposed visit, the visitor's date of birth and Social Security number, and a reason why I wanted that person to come into the prison. Normally it took about a week to get a clearance for a visitor. But my letters could be mislaid or lost. Sometimes the date of the visit would be approaching rapidly and I would have no clearance, although I had applied for it a month in advance. Maybe I was being paranoid, I thought, but I could see the head chaplain rubbing his hands and gloating over my apprehension. Once a visiting writer, W. R. Wilkins, came all the way from the state of Washington and did not get in, although his clearance had been approved in advance. The paperwork had not arrived on the proper desk. Several other times the necessary papers could not be found. Although I had copies in my hands, they were not honored at the gate. Looking back, I feel relatively sure that the head chaplain did not deliberately sabotage me in the matter of clearances, although I had given him every reason to. I learned enough about the general inefficiency of the prison system and of the Programs Administration office at that time to realize that I was probably not being singled out for inexcusable treatment, although these gross malfunctions in terms of clearances for visitors were inexcusable, and still are.

At the end of that first orientation session, I was fingerprinted, photographed, and presented with a green identification badge. The badge, like the necktie I was supposed to wear if I wore a necktie, clipped on, but I don't think the direction in which I was oriented had changed much.

The Cimarron workshop must have lasted for about eight years. As I remember it, it seems like more years than that. It met on Sunday nights, although in 1988, as soon as we decided to publish a magazine that was to become *Walking Rain Review*, I began going in on Saturday mornings as well, presumably to work with the editorial staff of the magazine, but often simply to work with individuals, to go over their writing. During those years the Cimarron facility had several deputy wardens, one after the other, and during those years the basic tone and strategy of the Department of Corrections gradually changed. The Cimarron facility went from medium to high-medium security, and actually broke down entirely at one point.

The Tucson complex is southeast of Tucson at the base of the Santa Rita Mountains, and in the winter it is usually colder there than in Tucson. A cold wind sweeps down the side of Mount Wrightson, nearly ten thousand feet high, and on those rare occasions when it snows in Tucson, it usually snows more at the Tucson complex. In spite of our normally hot, dry climate, many of my memories of Cimarron have to do with cold weather, probably because everybody had to ride a bus from the main entry point to the various facilities, and Cimarron was the most distant of the facilities. The bus service at night was undependable, and I spent a great deal of time waiting outside in the cold. It would have been much easier and more pleasant to walk from the staff entrance to the Cimarron Unit and back again, but the head chaplain had told us that if we did that, we would probably be shot by a guard. Not true, but enough to deter me.

From the beginning at Florence in 1974, I had adopted the policy that the workshop would meet every week regardless of holidays. Holidays are painful and difficult for people in prison, and I figured that having the workshop meet and do business as usual might distract them. In one of my first years at Cimarron, Christmas fell on a Sunday. The workshop met on Sunday nights. On Christmas Eve we had a snowstorm, rare in the southern Arizona desert, with big, wet flakes that transformed everything for a little while, melted on the highway, and then froze in the night. The interstate was closed—a sheet of ice. Thousands of travelers and truckers were stranded at small towns and truck stops along the way. Then it snowed seriously.

That Sunday night of Christmas day, I realized that I couldn't get to the prison by means of the freeway, as I usually did. By checking the map I was able to come up with another route, circuitous and involving some backtracking on city roads and freeway access roads. I wound up going under the freeway where hundreds of truckers and other motorists were stranded and where the hookers, wearing very little on such a night, were going from truck cab to truck cab, doing the best they could to keep the truck drivers warm.

It was cold and crisp, with about a half foot of snow on the ground at the prison, almost unheard of in this climate, and a bright moon. A miracle of a white Christmas. The guard in the control room at Cimarron seemed surprised to see me. The guard who unlocked the classroom door for me seemed even more surprised to see me. I got the classroom set up and the books out on the table and stood outside the door to watch the men coming, in twos and threes, as they were released from their cell blocks on the other side of the yard. They started to cross the huge patch of undisturbed snow, shimmering under the lights surrounding the yard. Then somebody scooped up a handful of snow and made a snowball, and the fight was on. It was a glorious snowball fight with the men whooping and shouting and everybody throwing snowballs at everybody else. The guards let it happen. I don't know if it was because they were too short of staff to stop it or because it was Christmas. I had never seen a group of inmates have such a good time. I had to get into it. The melee didn't last long, but it was intense. When we all got into the classroom, out of breath and steaming, somebody produced a little bag of hard candy that had come in his Christmas box, and somebody else had smuggled a box of homemade cookies under his coat, although the cookies had suffered some rough usage during the snowball fight. We all sat in a circle and ate cookies and chomped on the hard candy and they told me what had happened earlier that Christmas day.

One of the guards, grumpy because he had to work the holiday, said to a group of inmates from the workshop, "No creative writing tonight. It's a holiday and besides the freeway's closed. The professor couldn't get here if he wanted to."

"He'll be here," one of the men said. "He said he would be here."

"Would you care to make a small wager on that? Like maybe ten dollars?" The inmates were not supposed to have any cash, but many of them did, and the guard knew it.

"It's a bet," the inmate said.

"That was the easiest ten dollars I ever made," the guard said as he walked away.

Later I found out that the guard kept his part of the bargain, although I didn't like the way he looked at me from then on, as if I had somehow betrayed him.

I enjoyed that odd little Christmas gathering with its smuggled hard candy and crumbled cookies. Somehow it really felt like Christmas. Maybe it was the snow, but I think it was the company. When the men left the workshop that night and started back across the huge prison yard, with its snow now badly messed up from the snowball fight, I could hear them far in the distance shouting, "Merry Christmas!" It doesn't take much to make a Christmas merry, I thought, as I was waiting for the bus. After a half hour of waiting, I felt considerably less merry and much colder. Since it was Christmas and nobody was coming in or going out until the next shift change, the inmate bus driver had gone into the toilet at Santa Rita, where it was warm, and gone to sleep.

I think of those eight years at Cimarron and the next few years at Santa Rita as the "taking away" years. They and the next few years also happened to be the years Samuel Lewis and Terry Stewart, one at a time, were directors of the Arizona Department of Corrections. I think of both of them as characters in the contemporary Dickens novel I have been living, somewhere between Scrooge and Uriah Heep, but there have been no ghosts of the three Christmases to convert them and no Mr. Micawber to expose them. They are men who thrive on and make their livings out of bad news. They have never liked good news. I've never trusted people like that. As soon as Ellis MacDougall vacated the position of director of the Department of Corrections, the taking away began, and it continued relentlessly. The policy coincided with the reclassifying of the Cimarron Unit from medium security to high-medium security and ultimately resulted in another riot. When the current director, Dora Schriro, assumed that office, there was precious little left to take away.

Among the many other new restrictions on facial hair, radios, clothing, and commissary items after MacDougall left, two were met with a firestorm of disapproval from the inmates. The first was the removal of all weight-lifting equipment in 1995. The second, and much more devastating for the inmates, was the loss of their Christmas food boxes from home in 1997. Each inmate who was lucky enough to have a family who cared about him or her was permitted to receive a total of three boxes of food from home at Christmastime, each box to weigh no more than twenty-five pounds. Originally nearly all kinds of food were permitted, including baked goods, canned delicacies like special meats, pickles, cheese, candy, crackers, cookies. Those whose families showed largess shared with those who had no families. Next to a parole or release, the Christmas boxes were the most prized and sought after items in every prison. It was from these boxes the men at Cimarron smuggled candy and cookies into the workshop on Christmas night. Gradually the contents of the boxes became increasingly restricted until they could contain only foods in clear plastic baggies, usually home-made items. Ken Lamberton, a member of both the Manzanita and later Santa Rita workshops, author of *Wilderness and Razor Wire*, *Beyond Desert Walls*, and others, says that the best tamale he ever tasted came out of the food box of one of his Hispanic friends who lived on the same "run."

It was only the beginning of a policy so restrictive that "inhumane" is too weak a word to characterize it. In ensuing years the Department of Corrections removed from the inmates all typewriters, musical instruments, hobby-craft supplies, and prison law libraries. This last was devastating to many inmates who had been working on their own cases. Then the orange uniform was introduced. Today, no prison inmate in the state system wears anything but orange.

While I directed the workshop at Cimarron, as the situation became increasingly bleak and restrictive, several of the inmates told me that the guards were being deliberately repressive in order to incite a riot. The guards, they said, were writing inmates up for the most minor infractions, curtailing privileges, turning up the heat.

"Why would anybody want a riot?" I asked.

"The Department of Corrections has got to scare the bejesus out of the public so the public will put pressure on the legislature to come up with more money," one of the inmates said. "A good riot will get lots of publicity and put the fear into them."

By this time, I was well aware of the prison rumor mill and that a certain body of folklore was generally believed by many inmates. One of the most ubiquitous pieces of folklore is about the chicken served in the chow hall. I have been told by inmates on many different prison yards that they or some other inmate saw boxes of chicken being delivered to the kitchen that had NOT FOR HUMAN CON-SUMPTION stamped on them. Each time, I urged the inmate to bring me that section of the box with the message stamped on it. Many of the inmates I talked to worked in the chow hall and were adept at smuggling out various items of food. Surely they could smuggle a piece of a cardboard box out to me. In all the years I've been asking for this proof, no one has ever brought it to me. Because it doesn't exist. It may have happened in some prison long, long ago and then become legend, or it may never have happened. At any rate, it is one of the most persistent and broadly believed pieces of prison folklore.

In spite of the prevalence of rumor and folklore within the prison, however, I came to believe what the inmates were telling me about the Department of Corrections stepping up the pressure at Cimarron in order to produce a riot, and I came to believe it because of two things. One was the riot at Cimarron a few months later. The other was, for me, even more convincing.

Over many months at Cimarron I had become a little acquainted with one of the guards. She stood out from the others, and I had come to feel considerable fondness for her. She was a light-skinned, middle-aged black woman with one of the kindest faces I had ever seen. She was obviously very intelligent and she really cared about the inmates. They spoke highly of her. When an inmate says of a guard, "he's okay" or "she's okay," it is high praise indeed and suggests that the particular guard has treated the inmates fairly and with humanity. It's a mark of respect and indicates that the guard has respected them. For this particular female guard there was unanimous respect. I also knew that her feelings and interests went beyond her duties. Often while I was going in or coming out, we chatted, and she had shown a real knowledge of the writing and educational progress of various inmates in the workshop. "That man has come to *life*," she would say. "He reads all the time and he's writin' up a storm. He let me read one of his poems. It was *real* good. I'm so *proud* of him."

One evening as I came into the prison after I had been told by the inmates that the unit had been targeted for a riot, I was amazed to see that guard berating an inmate because his shirttail wasn't tucked in properly. She was really letting him have it and "writing him up," which would mean a loss of privileges. My shock must have shown in my face. After the inmate walked away, the guard turned to me and leaned close. She was terribly distraught. Her face was a mask of anguish. "They're making us do this," she whispered, and moved quickly on toward one of the cell blocks.

I never knew for sure who "they" were, where the orders were coming from, but the inmates were convinced that the orders to tighten the screws were coming from the director of the Department of Corrections. The same cell block that had taken the hit during the "orange riot," years earlier, blew up again. When it started, the guards left the building quickly and let the riot run its course. It was not racially motivated and the rioters did not attack one another, but they pretty well destroyed the building and nearly everything in it, directing their anger at the institution. It happened on a Friday night.

I arrived on Saturday morning, as usual, to work with the men who were editing the magazine, and for some reason the guards let me in, although the facility was locked down. (It was a period of great confusion at Cimarron, which would culminate in the deputy warden being fired.) I smelled the results of the riot before I could see them. There were smoldering mattresses and rolls of toilet paper strewn around outside the cell block. I wandered through them as if I had stumbled into the outskirts of hell and didn't have sense enough to leave. I went to the classroom where the workshop usually met, but the door was locked. Eventually a guard came along and told me the facility was under lockdown and I should get out as quickly as possible. I got out as quickly as possible.

One Sunday night in 1989 I arrived at the classroom in Cimarron to find three inmates waiting for me before the rest of the group arrived. This was not unusual since the prison unit nearby, Santa Rita, had agreed to transport those inmates who were interested and cleared to "travel" to the Cimarron workshop, and they were often brought over early, sometimes very early, and were either kept in a holding pen, like a cage, or stashed in the classroom until I got there. One of them was new. I had never seen him before. He was tall and thin, with dark, very curly hair, cut short. Good looking, pale, and reserved, trying, I could tell, to fade into the wall, to be inconspicuous in this new and possibly dangerous situation. When I introduced myself, I couldn't make out the name he almost whispered in response. Was it Anderson? His handshake was firm, but his eyes kept checking out each new member of the workshop as they arrived. He was quiet, cautious. He did not speak during the workshop, but I could tell he was following everything that went on with great interest. He was beginning, I thought, to realize that none of the people in this room would be a threat to him. His face relaxed a little and his eyes ceased to search the room constantly. As he was leaving, he said to me, low and hurriedly, "I think you know my wife, Karen," and he was gone.

I took a deep breath. Oh yes, oh yes. So this was Ken Lamberton, and suddenly I was able to put those eyes and that thin, handsome face into a story I had been told, a sad, sad story that could have been a Shakespearean tragedy except it took place in the last half of the twentieth century. Oh yes. I had been told his story, but I wasn't prepared for his haunted eyes.

Karen Lamberton had showed up as a student in an undergraduate workshop in creative nonfiction I was teaching at the university the previous semester. Most of the students were creative writing or

English majors, but Karen had graduated from Pima Community College as a paralegal and was working on an undergraduate degree in political science. She was bright, thin almost to the point of anorexia, and operating on a nervous energy so intense it was exhausting just to be around her. Some of the essays she wrote had to do with her situation as the faithful wife of a man in prison and the reactions her faithfulness had caused. She had appeared, for instance, on the *Phil Donahue Show*. She also wrote about her husband's crime and her adversarial relationship to the prison in general. When Ken showed up in my prison workshop, I suddenly realized that Karen's major purpose in taking my class had not been to learn to write essays or get three units of college credit, but to check me out so she could advise Ken whether or not he should attend my workshop at Cimarron. Evidently I had passed the test.

Years later, in my foreword to Ken's prize-winning book, *Wilderness and Razor Wire*, I tried to describe, as simply and directly as I could, Ken's crime. When he was a highly successful twenty-seven-year-old biology teacher in the public schools of Mesa, Arizona, he fell in love and ran away with one of his fourteen-year-old female students. His wife, Karen, was pregnant at the time with their third daughter. He was given a sentence of twelve years in the state prison and served every minute of it. Perhaps the most unusual part of this unusual story of a highly successful teacher who goes berserk and runs away with his fourteen-year-old female student, leaving a trail of credit card transactions all the way to Aspen, Colorado, where the two are discovered strolling down the street hand in hand like a couple of honeymoon tourists, is the behavior of Karen, the pregnant wife he has left behind. She went to Colorado immediately, where she found her unfaithful husband in the fetal position on the floor of the jail, incoherent and nearly catatonic because the girl had been taken from him. Karen began the long process of putting him back together. "Divorce is not an option in our family," Karen says.

Commenting on this in the foreword to his book, I say: "Ken's crime was love—disastrous, misplaced, and foolish—but love nonetheless. He and his lover were as star-crossed as Romeo and Juliet, and equally mad, in the sense of madly in love. The big difference was that she was a fourteen-year-old girl and he was twenty-seven, married, and the father of a growing family. Shakespeare never utilized this plot because in his day the liaison would not have been illegal, no crime would have been committed."

I was not much impressed with the work Ken turned in to the workshop at first—somewhat soppy religious, moralistic, short prose pieces that seemed to be aimed at the weekly bulletin of the Baptist church, which they probably were. It is not unusual for inmates, even those with a history of violent crimes, to turn to conventional religions for solace and support, and Ken had married into a staunch Baptist family and had been religious long before he was an inmate. I soon found out, however, that Ken had supplemented his bachelor's degree in biology with years of research before he was arrested, and that he was capable of doing another kind of writing based on his considerable knowledge of and passion for the things of the natural world.

He began to publish articles in various magazines dealing with some aspect of nature. I have two of those magazines in front of me now, both published in 1991. His "Species Profile" on the Harris' hawk in *Bird Watcher's Digest* is well written and informative. Ken had obtained much of the background knowledge required for such articles before he went to prison, and while in prison he corresponded with librarians and other researchers, but Karen did the remaining research for him, using the University of Arizona Science Library. There is no mention in the magazine that he is writing from prison. The other magazine, *Reptile and Amphibian*, is even more highly specialized. Several of its articles are written by herpetologists or zoologists associated with universities, including Duke and the University of Pennsylvania. Ken's article, "The Ubiquitous Side-Blotched Lizard," is undoubtedly the most readable of any in the magazine. The note about him at the end of the article is coy. "Ken Lamberton is an Arizona-based writer and artist." He was serving a twelve-year sentence in an Arizona state prison. How *Arizona-based* can you get?

Ken and Karen probably looked like Barbie and Ken dolls at the time they were married: Karen with long honey-colored hair and both of them tall, slender, and long legged. But beneath their stereotypical good looks lay his character flaw and her steel will, both since made public for everyone to see and comment on. When the American dream collapses into a Greek tragedy of illicit passion, betrayal, and scandal, we all line up to be the chorus. The one element that didn't fit the tragic pattern in this story was Karen. She simply refused to be tragic. She moved her children and herself into her parents' converted garage, went on welfare, went back to school to study criminal law, took her children to visit their father in the state prison, stared down the pitying or contemptuous looks of her neighbors and acquaintances, and eventually took on the whole prison system, including the Department of Corrections, in battle after battle to save her husband's life after the state had branded him "sex offender," that most dangerous of all names to have hung around one's neck in a prison.

Karen's struggles with the Department of Corrections and the local prison became Herculean, monumental, a day-to-day war that would quiet for a few weeks and then heat up to the point it drained her of energy, made her an angry, frustrated woman. She fought for her husband's life against a prison administration that seemed determined to allow him to be killed; she fought for her marriage; she fought to hold her family together. She helped other wives in their struggle to salvage their marriages and their families after their husbands were incarcerated. Any tiny concession on the part of the all-powerful Department of Corrections became a major victory.

Karen's legal research and political activity paid off in some changes in the law and in the fact that Ken's investigating officer requested that the severe sentence be reconsidered. Karen found a law firm that was willing to take Ken's case without pay and was so impressed with Karen's legal work that they hired her as a paralegal. Lois and I attended the resentencing in the Pinal County Courthouse in Florence where the judge said, "It is time for everybody involved to get on with their lives" and placed Ken on probation for the remainder of his sentence. He had served almost eight years. Ken went home to Karen and his daughters and entered the MFA program in creative writing at the university. Eighteen months later, after the state appealed the judge's decision in response to pressure from the family of the girl

Ken had run away with, a family that evidently did not agree that Ken should get on with his life, the Arizona Court of Appeals reversed this decision and Ken was returned to prison to serve out the remainder of his original sentence.

At the Santa Rita prison where I first encountered him, Ken had been relatively safe from the mindless brutality of those inmates, especially members of the Aryan Brotherhood, who take it upon themselves to punish all inmates labeled "sex offenders" without bothering to ascertain whether or not they are predators or people like Ken whose involvement was romantic, a matter of mutual consent, and a one-time aberration. One of the ironies here is that many members of the Aryan Brotherhood have had sex with underage girls, and I have heard several of them brag about it. Upon his return to prison, in spite of promises made by the Department of Corrections, Ken was not sent back to Santa Rita, but to Meadows Unit at Florence. Karen believes this was done deliberately and that what happened subsequently was planned by somebody in the Department of Corrections.

It went like this. As soon as he arrives at Meadows, Ken is threatened by a group of inmates. He asks to be put in protective custody. Two guards, a sergeant and a lieutenant, refuse his request and send him back into a cell block where he is immediately attacked and beaten unconscious by the inmates. Two of his ribs are broken and one ear is ripped or bitten nearly off. In the meantime, Karen and Ken's lawyer are frantically trying to locate him since he didn't return to Santa Rita as they had been promised he would. For twenty-four hours nobody seems to know where he is. He has dropped through the cracks of the system. When he is finally located, his lawyer drives to Florence to make sure he is sent back to Santa Rita. One can only imagine what would have happened had he not had a wife like Karen and a persistent and forceful lawyer.

Even with their vigilance, Ken was not out of danger yet. In 1998 Arizona's sexual predator law came into effect. It stipulated that all sex offenders were now to be considered violent and could be held in custody after their release dates for an indeterminate length of time. This depended on the whim of the county attorneys of the various counties. The place of incarceration was to be the state mental hospital. At this time, Ken, along with hundreds of other "sex offenders" was in the Tucson complex's minimum-security unit, Echo. Since all sex offenders in the state by the passage of this law had become "violent," the prison had a security problem. It could not keep "violent" inmates in minimum-security facilities. Ken and many others were reclassified as "predators."

The Department of Corrections' response to this problem was one of those bumbling, uncoordinated efforts for which it is famous, but this one was on a scale so large and "epic" that somebody should make a movie based on it with a cast of thousands. It wouldn't be as exciting as *Lawrence of Arabia*, but it certainly included great expanses of desert, some of the most severe desert on the continent. Hundreds of inmates, including Ken, were snatched up, loaded onto buses, and headed for Yuma, where the prison was out in the sand dunes three miles from the Mexican border. But Hurricane Nora, which the Department of Corrections had not taken into account, was also headed for Yuma.

Because of the storm, the inmate caravan was diverted to the Perryville facility, about thirty-five miles west of Phoenix. There the men spent the night in a lockdown unit, sleeping on the floor. The next day they were transported in waves to the Cheyenne Unit of the Yuma prison, where they were held in cages awaiting housing assignments. But Cheyenne proved to be Meadows all over again. Ken says, "Yuma inmates were confronting new arrivals about the nature of their crimes, asking for paperwork. Those who couldn't produce it, or wouldn't, were being assaulted and beaten in the shower, in their bunks, in the chow hall. Cheyenne wasn't supposed to be a 'political' yard. Officers said it would be safe for us. The gangs were here, however." Recently I asked Ken what he meant by "the gangs" in this passage, and he said "Aryan Brotherhood."

When those who were attacked refused to identify their attackers, they were threatened by the guards with being sent back to the dorms, only to be beaten again, or possibly killed. An assistant deputy warden told Ken that his refusal to identify his tormentors would result in increasing his risk score as a sexual predator. Under the new law, this meant that after he had served his entire sentence, he could be sent to the state mental hospital for an indefinite period. Scores of men went to the hole, solitary confinement, rather than face being attacked by the Aryan Brotherhood thugs. Ken spent two weeks in the hole before the Department of Corrections decided, reluctantly, that housing all sex offenders at Yuma was not such a good idea.

This time they decided to move all the sex offenders to Cook Unit at Florence in the same facility as Meadows Unit, where Ken had previously been attacked. They transported more than a hundred men and their property in three buses and trucks and vans pulling trailers, accompanied by chase vehicles to stop traffic at the intersections. A large contingent of television crews, newspaper reporters, and sight-seers waited outside the prison to see the "predators" on their way. When Ken arrived at Cook Unit, the determined efforts of Karen and his lawyer had again rescued him and he was returned to Echo Unit in Tucson, from which he had started this last hegira. Karen had discovered that when Ken had been returned to prison after being out for eighteen months, he was erroneously classified as a repeat offender, which led to his being gathered up in the entire grim episode.

Karen feels that the mistake was the prison system's way of punishing her and Ken for challenging it and winning his release in the first place. Ken thinks it was probably a careless error. It very nearly cost him his life. I keep remembering the 1970s at Florence when Warden Cardwell rewarded those inmates who flattered him and cooperated with him but refused to put others in protective custody, like Tony Serra, who was brutally murdered.

Ken's story leads me to some fairly obvious conclusions. When it comes to the term "sex offender," we have become a culture in the throes of hysteria. For example: A sixteen-year-old boy is found guilty of having consensual sex with his fifteen-year-old girlfriend and is given a short sentence in juvenile detention. Ten years later, he is found guilty of car theft and is sentenced to five years in prison. As he is about to be released after serving his sentence, somebody notices the earlier "sex offense" and calls it to the attention of the county attorney, who ran for office on a pledge to "get tough" on sex offenders. It's a small Arizona county with no major population centers and there really hasn't been all that much in the way of sex crimes unless one were to include certain indignities some of the local boys perpetrated on an unwilling cow, and the county attorney would decidedly not include that since he doesn't want to be laughed at. But with the new law, and using the previous conviction of a "sex offender" ten years earlier, an offense that occurred with a consenting partner, he can send the young man to the state mental hospital for an indefinite period, perhaps the rest of his life. *And by doing this he will gain political credit.*

Or there is the middle-aged man with a bladder problem who dashes in great distress into an alley to urinate and is arrested for indecent exposure. He becomes, forever after, a "sex offender." If he does not accept this quietly, he might be threatened with publicity. COMMUNITY LEADER ARRESTED FOR INDECENT EXPOSURE. Or the coach of the junior high school girls' basketball team who, while demonstrating a play, accidentally brushes his hand across the breast of one of the girls. With her unfounded accusation, he becomes a "sex offender." He may eventually, after much expense and mental anguish, be cleared of the charge, but once a person is branded a "sex offender," that brand can never be entirely removed.

The national hysteria concerning sex crimes has come into being because horrible sex crimes have been committed. Beautiful, innocent children have been raped and murdered by monsters who, if allowed to, will do it again. This group includes serial rapists. These people are criminally insane and should be kept in secure facilities in state mental hospitals. One of the problems is that many states, including Arizona, do not have mental hospitals with sufficiently secure facilities to contain these people. Consequently, they are dumped into the state prison system whose staff is not really trained to deal with them. They should not be a problem with which the prison system and the other inmates have to deal.

The recent murder in a Massachusetts prison of the notorious child molester and former priest John Geoghan tells the whole story. Although he was in "protective custody," he was murdered by a member of the Aryan Brotherhood already serving a life sentence. Because of the gang culture, prisons are simply not capable of dealing with this kind of notorious predator and shouldn't be expected to. Such people should be in a secure state mental hospital under the supervision of specialists.

Lately the category of nonviolent predators seems to be made up mostly of priests, although I'm sure it includes plenty of others. I suppose the question is, At what point does a person become a predator? Is it when the coach's hand accidentally comes in contact with the fourteen-year-old female basketball player's breast? Is it when the young man has sex with his underage girlfriend? Is it when the young teacher falls so in love with his willing underage student that he will throw away his entire future life to be with her? Is it when the priest lures one young boy after another into a sexual relationship and somehow keeps them from telling anybody about it?

In this area, where public hysteria is whipped into pervasive and ill-conceived laws by ambitious politicians, we need to be very careful to make fine distinctions. There is no way in which Ken Lamberton could be considered a sexual predator, and yet, when caught up in the coils of a vindictive judicial system and a careless criminal system, he very nearly lost his life at the hands of thugs who have appointed themselves the mechanism of moral vengeance, but who make no distinctions. Anyone with the label "sex offender" is a target for their brutality.

In the prison in the early nineties, when I saw some of the many articles Ken was publishing, articles on fish, raptors, toads, and snakes, I could see that he had a future in writing. I began to bring in books by successful naturalist writers, especially those who had written about the Southwest, like Joseph Wood Krutch, Janice Bowers, Alison Deming, Gary Nabhan, and Ann Zwinger. Ken devoured them. I stressed the genre of creative nonfiction. There was a way to write about the natural world with passion and personality without being tediously scientific or boringly environmentalist. It took only the slightest nudge and Ken saw what I was talking about. Gradually his work became more personal, more passionate, and he began to expose more of his feelings and his life.

During his year of freedom, Ken was able to meet some of those writers while he was taking courses in the Creative Writing Program at the university. Alison Deming was one of his teachers, and when Ann Zwinger came to town, I took him to have breakfast with her. Ann, one of the most dynamic women I have ever known, immediately became a champion of this terribly talented young man with the sad eyes who had come to the breakfast table, almost literally, out of hell. When he returned to prison after his eighteen months of freedom, he began *Wilderness and Razor Wire*. Since typewriters had been taken away from all inmates and they were not allowed computers, he wrote in longhand on lined pads I supplied each week in the workshop. I then brought the pads home, and my wife, Lois, typed their contents onto the computer. I would take the typed script in and Ken would proofread it and make revisions, whereupon I would return the sheets to Lois to make corrections. Then back to Ken. It was a slow, laborious process, but worth all the labor for everybody involved when *Wilderness and Razor Wire: A Naturalist's Observations from Prison* was published by Mercury House and subsequently won the John Burroughs Medal, the most prestigious annual award for a book of natural history published in the United States.

Since his final release in September 2000, Ken has completed his MFA degree in creative writing at the university and has published two more books. The most recent is *Beyond Desert Walls*, published by the University of Arizona Press. He continues to publish articles in such magazines as the *Gettysburg Review*, *Northern Lights*, and *Manoa*. He has functioned as a research assistant for several professors in the English department, including me, and is currently one of the editors of *Walking Rain Review*, the literary journal we produce showcasing the work of current and former inmates. He gives lectures and readings and is active in action groups aimed at prison reform.

Karen, after completing her master's degree in planning, took a job as senior transportation planner in Pima County, and now says she is attempting to distance herself from criminal law. All three daughters have been spectacularly successful and are lively and bright. The oldest is starting her senior year at the university on a $10,000 annual Baird Scholarship. The middle daughter is completing her junior year at the university, also with a scholarship. She was president of her high school's National Honor Society. The youngest, now at the University of Arizona on a Flinn Scholarship after turning down a scholarship at Harvard, publishes her poetry in important literary journals and, as a high school student, won national science fair competitions that took her to Washington DC and Hawaii. As the result of her success at a science fair, there is an asteroid named for her.

The other day I was crossing the parking lot on my way into the grocery store when I saw a family coming toward me pushing their shopping cart—obviously three sisters and their parents. While they were still at a distance and before I recognized them, I thought, *How wonderful to see a family like that, so happy, so much enjoying one another's company while they do the shopping together, laughing and talking and having a good time.* Then I recognized them. It was Ken and Karen and their daughters. I would have thrown my hat into the air if I had been wearing one. *Maybe it's Karen's victory or maybe it's everybody's victory, but this is one time,* I thought, *just one time, when the prison didn't win.*

In the recently published collection of essays called *Invisible Punishment: The Collateral Consequences of Mass Imprisonment*, edited by Marc Mauer and Meda Chesney-Lind, there is an essay by Donald Braman, "Families and Incarceration," which is the result of a three-year ethnographic study of male incarceration in the District of Columbia. Karen and hundreds of thousands of other mothers who wanted desperately to keep their marriages and their families intact could tell anyone pretty much what its conclusions are, even without reading it. The strain of incarceration on a family is so profound, economically, socially, emotionally, that the great majority of families cannot survive it intact.

Karen tells of her humiliations at the prison week after week as she tried to maintain her own and her children's contact with her husband and their father. At one point she was strip-searched in front of her children. Week after week I see wives and even mothers being humiliated and turned away at the main entrance to the Tucson complex because they are not dressed according to the arbitrary standards set by the Department of Corrections. Only the very strong can stand up to this treatment for long, especially when also suffering from the routine pressures of being poor and black or Hispanic. I see the incarcerated men, desperate to hear the voices of their wives and children, on the pay phones in the prison yards, and I know that they can only call collect, thus increasing the economic strain on their families, who are probably already on welfare. I see men sent to facilities far away from their families when they could be incarcerated in the local community.

There is no bus service to the Tucson complex. I see poor families coming to visit their husbands and fathers by taxi more than twenty miles from their homes in Tucson. For years in the Tucson complex, it was required that all visitors park about a half mile away from the main entrance and ride an open shuttle to the gate. Getting onto the shuttle was so difficult that only an able-bodied person could manage it. I saw tiny, elderly Mexican women, terrified and in pain, struggling and having to be dragged aboard by others. I saw the problems of women with several small children and an infant in arms trying to keep their children from falling out of the shuttle. No woman should have to undergo this kind of trial in order to attempt to keep her marriage intact and maintain the natural bond between her children and their father. In recent years the shuttle has been abandoned. Now the visitors still park in the same place and simply have to walk to the main entrance under the Arizona sun. I see the wives and girlfriends hobbling in their high heels because they want to look pretty for their men, often carrying infants and all the paraphernalia an infant requires.

Karen and hundreds of thousands of other wives, most of whom are not made of her kind of steel, can testify that incarceration is probably the quickest and most effective way to destroy a family permanently. And mass incarceration, as it is practiced in this country, is the quickest and most effective way to destroy the social fabric of entire communities, especially poor and minority communities. When most of the adult males are removed from a community, as is true in many black communities today, the result is a peculiar kind of ghetto where those left behind are stalled in hopelessness, transfixed, unable to move on, waiting forever.

IV *Watched by the Ravens*

Those of us on the outside do not like to think of wardens and guards as our surrogates. Yet they are, and they are intimately locked in a deadly embrace with their human captives behind the prison walls. By extension so are we.

—Jessica Mitford, *Kind and Usual Punishment*

18

The sprawling Tucson complex, made up of eight separate prisons, covers many acres of desert land at the base of the Santa Rita Mountains on South Wilmot Road. Across the road and a couple of miles closer to the I-10 freeway is the more compact federal prison, but an enormous new federal prison has just been constructed next door to the Tucson state prison complex. Between the new federal prison and the freeway, the Sonoran Desert, with its heavy growth of creosote bush, mesquite, ocotillo, cholla, yucca, and prickly pear, has been "developed" in the last few years. This means that manufactured homes, often with ornate facades and entrances, are now spaced at intervals where a few years ago there was nothing but open desert and a few scrawny cattle. The cattle were a major problem to those of us driving to or from the prison on Wilmot Road, especially at night, because the ranches on both sides of the road were not fenced, and herds of cattle crossed the road at all hours. It was not uncommon for a prison employee, hurrying to his or her shift, to hit a cow. Then the ravens and vultures would arrive quickly to begin to feast on the dead cow. Lately most of the cows are gone, and manufactured homes or two-story ticky-tacky have taken their place. Most recently a few cows can be seen browsing on the prison grounds, and I have been told they are the property of the complex warden. Perhaps this is not true, but knowing the extent to which irony rules the prison, I suspect that it is.

I have never seen so many ravens congregated anywhere else as I see each week at the Tucson complex. It's probably because the prison complex was built near the county landfill, referred to in this area as "el dumpo," although it would almost seem that the ravens enjoy life in prison. I think of them as a kind of Greek chorus commenting on everything we do.

Of the various prisons in the Tucson complex, Rincon (which was the first unit built in the complex and was originally Arizona Correctional Training Facility for men eighteen to twenty-four) seems to be the favorite of the ravens. It has a large open area with grass, something rare at the Tucson complex, and several enormous cottonwoods. Cottonwoods grow fast, but still it makes me feel ancient to realize I was directing a workshop there when they planted those trees. In the winter when the cottonwoods are leafless, one can often see dozens of ravens perched like dark, sinister fruit on the branches. They call to each other or perhaps to the humans below with a harsh croaking. They also produce a low throaty chuckle as if they have just found out something nasty and unspeakable about us and find it very funny. At the Cimarron and Santa Rita Units they hang around the dumpsters, quarreling over scraps and often hopping around on the ground, but at Rincon they seem to be watching everything and commenting on it from their perches in the cottonwoods.

At the Tucson complex it sometimes seems that everything depends on the buses driven by inmates from the minimum-security unit. Most of these drivers are very helpful, but over the years several of them have been mad kamikaze pilots whose purpose in life was to terrify their passengers. One I remember best, for several months during the winter, wore a stocking cap that completely covered his eyes. I have never figured out how he could see anything at all, but he rocketed around his appointed route as if it were a racetrack. Presently all pedestrians—visitors, employees, volunteers—enter the prison at what is called the "main point of entry." After going through the metal detector, being sniffed by the drug dog, and, if they are visitors, often being harassed about how they are dressed, everyone goes through a sally port and winds up outside, which is now inside the complex, waiting for one or the other of the buses, each of which is marked with the units it is going to.

All of the buses are old and dilapidated, but several of them are ancient school buses, Bluebirds that have long since given up any pretense to a suspension system and whose exhaust is deadly. The buses, probably like many of their drivers, have been abused since infancy. They are noisy, uncomfortable, and in danger of breaking down at any moment. Each has a set route. Usually the drivers ignore all stop signs along the way. Just last week the bus I was on came within inches of a high-speed collision with another bus as both made a sharp turn. The standard question people ask me is, "Aren't you in danger in the prison?" My stock response is, "Only when I'm on the bus."

We pile onto the buses in any order: guards with their equipment and transparent plastic backpacks containing their lunches; mothers with their infants and diaper bags with bottles and blankets; other visitors clutching transparent coin purses with cigarettes and coins for the vending machines in the visitors' area; excited children, scrubbed and dressed to a fare-thee-well; the elderly parents or grandparents arriving for the first time, frightened, in highly pressed polyester and white shoes; the friendly young wives who have been coming in for months and know all the bus drivers; four-generation Chicano families who will turn the visit, with the help of the vending machines, into a huge picnic while their children run through the room charming everybody; the male religious volunteers, usually preachers or lay preachers in suits and ties, carrying their Bibles; and me with a large box of books that gets in everyone's way and is a great hassle.

Sometimes some of the women on the bus have on so much perfume I can hardly breath. The children are miracles of energy and beauty. They realize that I am somehow different from the visitors because I have that big box of books while their mothers aren't allowed to carry anything in except a transparent plastic coin purse, and because I have on an identifying badge, but they don't understand the nature of the difference. They stare at me, not knowing whether I am one of "them" or one of "us," and generally their mothers don't know either. The important thing, I guess, is that I know. And I do know. I have known for many years.

There are human dramas on the buses every weekend when the visitors come. I keep thinking I'll get used to it, but I don't. One Saturday afternoon I caught the bus at Santa Rita, where I had just finished a workshop, and it went by Cimarron on its appointed rounds. An attractive young girl got on at the Cimarron Unit, probably eighteen or so, and the driver seemed to know her from previous visits. "Hey," he said, "I just let you off a few minutes ago. What's wrong? Won't they let him have a visit today?"

"He's got some other bitch with him," she said with great bitterness but with her head held high, and marched down the aisle to take a seat in front of me. I admired her for her tough stance, and then as the bus lurched on toward the main point of entry I could see that her head was no longer high and she was sobbing.

Women, and sometimes men, cry on the buses fairly often, usually as quietly as possible. A "Dear John" visit is considered more humane than a "Dear John" letter, especially when it is a wife bringing the children to say good-bye for the last time. After such an ordeal the wives and older children sometimes cry on the bus. Elderly parents cry on the bus when they have come hundreds of miles for a visit, and it is over, and they sense it will be the last time they will see their son or grandson. Guards banter among themselves on the bus, while the visitors listen. "I told the son of a bitch he was out of his fucking mind, but he did it anyway. They're all alike. He's a crazy fucker, so I wrote him up. What are you and Joan doing Sunday? Why don't you come over and we'll have a barbecue and drink some suds? Okay?" Recently an older guard called out, "Watch your language. There are children on this bus."

One cold morning while a group of us were waiting for our various buses, a woman leaned close to me, whispered the last two lines of one of my poems about the desert, and leaped on a bus that was departing. I had never seen her before and I never saw her again.

Cimarron, judging by its history of riots, hasn't been the best run facility in the complex, although it wasn't too bad when I first started the workshop there in 1988. At that time the deputy warden, John Hallahan, was a good manager and really believed in the creative writing workshop, but he was soon moved to another facility, and things at Cimarron began to go downhill. After several deputy wardens came and went, I never knew what to expect from one week to the next. The facility began to spiral down into a chaos of general mismanagement and conflicting signals from the administration, and I began to have the feeling that I was pretty much on my own. In some ways I liked this, but it was also frustrating because the rules had a tendency to change from week to week, depending on who was on duty that week, and without warning.

I find some ominous sentences in one of my reports to the Lannan Foundation written during the fourth year of the Cimarron workshop. "We have recently had two murders at Cimarron, one week apart. . . . In between, one of the members of the workshop went insane, probably because his medication was being tampered with, and dived head first off his top bunk onto the concrete floor. They patched him up and brought him back to his cell because everything else was full. He immediately did it again, this time nearly killing himself. He is twenty-four years old. They shipped him to the prison psychiatric hospital and I shall probably never see him again."

At that time, while the Arizona judicial system was handing out the longest and most severe sentences of any state in the Union, Arizona prisons housed about sixteen thousand inmates, one thousand more than it had space for. The total number was increasing by almost a hundred inmates a month. Two prisons were housing inmates in tents.

It was during this period that I met the "contractual volunteer." In the late 1980s, the Tucson complex made use of two different categories of volunteers. The members of one group, called "contractual volunteers," were hired by the prison to perform some service—usually teaching a class—that no regular employee of the prison was equipped to do. I suppose these people were called "volunteers," in spite of the fact that they or the organization they came from were paid by the prison, in order to distinguish them from the regular prison staff. Volunteers in the other category, like me, were unpaid. Nearly all the unpaid volunteers were religious volunteers. As an unpaid educational volunteer with university credentials, I was an anomaly, and the prison administration didn't know exactly what to do with me or how to treat me. That was exactly the way I liked it.

I struck up a conversation with the "contractual volunteer" while we were both waiting for the bus to Cimarron one night. I will call him Mahmoud because I can't remember his real name, and it's probably just as well. He was a Saudi in full regalia—magnificent robes,

brocade cap—and he was handsome, a young scholar in Islamic studies at the university, with huge dark eyes and skin like glowing amber.
Everything about his manner impressed me with the fact that he was
a serious and successful scholar, a true intellectual from a background
of privilege and luxury. He had been hired by the prison, he told me,
to teach a course in Islamic studies, and he was excited that night
because he was going in to teach his first class. He asked me many
questions about the inmates and the prison routine.

Already I felt a little apprehensive, but tried to be as enthusiastic
as he was. "Do you know anything about the group you will be teaching?" I asked him.

"No," he said, "except that they requested the class, so they must
be motivated."

"Yes, but what kind of class, exactly, did they request?"

He assumed it must be a class in Islamic studies. I told him I
hoped so, and I did, fervently. What he encountered when he walked
into the classroom that night were fifteen militant Black Muslims
looking for a leader. Most of them had read *Malcolm X for Beginners*
and not much else on the subject. I was aware of this because I was
the one who brought *Malcolm X for Beginners* into Cimarron, where it
had circulated like the only copy of the hottest best-seller at a branch
library. Looking back on it, I can defend myself by saying I am an educator, not someone who suppresses books. On the other hand, there
is some truth to the old saw, "A little learning is a dangerous thing."

It soon became obvious that Mahmoud was not going to meet
the expectations of his students and that his students were going to
disappoint him grievously. Each Sunday night on the bus, going and
coming, he poured out his tale of frustration to me, and there was
very little I could say to encourage him. He was attempting to teach
the historical, philosophical, and doctrinal elements of an ancient
and complex religion. That was what his background and training had
prepared him to teach. What his students wanted was Black Muslim
social activism, and they wanted it *now*. Several of the men in his
class were also in the creative writing workshop, but since the two
groups met at the same time, they had chosen to attend the Muslim
class for a semester while they had the chance. From them I was get-

ting their side of the story—unmitigated frustration, although they were patient and hoped they could "do something" with their young teacher. As one of them said, "He's smart and he's read lots of books, but he don't *know* nothin'."

I wondered how the prison administration could have been so naive as to bring about this problem. Or did they think Mahmoud would magically defuse the potential radicalism of the Black Muslims? Or did they want a confrontation in order to send this group of men, or some of them, to the unit at Florence, Special Management Unit (SMU), for those violent men who are perceived to be very dangerous. (I usually refer to it as Southern Methodist University, but nobody thinks that's very funny.) I didn't want to believe that the prison had deliberately engineered the confrontation, but as the weeks passed, I came to feel it was the explanation that made the most sense.

Mahmoud's class met next door to the writing workshop. Our doors opened onto the same courtyard, and since it was warm, we usually left them open. One Sunday night, about an hour into the class, I heard a call from next door, and there was no mistaking what it was. "Help!" It was repeated immediately. "Help! Help!"

"Stay put!" I said to my group, and dashed out the door. When I entered Mahmoud's classroom, fifteen mostly very large, very black men had him up against the blackboard, although they were not touching him. They were shouting at him and gesturing toward him. Some of them were gesturing with their fists. His beautiful amber face was several shades lighter than usual.

"A guard is on the way," I told them with all the authority I could muster, although I was by no means sure that a guard was on the way. "You guys sit down quick and shut up."

As they sat down, one of them said, "We didn't touch him."

"I know," I said, "but he's the only one they'll believe. It could be big trouble for all of you."

Just then a young guard rushed in with his radio in his hand and halfway to his mouth, clearly alarmed. When he saw the men in their seats, the teacher at the blackboard, and me standing in the back of the class, he was confused. "Who yelled?" he said. I looked at Mahmoud; the inmates all looked down at their desks like guilty school-boys.

Finally Mahmoud said, a little shakily, "We heard it too. It must have come from outside somewhere." I agreed with him. The guard was not totally convinced, but he wasn't eager to call two volunteer teachers from the university liars in front of fifteen Black Muslims.

"I came in here," I told him, "to invite this group to join the writing workshop for the rest of the class period, since Mr. Mahmoud has to leave early tonight. We're doing readings of our work, and we'd like this group to be our audience. Is that okay?" I could hear myself chattering like a moron, but anything was better than letting him use that radio to call for a backup.

"I guess so," he said doubtfully.

Mahmoud began gathering up his books to leave. I directed the men in his class to go next door. The guard stood outside, watching. Under the pretext of helping Mahmoud with his books, I said to him so that no one else would hear, "You know you can't come back. Your usefulness is over here." Then, in response to his stricken, defeated look, I added, "It's not your fault. It's not the men's fault. It was a bad idea from the beginning and they suckered you into it. It's a rotten system." The guard watched as I went back to my classroom and Mahmoud trudged off to catch the bus for the last time. I never saw him again.

One Sunday evening just before dusk I arrived at the staff gate through which, at that time, all volunteers entered the Tucson complex. The deputy warden of the Cimarron Unit was there ahead of me, just about to go through the gate, affable and relaxed. He called to me, "Hey, Professor, we've had a stabbing. Come on with me." On the other side of the gate an electric golf cart was waiting, and we climbed in. I had no idea where we were going or why I had been invited, and although I soon found out where we were going, I don't know to this day why I was invited

We were going to the Cimarron chow hall, in front of which a small group of guards was gathered while others escorted the inmates out of the chow hall and back to their cells. There was an inmate lying on the ground and another man in white, evidently somebody on the medical staff, kneeling over him. We got out of the golf cart. The man on the ground appeared to be unconscious, and I could see a pool of blood spreading under one side of his upper body.

"Where's the ambulance?" the warden asked.

"At the gate," one of the guards said, pointing vaguely northeast. "They won't let him through the gate until they search the ambulance. I talked to them. They are afraid the ambulance driver might bring in drugs." The only entrance to the prison compound for automobiles of any kind was a complicated set of gates and a guard house near the Rincon facility, about a half mile from Cimarron. The deputy warden got on the radio and ordered the guards at the vehicle gate to let the ambulance through immediately. Then we could hear its siren as it approached Cimarron, where it had to negotiate another gate that was not electronic, but fastened with a padlock for which nobody seemed to have the key. By the time the ambulance arrived in front of the chow hall, the stabbed inmate was dead. The guards shackled the hands and feet of the body anyway, and loaded it into the ambulance. This, I already knew, was standard procedure when transporting any inmate's body.

The deputy warden seemed to have forgotten I was there. As the ambulance pulled away, the warden and a guard captain took off in the golf cart toward the administration building. It was getting dark. I walked across the deserted prison yard to the classrooms, where a guard told me that because of the "incident" the prison was under lockdown and the workshop would not meet. I went out the main entrance of Cimarron, caught the bus that took me to the staff entrance to the prison compound, and drove home.

I was baffled and troubled by the fact that the deputy warden would invite me to witness this death, almost in the cavalier manner someone would invite a friend to a hanging in the nineteenth-century West or in sixteenth-century London, and it must have been about this time something else happened that baffled me, something having to do with a member of the prison administration. I decided later that it was sufficiently ludicrous and bizarre to be considered surrealistic.

A colleague in the English department at the university wanted to start up a journal-writing class in one of the prisons in the Tucson complex. I had promised to help her try to establish it. I got an appointment and went to see the man who was in charge of all educational activities at the complex. I don't remember his title, but he was very high up the prison's administrative ladder and his office was impressive.

He sat behind his massive desk listening to my recommendation for the new course and then, in reply, said, "Let me show you my eagles." With that, he stood up, whipped off his shirt, and turned around so I could see his back, which was completely covered with tattoos of several large eagles. I was dumbfounded. I didn't think he was trying to sidetrack the discussion; I think he just wanted to show me his eagles in order to prove himself a real man in the presence of anything or anybody even vaguely "literary." Since I had no such embellishments to show him in return, I guess he felt he had somehow outmaneuvered me. He never approved the proposed course. Later, I thought of a plan that might help if I ever had to get another appointment with him. I would first get a large, flashy tattoo on my ass. As soon as I walked into his office, I would turn my back, drop my pants, show him my tattoo, and say, "Now that we've gotten that out of the way, let's talk business."

Even beyond some members of the administration, like the man with the eagles, I have always felt there is something intrinsically surreal about prisons. Many times, when I was crossing the Cimarron yard at night, with its amber lights, massive blocks of concrete with little slits for windows, and great silent, empty distances, I have thought, *This is the landscape of a dream. This isn't real.* Perhaps that is how I have managed to stay afloat in those dangerous administrative waters all these years. While the inmates I have worked with have been very real to me, most of the rest of it seems like a dream, a nightmare more often than not, but certainly not real. To the inmates, of course, it is the most bitter of realities.

To others who might want to go in as volunteers, I know all of it can be very real, perhaps too real. Or perhaps their imaginations make it too real. Some people seem to be accompanied by the shadow of fear wherever they go. I saw this all too clearly one night at Cimarron in the late eighties. I was taking in a graduate student who had sought me out and asked if he could be of any help in the prison workshop. He was an excellent writer with a successful career in journalism, a sturdy kind of guy, married, and probably in his midthirties. I was hoping that after a period of training and experience, he could become my backup. One of the things that seems to have remained constant over the years is that I am always looking for a backup since I can't bear to break the continuity. The workshop must meet on an absolutely regular basis regardless of how I am or where I am.

We went into Cimarron on Sunday night, and I think my graduate student friend was favorably impressed by the men in the workshop and willing to continue to go into the prison with me. As we were leaving, however, passing down a narrow hallway toward the Cimarron control room, which was separated by bulletproof glass from everything else, all hell broke loose. A deafening siren began to shriek its wavering warning. We must have been very near the source of the sound. It was almost unbearable. At the same time a flashing red light strobed the hallway and an excited male voice began to shout over a loudspeaker, "CODE ALERT, CODE ALERT, CODE ALERT." A guard ran past us, not even pausing in his headlong run but pointing at a spot on the wall as he passed and shouting, "Stand there!" We stood there, our butts pressed against the wall, as a line of male guards, maybe eight or ten, in helmets, bulletproof vests, and carrying high-powered rifles ran past us and out the door to the prison yard, the door through which we had just entered the hallway. I looked at my friend. Even with the red light flashing on him, he seemed very pale.

I said to him, "It's okay. We aren't on the yard now. Any problem will be on the yard or in the cell blocks. That's where those guards are going. We're in the administration building now. We're perfectly safe here. All we have to do is stay out of the way."

"What if it's a riot?" he said. His eyes were twitching and his hands were trembling.

"It's not a riot. The guys in the workshop would have warned us to get out if there was going to be a riot. It's just some screwup. Probably an escape. It's nothing for us to worry about. And no matter what it is, we're in the safest spot we could possibly be."

"Except home," he said, rolling his eyes.

My major concern was that he was going to go into shock or pass out, and I didn't want to deal with either of those problems in a narrow hallway with prison guards in full riot gear running down it. I kept talking to him, reassuring him that we were safe. Eventually, after what seemed like several years, a guard in Cimarron control tapped on the glass and motioned for us to enter the sally port that had just opened. From there we were motioned through the exit that led into the visitation room, and the sally port door closed behind us. I guess by this time somebody had noticed that two volunteers were standing at attention in the hallway and one of them was shaking. The inside visitation area at Cimarron is a large, long room with a glass wall that looks out on the desert. It has many square tables, each with four chairs. Along the inside wall are the usual vending machines found in all prison visitors' areas, making one wonder about the financial arrangements between the prison and the suppliers of coffee, sodas, and potato chips.

When we entered the visitation room, another volunteer was already there. He had been evacuated from the other wing of classrooms on the yard. He was a young representative of The Door, a religious group that had recently been very popular with inmates. He was a laid-back tatterdemalion saint, a recovered veteran of the drug scene. I liked him at once and knew I could depend on him to help me if things didn't go well and my friend's terror escalated.

All the chairs in the visitation room had been put up on the tables so the floor could be cleaned and buffed. In prison, buffing the floors is a constant, ongoing process, whether the floors need it or not. I don't think I have ever been in a prison since Florence, which was generally a pigsty, that several inmates were not buffing the floor nearby, often just outside the door where I am trying to conduct the workshop. So the chairs in the visitation room were up on the tables and the floors were waxed and buffed until they reflected like mirrors. I took three chairs off the tables and got sodas out of the vending machines. It seemed to help. There's something about having a chair to sit in and a 7-Up in your hand that says things can't be totally hopeless. We sat in the visitation room for a couple of hours. My friend began to calm down—perhaps it was the sheer boredom of it.

We could see white pickups searching along the outside of the perimeter fences to the north, shining spotlights onto the area known as "no man's land" between the two fences. There are parallel chain-link fences about six feet apart and topped with concertina wire around most prisons built since the 1970s. The era of high stone walls, as far as prison construction goes, has been over for decades. Between the two fences an electronic beam sends a signal if it is interrupted by the passage of anything—a rabbit, a coyote, a raven, a man, a woman. This ground between the two fences is carefully raked so that anyone crossing it will leave tracks. I knew when I saw the trucks and spotlights checking for tracks that what they were dealing with was an escape. That turned out to be what they thought they were dealing with. What they were actually dealing with was a mathematical error. The "count" was off. Somebody had made a mistake in addition, and for several hours it appeared that the prison didn't contain as many inmates as it was supposed to. When they had corrected the count, they sent all three of us trapped in the visitation room on our way. With no explanation, of course.

The last thing my friend said to me as I dropped him off at his apartment in Tucson was, "What am I going to tell my wife? She'll be worried sick that I didn't get home hours ago."

"Tell her you missed the bus," I said, and thought, *Damn! Scratch one more possible backup.*

I took many established writers into the Cimarron and Santa Rita workshops, but the two visits I remember best were by Patricia McConnel and Terry McMillan. Patricia McConnel had spent several years in prison when she was a very young woman for having functioned as a drug "mule," smuggling heroin into the United States from Mexico. Many years later she published a memorable fiction work based on her prison experiences, *Sing Soft, Sing Loud*. When she visited Cimarron she talked to the men in the workshop and read from her book with an intensity I had seldom seen. We were all mesmerized. She wasn't talking theory. They recognized the degradation she had experienced and what it had done to her, how it had affected her for the rest of her life, crippling her emotionally. She bridged all the chasms between gender and age. She exposed the raw edge of what it meant for anybody to be in prison. Before she finished, several of the workshop members had tears in their eyes and were trying to hide them. These men had seen inmates drop dead on the yard and get stabbed in the chow hall. Only something very powerful could make them respond as they did to Patricia McConnel. Again, as it had been years earlier with W. S. Merwin, I had to almost drag her out of the prison. They didn't want to let her go, and she didn't want to go.

Terry McMillan's visit to the workshop was also electric, but for different reasons. Her novel *Disappearing Acts*, published in 1989, had garnered a great deal of attention, and it wasn't all positive. In the book she portrays the protagonist's lover, a black man, in a less than flattering light. In fact, it was such an unflattering portrait that Terry's real-life former lover sued her, only adding to the book's publicity. The suit was not successful because there was no way her former lover could prove that he was the model for the fictional character. As I tried to do in each case when we had a visiting writer come in, I had circulated several of Terry's books, including *Disappearing Acts*, to the men in the workshop. I might as well have tossed a wasp nest into the middle of the room. The black men in the group were offended, especially Cedress, who was furious. They discussed this the week before Terry arrived, and I braced myself, not knowing how far they would go. Terry read a passage from one of her other books, talked about writing for a little while, and asked if there were any questions. Cedress let her have it. He said that he and his brothers felt that her characterization of the black man in *Disappearing Acts* was a slur against their race and their manhood. It was a daring thing to do, verbally attacking the creative work of a highly successful writer who was a guest in the workshop. It had never happened before in any of my workshops, but I didn't have a chance to object. Before I could respond, Terry was on her feet and in Cedress' face, forcing him back in his seat.

"Don't you shuck and jive me, boy!" she said in a tone so heavy with significance that everybody in the room, including me, became silent, focused. "If you had any right to criticize my characterization of a black man, you wouldn't be here. My brother is in prison. You've bought into the same lie he did. You think because you're a black man you don't have to make it. You can just lie back and deal drugs and mistreat your 'hos' until you get caught and go to prison, and then the state will take care of you. What about the women and your children you leave behind? How dare you jump on me for creating a character like you in my novel. Don't I have the right to show you for what you are? Only a black woman can show you for what you are because only a black woman knows how worthless you are."

Terry sat down. Cedress was stunned. So were the rest of us. I don't remember who broke the silence, but somehow we went on to someone else's work, although we were shaken by what she had said. She seemed to have knocked all the wind out of Cedress. Most of us had known it was just hot air anyway.

19

At Cimarron and later at the Santa Rita facility, the workshop had to have an inside sponsor, a full-time employee of the prison to see that the "turn out" sheets got into the right hands so the inmates would be allowed to come to the workshop. I think the inside sponsor had a couple of other functions as well, although they were never spelled out to me. One of them was probably to keep an eye on me and the members of the workshop and make sure we didn't get too subversive. Another was simply to be in place in case something went wrong so the deputy warden could have someone to blame. Since I was not on the payroll, I was largely beyond the administration's control, so somebody who *was* on the payroll needed to be made responsible for *me*. My major concern was that "turn out" sheet each week. If it didn't get done, the inmates couldn't come to the workshop.

The first sponsor assigned to the workshop at Cimarron proved undependable. Such additional duties are often simply dumped on an already overworked staff member who has no real interest in creative writing or the workshop or much of anything. I complained. Then I got a call from a man named Roger Jenson, a counselor at Cimarron, who had agreed to be our inside sponsor. Roger turned out to be a big, easygoing, solidly dependable man, exactly what we needed. He inspired trust on sight, and his laughter would shake the room. He was not a spy for the head chaplain or anybody else, and he was a great favorite with the inmates, who trusted him. He was disorganized, but his terrific instincts and sense of fair play usually got him over the rough spots. He saw us through the good times and the bad times and the first issue of *Walking Rain Review*, published in 1989. The second issue was dedicated to him.

As is often the case in the Arizona state prison system, however, Roger was soon transferred to another unit, and the workshop was left without a sponsor. One of the assistant deputy wardens took over the responsibility of processing the all-important "turn out" sheets temporarily until a new sponsor could be chosen. I knew how important it was to find the right person, so I stalled for time. After about a month, during which it became increasingly difficult to get the necessary "turn out" sheets through the necessary channels, one of the teachers in the prison's GED program sent me word that he would like to be considered for the inside sponsor position. The Tucson complex had a three-tier educational system. Inmate teachers, called teachers' aids, as well as regular teachers employed by the prison, taught the high school equivalence (GED) courses and the English-as-a-second-language courses. These courses are mandated by law. The prison also had a contractual arrangement with Pima Community College by means of which teachers from the college taught courses above the high-school level, and these courses offered college credit, although in recent years there are precious few of them.

The teacher who wrote to me was employed by the prison, a middle-aged man whom I had never met, and no member of the prison administration had recommended him, so I asked the men in the workshop if they wanted him to be the sponsor. There was marked hesitation. No one said anything bad about him. Several of the men just looked at the floor and said nothing. A few shook their heads and said they didn't think it was a good idea. I told them I would hold off and try to find somebody else, but the pickings were slim, and if we didn't have somebody on the inside to prepare the "turn out" sheets, the workshop couldn't meet. Did they know of anybody?

The next week when I came in and was going through the rigmarole all volunteers had to go through in front of the glass cage that was called Cimarron control, I was aware of somebody behind me. I didn't pay any attention and started down the hall toward the door that led outside to the classroom wing of the building. I could hear someone shuffling along behind me and trying to get my attention with a series of little sounds, throat clearings, ahems, and um's. Finally I stopped and turned around. He was a small man, and seemed to be crouched, almost apologetically, looking in all directions but at me. I could barely hear what he was saying. He gave me his name and told me he had contacted me about being the program's inside sponsor. Had I given it any thought?

"No, I'm sorry, I haven't had a chance to make a decision yet. But thank you for applying, and I'll let you know as soon as I can."

After I had met him, I thought I realized why the men in the workshop had been hesitant. I didn't think this gnomelike man would be forceful enough to help us if we had real problems, and I was already aware of a terrible problem that was getting worse each week. A few weeks later, after we had found the perfect inside sponsor, or actually after she had found us, the deputy warden suddenly and quietly fired the little man because somebody had opened the wrong door at the wrong moment and discovered him on his knees with a considerable portion of an inmate's penis in his mouth. Evidently this had been an informal but not uncommon part of the curriculum with some of his students for some time. True to the inmate code, the men in the workshop had been unwilling to rat on the little man, but by their reaction they had saved us from what could only have been a disaster for the workshop.

Then Anne Reeder (her friends call her Annie) arrived like a whirlwind. She came as a counselor to the Cimarron Unit, and when she found out there was a creative writing workshop, applied to be its inside sponsor. She had been an English major. She wrote a little poetry. She was full of life. She was zany. She was wonderful. She was exactly what we needed. She was Annie, all the way from *Little Orphan* to *Get Your Gun*. She was a big woman in every way I can think of—about 6'3", rawboned, strong, surefooted, and with a heart as big as they come, very blonde hair, very blue eyes, and a sweet, kind face. She had been working in the Special Management Unit at Florence. I was told there is a film of her going into a cell unarmed and alone and subduing a powerful and insanely violent man, although I never saw the film.

Anne and I became friends immediately, and we still are. I was impressed by her, just everything about her. The last place in the world I would have expected to meet such a woman was in the state prison system, but there she was, moving up the ladder and obviously being groomed to become a warden. Later, when she went into labor with her first and only child, she called Lois and me and said, "You guys get your butts on up here to the hospital right away. We're having a party."

She was a joy. She came to several of the workshop sessions and even presented some of her own poetry. The men were markedly kind to her work because they liked and respected her. She had the notion, increasingly bizarre for an employee of the Department of Corrections, that she was there to help rehabilitate the inmates, in spite of the fact that the administration of the Department of Corrections and about 99 percent of the prison staff had, years earlier, given up all pretense of attempting to do such a thing. In that regard, she was an anachronism, and proud of it. I guess we both were, and maybe that's why we became friends.

Sometimes I think Anne was sent to that facility for the express purpose of helping us when we needed her most, and I don't mean sent by the prison administration. She got there just in time, one of those angels who always seem to arrive exactly when I need them. I am not superstitious, but I have a firm belief based on past experience. When I need help, when I really need help, someone will arrive to help me, and it will invariably be a person who is capable of providing the kind of help I need at that particular time. This applies to everything from a breakdown on the highway to a serious obstruction in the prison workshop. I try to do the best I can and not depend on anybody, but when I get into a situation beyond my ability, I look around and there is an angel. This one even looked like an angel, although it would have been one of those large, muscular, athletic-looking angels above the altar at the mission San Javier del Bac outside of Tucson. Those angels look like they are quarterbacks on the heavenly football team when not otherwise occupied with their angelic duties. Different situations call for different kinds of angels, and Anne was exactly what was called for to get the workshop out of the mess I had let it get into.

Between the time Roger Jenson transferred out and Anne Reeder transferred in, while we floated without a real "inside sponsor," big trouble arrived in the Cimarron workshop. As the security level of the unit was raised, daily it seemed, the makeup of the workshop began to change. It happened gradually, over a period of weeks, and I must have been asleep. I didn't really notice it until there were no more African Americans in the group, which had increased in size alarmingly, even though it had been too big in the first place. There were also very few Hispanics, although Roberto Gonzales, our star poet, hung in there. He was too big and too determined to mess with, and he was also enormously talented. As I looked around the room, I began to notice the nature of some of the many tattoos I had been seeing but not paying much attention to. There were several swastikas, and one man had two tattooed tears hanging from the corner of his eye, although he wore a stocking cap very low to hide them. Suddenly, like a bucket of ice water down the back of my neck, I realized what was happening. The workshop was being taken over by the Aryan Brotherhood.

By the time the inmate called "Stretch" shot Larry six times at Florence in 1976, the High Wall Jammers were rapidly becoming the Arizona arm of the Aryan Brotherhood. Stretch's brazen shooting in front of hundreds of inmates and staff was a move to become the leader of that organization, which would soon control the sale of nearly all drugs and other contraband within the prison. With the importation of more leadership, mostly from California, the Brotherhood spread out to other prison units as those units were built throughout the state. In fact, it was not unusual for the leadership of the Brotherhood to have one of its members on the outside commit a crime in order to be sent to a particular facility to recruit members for the organization. By the late eighties the Brotherhood had pretty much won in the struggle between the racial gangs and had become a feared and fearful force throughout the state prison system.

The Aryan Brotherhood, or Aryan Nation, combines the beliefs and attitudes of Nazi Germany with the methods and commercial ambitions of the Mafia. Only in prison could such an organization develop and flourish in this country. The Aryan Brotherhood is one of the major reasons why the American prison system as it presently exists must be abolished. The Brotherhood is a cancer, and its host must be destroyed or radically altered or the cancer will continue to spread throughout free society.

Because of all I had seen and endured at Florence and all I had heard, I hated the Brotherhood; and that hatred was tinged with more than a little fear, not for myself but for the other members of the workshop. Not only were its principles of racial superiority repugnant to me, its methods were terrifying. The tears tattooed on the inmate's face represented the number of people he had murdered in order to prove his loyalty to the Brotherhood. I didn't know for sure how many members had infiltrated the workshop, but I knew we were facing perhaps the most serious threat the workshop had ever encountered. Since the security level of the Cimarron facility had been raised from "medium" to "high medium" and the facility had become a "closed yard," members of the Brotherhood had little opportunity to be in direct contact with one another, to disseminate orders and information and to transfer drugs and other contraband, including money, along the necessary channels. The Brotherhood, like the Mafia, is a very large and complex business enterprise depending on a communication network. If the key players could meet in the workshop and communicate with one another, their problem was solved.

As soon as Anne Reeder became our "inside sponsor," I went to her and told her what I thought was happening. She said it was the inevitable result of a recent Department of Corrections policy. The deputy warden at Cimarron had already told me that the department had decided to use Cimarron as a dumping ground for members of the Aryan Brotherhood in order to break their stranglehold on the other facilities. Many of the men being transferred in were members, and often leaders, of the Brotherhood. This, in part, explained the heightened security level at Cimarron.

"We've got to get them out of there," I told Anne. "The workshop can't become a front for a bunch of Nazi thugs. I'll cancel it before I'll let that happen."

"We can do it," she said, "but they'll scream bloody murder and maybe get nasty. We've got to do it so I take the heat, not you. That's what I'm trained for and it's my job. So let's work out a plan."

The plan we worked out was possible because Anne controlled the "turn out" sheets that authorized the guards in the various cell blocks to release men for the workshop. First, I was to identify all the men I was sure were members of the Brotherhood, based mainly on tattoos or things they had said or written in the workshop. These men were to be dropped from the roll immediately. When they asked why, they were to be told to see CO3 Reeder, because she was the one who had excluded them. Anne would also drop others on the basis of the history in their files. This, we thought, would get rid of the core group and possibly discourage others. Anne was obviously placing her ample body, armed only with a radio, between me and any danger that might result from our plan. You have to admire a woman like that.

In addition, Anne gave me the option of interviewing all applicants to the workshop in the future. I would go into the prison on a weekday once or twice a month, depending on how many men had applied, to interview applicants. Anne would have the interviews scheduled, and they would take place in her office. Since the workshop was too big anyway, I now had the option of admitting only those for whom I thought it would be most useful, and I could also exclude anyone I suspected of being a member of the Brotherhood. The plan worked. The minority members returned, and the leadership of the Brotherhood evidently decided, after putting considerable pressure on Anne, that it wasn't worth the trouble they had to go through to use the workshop as their private club. Eventually many of them were sent to the Special Management Unit at Florence.

Several years later, in the mid-1990s when I was conducting a workshop at the Santa Rita facility, I was reminded of our brush with the Aryan Brotherhood and of how much I owed Anne for engineering our deliverance. Members of the workshop were sitting around the long table at Santa Rita one Saturday morning when suddenly a guard and another man in civvies but with a badge, possibly a detective, burst into the room.

"Everybody stand up and take your shirts off!" the guard said in a tone that meant business. Completely confused, I stood up and started to unbutton my shirt. "Not you," he barked. I stopped unbuttoning my shirt.

"Now everybody hold your arms out in front of you!" The guard and the man in civies then inspected the chests, arms, and backs of all the Anglos and had them turn their arms so that all surfaces could

be examined. Their examination of the minority members was per-
functory at best. When they were through, the guard growled, "Put
your shirts on!" and the two men left without another word.

"What was that all about?" I asked, and the story came out. A
young inmate who had been a member of the Aryan Brotherhood
had a large swastika tattooed on each cheek of his butt. Sometimes
tattoos in that particular location indicated that the wearer was what
they called a "woman" and the sexual property of somebody in the
Brotherhood. I don't know whether or not that was true in this case.
Recently the young man had had a change of heart and wanted out of
the Brotherhood, whose leadership was not happy with his defection.
During the night, several men had held him down while somebody
cut the tattoos off his butt. They flayed him. He was in the hospital,
having nearly bled to death, but he wisely refused to say who had
attacked him. Since he had put up a struggle, the guards who came into
the workshop were looking for scratches or bite marks on the chests
or arms of the inmates that would suggest they had been involved. I
wondered where the guards had been when the flaying took place. I
suspect that every white inmate in the prison was examined, but if
anyone was charged with the crime, I never heard about it.

By 1993 the Cimarron workshop had put out two
issues of its literary magazine, *Walking Rain Review*. Both were
physically fairly crude, and the artwork, all black and white, was not
always well reproduced, but the literary level of the work was good.
Both issues, and the third issue as well, were printed in the prison
print shop at the Rincon Unit, a fine vocational training program
for inmates run by Pima College, but later abolished by the Department of Corrections in its crackdown on all educational programs
and everything else. The deputy warden of Cimarron, John Hallahan,
provided funds for the printing of the first issue.

I had approached the publication of the magazine with considerable trepidation, at first resisting while the members of the workshop
urged us to do it. Finally I decided that a magazine would not only

be a good showcase for the inmates' work, but the act of producing it would be good experience for them. Prison takes away most of an inmate's chances to make decisions. Inmates are told when and what to eat, what to wear, when to exercise, where to walk, when to go to bed, and so on. This isn't really the best way to prepare anyone for a responsible life on the outside, a life in which one is constantly faced with decisions. My plan had been that the men in the workshop make all decisions concerning the acceptance or rejection of submissions, size and format of the magazine, and that an editor, chosen from someone in the workshop, would handle, as much as possible, all the details of record keeping. The biggest problem we faced, it seemed to me, was the prison policy that no inmate was allowed to correspond with any other inmate. This meant, I realized, that I would have to do all correspondence myself. This was the major reason I hesitated. I was already corresponding with what seemed at times like half the Arizona prison population as well as many former inmates. I didn't look forward to increasing that correspondence, but set about devising some way to minimize the load.

For the first two issues, I set up an editorial board made up of everybody in the workshop who wanted to be involved, and chose one of them as editor. The problem that presented itself immediately was pressure, with a capital P. Somebody's cell mate wanted to get his dreadful poem into the magazine in the worst way, and he was leaning on one of the editors in the worst way. I saw that this could lead to sticky and even dangerous situations in an institution riddled with gang pressures and embedded with hidden animosities and alliances like a minefield. To get around this problem, we adopted the policy that nothing went into the magazine without the final approval of the editor and me. Then I was careful to appoint a strong editor who would not cave in to pressure.

And thereby, when we came to the third issue, hangs a tale. There was a man in the workshop named Steve. He was intelligent, pleasant to work with, and he wrote well. He was also big, tough, and covered with tattoos. Anne Reeder recommended him for the editor's position for *Walking Rain Review* III. She said she knew he had once been a member of the Aryan Brotherhood, but that from his file and from talking to him and working with him in her office, she was certain he had cut his ties with that organization. I talked to him and was also convinced that he was no longer a member of the Brotherhood. It isn't easy to break one's ties with that organization and survive. I admired him for doing it. When I asked him what he would do as editor if someone pressured him to include their work in the magazine, he placed his index finger firmly on the tip of my nose, leaned his face to within about three inches of my face and said, "No!" I was convinced, and Steve became the editor.

The volume of submissions was growing with each issue. We advertised on the prison's closed-circuit television and received submissions from the various prisons all over the state. Most of the work sent in was very bad. I devised an elaborate system of keeping track of the submissions and responding, a system designed to avoid the editor writing directly to anyone in prison. We printed up rejection and acceptance slips from "The Editors," which it was not necessary for anybody to sign.

We wanted the editorial board to judge the work blind, and that was more of a problem. The work came to a PO box in Tucson, where I received it and took it to Steve. He deleted the names of the writers from each submission and passed it on to the editorial board, and we discussed it in our Saturday morning meetings. If we requested changes, I took notes and wrote to the inmate or former inmate who had sent the material. Otherwise, it was an easy matter for me to mail either a printed acceptance or rejection slip.

But there had to be a record, somewhere, of everything coming in with the addresses to respond to, and which pieces were accepted or rejected. I feared that in the crush of submissions, and passing them from hand to hand, some of the blind submissions would fall through the cracks. Correspondence for people in prison takes on a significance most of us cannot begin to understand. I did not want to be involved with a magazine that solicited work and then did not respond, one way or the other.

To avoid this, I designed a system that I thought was very clever. I learned from it that clever is the last thing you want to be in prison. Even the hint of clever can cause hideous problems. I bought Steve a ledger book, one of those old-fashioned tall gray things with hard covers and lined paper. A spiral notebook would have been simpler, but spiral notebooks are not permitted in the prison, and for our purpose the ledger book worked fine. The main purpose of the ledger book was to keep track of each submission. First, because the names of the writers were removed from the work submitted, each submission was assigned a number next to the author's name in the ledger. Then the date of submission. Then a brief description of the work submitted and brief titles. All this to make sure we didn't get the submissions, now without names, mixed up. Then several spaces in the ledger to indicate who on the editorial board currently had, and hopefully was reading, the submission, indicated by their initials, and then the final disposition: rejection, acceptance, or returned for revision to me.

Such an entry, translated, would mean that William Aberg's submission was listed as number thirty-three so it could be matched up with his name later in the ledger. His submission had been received on July 13, 1993, and consisted of a poem of two pages and the title was "Bicycle Messenger." The submission was currently in the hands of John Arnold or Tony Dunn and ultimately accepted with changes suggested by Richard Shelton.

I should have known better. Once the names were removed from the submissions, the ledger was our only record of who wrote what, and the ledger was *in the prison*. Suddenly Steve was "rolled up." That meant, in this case, taken in the middle of the night and sent to the Special Management Unit at Florence, where only the heavies go. I was never told why. That ledger we worked so hard to design, in the hands of an inmate whose background identified him as once a member of the Aryan Brotherhood—could it be a code of the dealings of the Brotherhood's drug transactions, or even worse, their hit list? What could one make of an entry like "Aberg, B. #33, po. 2pp, Bi Mess, J.A, T.D. acc w c Sh"?

When Steve was rolled up, they took everything with him, both the ledger and all the submissions to the magazine he had, which included the majority of them. Both Anne Reeder and I appealed to the deputy warden of Cimarron to have the materials returned, so that the workshop could continue with the production of the magazine. Both of us were told that the materials were being examined by the Internal Investigation Division at the prison. None of the materials, including the ledger, were ever returned. It is possible that the Internal Investigation Division is still, many years later, poring over that ledger book trying to break the code. I offered to break it for them, but they chose not to accept my help. Perhaps the ledger book is still in a file somewhere, waiting for some new member of the Internal Investigation Division to stumble upon it and have a go at cracking the code. I wish them well.

We got that issue of the magazine out, but there were many inmates and former inmates who had submitted work but to whom we never responded because we had no record of their submissions. Starting with issue four, I set up new policies to keep all submitted materials out of the prison. It severely curtailed chances that the men in the workshop could make decisions concerning *Walking Rain Review*. The prison had won again.

In May of 1991, another angel arrived, and it eventually changed the scope and quality of the prison creative writing workshop program more profoundly than anything ever has. It started quietly, over the telephone, with an unexpected call from Jeanie Kim, then assistant director of the Literature Program of the Lannan Foundation in Los Angeles.

"Jimmy Santiago Baca was in LA recently and did a poetry reading for us," she said in her quiet, charming way. "He told us you had a wonderful creative writing program in the prison. I believe he was once a member of your prison workshop. Patrick Lannan and I were wondering if you might like to apply for a Lannan Foundation grant to help you with the program."

"Y-y-yes," I stammered, hardly believing what I was hearing because it sounded like that angel we had all been waiting for was finally landing on the roof of the prison. And that's what it has proven to be. The grants were small at first, but any support at all seemed too good to be true, and I was afraid to ask for more, afraid the foundation would consider me greedy and stop the grants. Evidently I had nothing to worry about on that score. The next year Jeanie hinted that some members of the foundation's board felt I should ask for more than I did.

With that encouragement, I began to see the possibility of expanding the program. I began to dream a little bigger. For years I had wanted to establish a writing workshop in the women's prison. It started with a story somebody told me—I can't remember who. It might have been Roger Jenson, our inside sponsor, or some other employee in the Tucson complex. The power of a story is amazing, even a little story, and it doesn't have to be literally true; it can be true in the lesson it teaches. The person who told me said that the Department of Corrections had just supplied the prison facilities that were housing male inmates with several computers for the classrooms in each unit, depending on the size of the unit. They had supplied the women's prison with a comparable number of sewing machines.

Whether it was true or not, this story caused me to fly into a rage. I am not usually given to rages, but this story, with its broad implications too obvious to be ignored, pressed my button, and I vowed I would get a creative writing workshop into the women's prison somehow. I think the story was true because when I finally got into the women's unit and established the first workshop there, I found that the industry the women worked at was sewing, that they had a special room fitted up with many sewing machines where they produced underwear, mostly brassieres and men's boxer shorts. Later, after I got to know the women in the workshop and realized most of them felt they were in prison because of some man or men with whom they had been involved, one of the women told me that sometimes they got great pleasure out of sewing the fly shut on the boxer shorts. A small gesture, but it made them feel better.

Most of the women inmates in Arizona were housed at that time in the Manzanita Unit of the Tucson complex. I began negotiations with the deputy warden there and cast about for a woman or women to run the workshop on a weekly basis while I oversaw it and visited it from time to time. That year the Lannan Foundation gave me twice the amount I had asked for in my grant proposal, and I knew it was the green light I needed for the women's workshop I had wanted to start for years.

I chose Deidre Elliott and Lollie Butler to direct the women's workshop that met one night a week in the library of the Manzanita Unit. Both held MFA degrees from our Creative Writing Program at the university, Deidre in creative nonfiction and Lollie in poetry, and both had teaching experience. Lollie also wrote children's books, and Deidre had taught for us at the university undergraduate level. The most difficult thing both of them had to do was go through the volunteers' orientation program before they began the workshop. I warned them about the head chaplain and we all went to the orientation program together, but their reactions were even stronger than I had anticipated. I feared that these two kind and gentle women would become violent before it was over. If so, I hoped they would direct their violence at the head chaplain rather than at me, the one who had got them into that ordeal.

Many of the Lannan Foundation's board and staff members have changed in the last fourteen years, since the foundation awarded me a grant for the first time, and the foundation has moved its headquarters to Santa Fe, but its stalwart support of the various creative writing programs in Arizona prisons has never faltered. That support has made it possible for me to run as many as four workshops simultaneously, each in a different prison and some as far as 150 miles from Tucson. I can buy writing supplies and books for all the inmates in the workshops—sometimes more than sixty—and see that they have dictionaries and the reference tools they need. I can help them get their manuscripts ready for publication in a professional-looking format and defray the cost of submissions. We can produce an issue of *Walking Rain Review* each year, now undoubtedly the most beautiful and high-quality literary magazine to come out of any prison in the United States, and we can distribute it without charge to those who are interested. I can actually pay someone a small fee to cover a workshop if I am not available. I have the luxury of going out of town once in a while. I even have the luxury of being sick. I have a backup.

20

After the Cimarron riot on Friday night, the results of which I wandered through the next morning, I was told that the deputy warden of Cimarron was fired. This was unusual. Usually after an escape or riot or some big problem, a deputy warden was sent to the Department of Corrections equivalent of Siberia for a few years, like Fort Grant or Yuma, and sometimes demoted, but almost never fired outright. And still later, the confusion at Cimarron continued to grow. The entire system was breaking down into chaos and confusion. I was sorry, but not surprised, when Anne Reeder, at the request of the deputy warden of the Santa Rita Unit next door, transferred there. She begged me to go with her. "Even rats leave a sinking ship," she said. "Let's go together." The deputy warden had requested my program at Santa Rita, but I couldn't leave the men at Cimarron where things were going from bad to worse. I couldn't leave them there while that facility collapsed around them. If I couldn't help them, I could at least record and possibly expose what was happening to them. But even that opportunity soon became closed to me.

For three consecutive weeks I appeared at the front door of Cimarron to be told that the "turn out" sheet had not been taken care of and the workshop could not meet. The third week when I was refused entrance, I told the guard that if the workshop didn't meet that night, I would never come back. It was an empty threat. I knew that the Cimarron administration would prefer that I not come back because they didn't want to be bothered with me and they didn't want anybody to know what was happening inside the unit, but I thought I might bluff the guard. It didn't work. I didn't get in that night and I never went back. I transferred my program to the Santa Rita facility, where Anne was waiting with a large group of inmates for the workshop, including those, like Ken Lamberton and several others, who had previously been bused to Cimarron.

It wasn't the worst or the most wrenching break with a well-established and functioning workshop I have ever had to make. That was yet to come. But this one was bad enough, and like the later more severe ones, it was caused entirely by the Department of Corrections. It made me increasingly aware of how little the department cared about programs, rehabilitation, or any of the fine phrases that were still part of their public rhetoric. Moving the creative writing program sideways, like a crab, kept it alive, but somehow it didn't feel like progress. I was reminded, if I hadn't learned the lesson earlier at Florence, that as far as the Department of Corrections was concerned, volunteers were shit and educational programs, even those bringing their own funding and making the prison look good, were of no importance. The fewer of them the better.

The Santa Rita workshop was successful from the moment it started, partly because it included several inmates from earlier workshops. Even Greg Barker from the original Florence workshop was in it for a while. At the first meeting of the workshop a handsome inmate approached me and said, "You don't remember me, do you?" I concentrated on his face, but came up with no memories. He was fairly young, fine featured, compactly built, and with prematurely silver hair. He must have been in some previous workshop, I thought, but I couldn't place him.

"My name is Gerald Gordon," he said. "I was a member of the English department faculty at Yavapai Community College in Prescott when you came there, years ago, to do a poetry reading. I introduced you."

I had only the vaguest recollection of doing that reading—it must have been in the midseventies—and none at all of somebody introducing me, but I was impressed with this distinguished-looking professional educator. He was now an inmate, there was no mistaking that, and I later found out that he had been convicted of killing his wife and her lover and was serving a life sentence. His poetry turned out to be stiff and formal and much influenced by late-nineteenth-century models, but he was very bright and willing to read contemporary work and revise his own. He has since been transferred to a facility at Florence, but I am still working with him through correspondence. Three years ago he won first prize in poetry in the annual PEN Prison Writing Contest. He is writing hard-hitting, contemporary poems, often about the prison experience.

Gerald is a good example of the kind of diversity one encounters in a prison. At the university we use the term "diversity" in a somewhat different way. When we talk about increasing the diversity of the university, we mean increasing the ratio of underprivileged minority members. Since underprivileged minority members are the majority in the prison, Gerald Gordon, a white, well-educated, former professor is a minority member increasing the "diversity."

Five percent of all inmates in Arizona have a college degree. I suspect that the majority of those degrees are two-year degrees, but one of the recent members of the workshop had been well on his way to a PhD in physics when he was sent to prison. After about a year in the workshop, he was sent, without warning, to Yuma, far from his entire support system here: his friends in Tucson and the workshop. His letters from Yuma, the equivalent of Siberia for Arizona prisoners, are truly piteous. The fact that 36 percent of all Arizona inmates have an eighth-grade education *or less* makes it difficult for those with college educations to find friends in prison, although such men as Ken Lamberton and Gerald Gordon have been major exceptions. They have spent much of their time teaching others, and it may be what kept them sane.

The Santa Rita workshop was one of the most exciting and productive groups I have ever worked with. Again, as with the first workshop at Florence, the energy level was so high I felt that I was being carried forward by a whirlwind. I could only hang on and hope we were moving in the right direction. A good portion of that energy was coming from a big barrel-chested redhead named Joe Barlow, who was serving a very long sentence. Joe is one of the most remarkable men I have ever worked with, inside or outside the prison.

At first Joe was fairly quiet and tentative about the whole situation, intimidated by people like Ken Lamberton who had better educations than he did, but willing to give the writing thing his best shot. Like most of the other newcomers, he had to either get over his penchant for sentimentality and worn-out language or take a beating from me every week. He took plenty of beatings, and he took them with dignity, but he learned. He is one of those people who learn slowly and painfully, but never stop learning, and once they have learned something, put it into practice immediately and never forget it. He became increasingly excited about writing and began to take a leading role in the workshop, but it was the parole board that really turned him around.

Twice a year, after serving a set portion of their sentences, inmates are permitted to write to the parole board and ask for clemency. Usually these requests are turned down out of hand. Many inmates serving long sentences don't even bother to write, and for others the letters are not worth the paper they're written on. When it came time for Joe to write his semiannual letter, he decided to include a poem he had been working on in the workshop. It was a poem about the searing guilt one can feel after committing murder. I had suggested the title for it—"Having Taken a Life." In response to this very moving poem, the parole board knocked six years off Joe's sentence. That did it. Suddenly he realized the power of words and that he had access to the power. He has been a poet and a good one ever since, and he will be a poet for life. He has also become one of the most impressive teachers I have ever encountered, in spite of all that the prison system can do to stop him. He was born to teach. His inmate students have set records for achievement and high GED graduation rates. I use, both in the university classes and the prison workshops, educational exercises he devised.

Most people who work in prison for any period of time develop a different attitude toward murderers than they had previously. They begin to make finer distinctions between the various kinds of mur-

derers. There is an enormous difference, almost a difference in species, between the psychopathic serial killer, the executioner or assas-
sin killer, the person who panics and kills someone in the process of
a robbery, the manslaughter or "accidental" killer, and the "crime of
passion" killer. Of all of these, the "crime of passion" killer is least
likely to be dangerous and most likely to be just anybody we might
know or live next door to. There is a saying: "My crime was my cure."
It does seem, in some cases, that once the crime is committed—the
unfaithful wife or husband is murdered, for instance—the murderer
reverts to his or her normal nonviolent pattern of behavior and is
never tempted to harm anyone again. Or even to run a red light.
When in prison, such people are usually models of behavior and often
placed in positions of trust and responsibility. The severity of their
crimes results in very long sentences, but unless they are totally brutalized by the prison experience, they are probably the kind of inmate
least dangerous to society.

There are always exceptions, like Bunny in the women's workshop.
Bunny had killed *two* husbands, both of whom abused her physically.
Her problem seemed to be one of making the wrong choices in regard
to husbands rather than one of murderous intent. I liked her very
much, and when she got out I did the best I could to help her get a job
she wanted in a shelter for battered women. But I wouldn't want to
be married to her.

What does it feel like to know that some of your best friends
are murderers? I can't really think in those terms. I can think only
in terms of Gerald Gordon and Joe Barlow, my friends, whom I
admire. They are wildly, radically different from each other, and yet
they are both poets, and good ones. They are also both murderers. I
would trust either of them with my life, my wife's life, my son's life,
my property, or my reputation. I think we have all, at one time or
another, been brought to the edge of murderous rage, or perhaps I am
merely projecting my own passions on everybody else. Some kind of
governor controlled us at that moment, or was it simply the fact that
no weapon was available? It is highly unlikely that most of us would
ever become bank robbers—that requires considerable daring and a
degree of skill—but it is entirely possible for many of us to commit a

crime of passion so severe that we would wind up in prison for perhaps the rest of our lives.

If you should meet Gerald Gordon and Joe Barlow at a PTA meeting or a Fourth of July potluck, you would like them. They would
be very much a part of the community. Joe, who has never met a
stranger, would charm you with his friendliness and good humor.
His love of humanity would spread out in waves around him. Gerald
would impress you with his quiet reserve, wisdom, and deeply held
religious beliefs. You would listen carefully to his political views and
his ideas in general. Unless you were told, you would never know that
both these men are murderers. And are they likely to commit murder
again? Probably less likely than you and I are, since they have the
long memory of their long punishment, and you and I have no such
memory.

The workshops never blur or run together. I have
only to focus on the room, the setting, and it all comes back, with the
faces around the table and even the voices, some so soft and hesitant
I could barely hear them and others shrill, near the breaking point.
Perhaps I am haunted by those voices.

The administration at Santa Rita couldn't seem to make up its
mind where or when we were going to meet. At first we met on Sunday nights in the visitation area with the vending machines we were
not allowed to use humming and clicking in the twilight zone behind
us. There were two toilets at the end of the room, one for inmates and
one for everybody else, but for months the guards refused to unlock
them. It became a running battle. One of the members of the group
had recently had bowel surgery, and without a toilet near he simply
couldn't attend our meetings. Then they moved us to a classroom out
in the middle of the complex, far from the main entrance, and the
administration decided that for security reasons, no programs would
meet at night. So we changed our meeting time to Saturday mornings, officially from 8:00 to 10:00, although I was permitted to stay
as long as I wanted to if the men wanted to work on the magazine

or if individuals needed help with their work. Then they moved us
to another classroom much closer to the main entrance, a peculiarly
shaped room with one glass wall. The view across the Santa Cruz Valley was spectacular, and the ravens, swallows, and grackles carried on
just beyond the glass. Then our meeting time was changed to Saturday night and we were moved to still a different room. I can't remember why, if I ever knew. Each time a new deputy warden took over,
new policies were put in place. It was because of all this moving about
that I started calling the workshop a "floating crap game."

During most of the years at Santa Rita I was lucky to have excellent people ready to go in for me if I were ill or had to be out of town.
During the three years that the women's workshop met at Manzanita, Deidre Elliott was available to fill in for me, and then I relied on
Mark Menlove, the graduate student who had been my assistant at
the university. During a two-year period Mark went into Santa Rita
with me nearly every week. He was a good sport about the fact that
I referred to him as my "mule," although instead of carrying drugs
he carried the big box of books. Then Joni Wallace began attending
the workshop with us and I had two backups. Ultimately, when the
women were moved to Perryville, 135 miles to the north and west,
Joni and I started the women's workshop there and she directed it.

Things went fairly smoothly for the workshop at Santa Rita until
about 1999, although the storm clouds were gathering. The prisons
in the Tucson complex had received an influx of Mexican national
inmates, Mexican nationals who had committed crimes, often serious and usually involving drugs, while in the United States. Eventually, as this population rose beyond two thousand inmates scattered
throughout the various state prisons, war broke out between them
and the Chicano population over turf, drugs, and booty. The Chicanos
were no match for the ultra-tough Mexican nationals who roamed
through the prisons in bands, attacking any Chicano they happened
to find. I was surprised at this. The only Mexican national who had
been in the workshop at Cimarron, Alberto, was as gentle and peaceful a young man as I have ever known, and the other inmates in the
workshop were very fond of him. I would assume from this that not

all the Mexican nationals were involved in the war, but nobody bothered to find out which were violent and which weren't.

One of the Chicanos in the Santa Rita workshop was on a gardening detail when he was attacked by a band of Mexican nationals. He hit one of them with a shovel and killed him. The Chicano had been nearing the completion of his sentence. I heard that a much longer sentence was added, although he had killed the Mexican national in self-defense. Most of the Chicanos were afraid of the Mexican national thugs, who were incredibly daring and tough. The Anglo inmates were terrified. The situation had been festering for a long time, and the prison administration seemed to take no steps to control it until it became open warfare.

"We've never seen anything like them," one of the men in the workshop said, meaning the Mexican nationals. "They're crazy. They don't give a damn. They'll stop at nothing. It's happening on every yard and nobody's safe."

At Santa Rita the administration's first reaction was to lock the prison down for three weeks, during which the workshop couldn't meet. All the inmates were locked in their cells. Then they segregated all Hispanic inmates, both Mexican nationals and Chicanos. One of the members of the workshop who was Greek and fairly dark skinned, was caught up in this operation and put in segregation with the Hispanics. He was able to extricate himself only with great difficulty. When the segregation went into effect, the workshop temporarily lost all its Chicano members.

By this time there were fifteen Anglo and black members left in the workshop. Joe Barlow was the obvious leader, having published more than twenty poems in well-established magazines. Ray and Matthew were coming up the ladder fast. For wisdom and patience we relied on two older inmates, Tom and a man serving a life sentence and known affectionately throughout the prison as "Uncle Ed."

One Saturday night in early January of 2002, Mark Menlove and I arrive in the classroom at Santa Rita and start putting several tables together to make one long table, as we always do. The men come in all at the same time like a human whirlwind, but they don't sit down at the table as usual. They gather around Mark and me, distraught, several talking at once while others just stare glumly at the floor. Something is terribly wrong. Then I see Joe Barlow, the big, red-faced redhead with a huge plastic bag over his shoulder, looking like a young Santa Claus in an orange suit.

"We gathered up as many books as we could," he says, looking away from me. "I think I got most of them. Except the ones Ray had. They took him yesterday. We're all being transferred. Nobody knows where we're going for sure. The yard will be all Mexican nationals. I'm sure glad Mark came with you tonight. I was worried about you carrying all these books out by yourself." He says all this in a great rush.

"We're going to be scattered all over the state," Uncle Ed says in his quiet way. "Some to Florence, some to Buckeye, probably some to Safford or Douglas or Yuma." I have never known Uncle Ed to say anything that wasn't accurate.

We go to work frantically, trying to critique as much of their writing as possible in the little time we have left, trying not to think about what's coming. Then we have to say good-bye, the thing we have all dreaded. I try not to look at Joe. Big, tough Joe is in trouble. I'm afraid he is going to break down. Matthew too and several others. I'm having more trouble than anybody, and I know I must not show it or the others will break down. You don't cry in prison, or at least you aren't supposed to. You don't cry when you get word that your mother has died. You don't cry when your wife writes that she is filing for a divorce. You don't cry when your parole is denied. You don't cry in prison. So we shake hands and say good-bye. I see tears in several eyes. I look the other way.

Uncle Ed was right. They were scattered all over the state, and the pathetic letters began to arrive. Joe went to Safford, 150 miles to the northeast. Matthew went to one of the units at Florence. Tom went to Buckeye. Ray wound up at Yuma. They were scattered to seven other compounds throughout the state, hundreds of miles apart. Both Santa Rita and Cimarron Units would house Mexican nationals only. The Chicanos were returned to the general population and scattered among the various complexes around the state, but not, of course, to Santa Rita or Cimarron Units. It was the end of the workshop at Santa Rita after eight good and productive years. We had put out several issues of *Walking Rain Review* and bonded as a group. Now it was over. I was going to have to take my floating crap game somewhere else because few of the Mexican nationals would have sufficient English to participate in such a program, and anyway, I was afraid of them. I was thoroughly discouraged and more than a little angry. *This damned system,* I thought. *You can't beat it. It leaves you alone for a little while until you get complacent and then WHAM it gets you.*

Instead of being discouraged, I should have remembered that every ending is a beginning. As it turned out, this one proved to be one of the biggest beginnings the workshop program ever had.

21

After the dissolution of the Santa Rita workshop, it seemed like all I had done for twenty-five years was start over. Each letter I got from the men who had been in the Santa Rita workshop made an appeal for me to start a workshop in their present facility, but I knew I couldn't start driving long distances and continue to teach full-time at the university. I decided to stay in the Tucson complex, if I could, at least for the time being. I still had several units to choose from in spite of the fact that Santa Rita and Cimarron were no longer viable possibilities. I began to eliminate the various units one by one, trying to focus on one.

There was the Rincon Minors Unit, a special prison for minors who had committed murder or some other very serious crime and were treated by the courts as adults. The Minors Unit was by that time a large, full-fledged prison, but I remembered it in its beginnings. When I was directing the workshop at Arizona Correctional in the late seventies, the deputy warden had asked me to stop by and talk to him, which I did. He wanted to show me something. It wasn't necessarily something I wanted to see, but I saw it. At that time the Minors Unit was just a small wing of Arizona Correctional with about ten male juvenile inmates. I was told that all of them were murderers. The unit was not highly advertised. I had been going into the prison for several months and didn't know the Minors Unit existed.

"We have no programs for the minors beyond some basic schooling," the deputy warden said. "Nothing to occupy them. I wonder if you would consider just going in to look them over and see if you might be interested in getting them to do some creative writing. Your program with the adults has been very popular here."

The warden took me down a couple of hallways and through a sally port into a long narrow room. At the far end of it, bunched together as if for mutual protection, were ten boys. I would guess they ranged in age from about fourteen to sixteen, and most of them were probably sixteen. What struck me first was that they all looked alike. They were all Hispanic, slender and fairly short, and they all had patent leather hair cut in exactly the same way. They were all dressed alike in Levi's and white T-shirts. But it wasn't just their physical similarity that struck me; it was also their expression. They were all looking at me and the deputy warden with the same expression: bitter hatred and distrust. I immediately thought of the movie *The Boys from Brazil*, which includes a group of boys who are Hitler's clones and all look alike. I was ashamed for thinking of that film at just that moment, but I couldn't help it. The deputy warden told them who I was and what I did and then left us together so I could talk to them alone.

For the next half hour I tried desperately to get any one of them to say something or change his facial expression, to show some degree of interest or acceptance. Nothing! I kept having the feeling that I was talking to only one person or thing, that they had ceased to be individuals but had somehow merged into one entity. The experience rattled me and made me feel eerie. On the way out I stopped at the deputy warden's office.

"Sorry, but I can't do it," I told him. "It would take years to get them to trust me enough to do any meaningful writing. It wouldn't be a good use of my time when, during the same period, I could be working with adults who would be willing to accept me and start writing right away."

The deputy warden sighed, but he knew exactly what I was saying and he couldn't argue with it.

So in early 2001, when I was deciding which of the Tucson units I should try to get into, the Minors Unit didn't even make it onto my radar screen. *I know there are people who work well with juveniles,* I thought, *but I'm not one of them. I was successful when I taught in the seventh and eighth grades in Bisbee, but those students weren't murderers and I was only twenty-five years old.*

Finally I decided on Manzanita, now a medium-security unit for men, since the women had all been moved to Perryville. Getting in and getting the program set up wasn't too difficult. By this time I had been working in the Arizona system about twenty-five years, and many of the wardens and deputy wardens, most of whom had been in the system far fewer years, recognized my name. I think they had come to the conclusion that after twenty-five years I wasn't going to start smuggling in heroin or help an inmate escape, although some of them were not yet convinced. Maybe their doubt about my helping inmates escape, at least temporarily, was justified. Dozens and dozens of inmates had told me that for two hours a week, while the workshop met, they were free.

The Manzanita workshop started out slowly. It didn't look too promising. I was starting over for sure. It seemed like digging ditches, having to unteach all the bad stuff about how to write that the men had already learned and which, like sentimentality and clichés in poetry and trick, clever endings in fiction, were so deeply embedded that in some cases it was impossible to get rid of. Since Mark Menlove had moved to Utah, I chose Mac Hudson, who was working on his master's in Indian American Studies and had a background in creative writing at the university, to replace him, and Mac met with us each week. The prison staff at Manzanita, often young women, was cooperative and helpful. Mac Hudson and I went in on Saturday mornings at 9:00. The facility was obviously shorthanded, especially on weekends, but the staff was trying to make things run as smoothly as possible for us.

During early 2001, while Mac and I were struggling at Manzanita every Saturday morning with little success in terms of improvement in the men's work, Joe Barlow was writing to me regularly from the Tonto Unit at the Safford prison, where he had been sent after the breakup of the Santa Rita workshop. His letters expressed more and more excitement. At the Tonto Unit he had landed a job in the library, one of the most desirable work assignments for an inmate, especially for a writer who loves books as much as Joe does. Such a job often gives an inmate access to a typewriter (personal typewriters had been taken away from the inmates throughout the state years earlier) and duplicating facilities. In my correspondence with Joe, I teased him about being a "Rosie," someone who can fall into a bucket of manure and come up smelling like a rose.

Actually Joe's success, then and subsequently, reflects the fact that he is hard working and very smart, that he has been in prison many years and has learned how the system works, and that he loves working with people and is very good at it. But it was even better than just a job in the library. His letters contained repeated references to his boss, the librarian for both units at Safford, Mrs. Swerline, as the inmates referred to her. She was, evidently, a remarkably intelligent and progressive woman, deeply interested in the intellectual and creative development of the inmates. This, in itself, was so unusual for a Department of Corrections employee that it made me suspicious, but the next development was mind boggling. John had told Mrs. Swerline about the Santa Rita workshop and provided her with copies of *Walking Rain Review*, and she was interested in starting up such a workshop in the Tonto Unit at Safford. Could I help?

Joni Wallace, who had assisted with the workshop at Santa Rita and was directing the women's workshop at Perryville, went with me to Safford to meet Mrs. Swerline and the men in the fledgling workshop, and to have a grand reunion with Joe Barlow. Tamara Swerline was obviously the key to any possible workshop at Tonto. Safford is about 140 miles from Tucson. I had learned from an early experiment with a workshop at Douglas back in the seventies that the farther away a workshop was, the less control I could exercise, and the more it depended on some local figure of authority to keep it going. Everything depended on who that local figure was. I was counting on Joni's hard-headed female assessment of Tamara Swerline. Joni and I were much impressed with Tamara and what she and Joe Barlow had been able to accomplish with the fledgling workshop in the Tonto Unit. It was wonderful to see Joe again. He was writing, working in the library, and leading the workshop while Tamara sat quietly behind her desk, keeping an eye on things and following the discussion with great interest. Joe, the orange pumpkin, was in his element, and Tamara turned out to be what every librarian should be—an educator. She is also smart, careful, sly, and witty. When an inmate tries to con her, she has been known to say, "Notice those dark roots at the base of my blonde hair. Don't assume anything." She also tells about the young inmate so hungry for language that he comes into the library and reads the unabridged dictionary.

The result was a very active workshop in the Tonto Unit that expanded to include a workshop in the Graham Unit at Safford as well. Both met on Sunday, and eventually I turned them both over to Mac Hudson, while I supplied them with writing materials and visited them fairly often. The Lannan Foundation grant paid for Mac's mileage—three hundred miles a week.

Something else had happened before the blowup of the Santa Rita workshop that now took on added significance. It started gradually and then burst into a major activity and is still going strong. I call it "Operation Books." When I was a child, books saved me from an otherwise nearly unbearable situation. I think there are many of us for whom that is the case, and we never forget the importance of books, especially the novels we read as juveniles to escape a reality we were not yet mature enough to deal with. Maybe it was our first encounter with Tom Sawyer or the March sisters, Meg, Jo, Beth, and Amy. They all lived for us and kept us from the despair of our situation while we turned the pages. We chose to live in Rudyard Kipling's jungle, Dickens' French Revolution, or on Emily Bronte's haunted heath. With the help of books we survived until we were old enough to go our own way, but we never got over our love of books.

I started Operation Books because of Anne Reeder, who had been flying through the prison system on a trajectory that was not unusual, although baffling to outsiders. She was briefly at Buckeye, the ill-fated prison in the middle of nowhere west of Phoenix and south of the Perryville complex, truly the most bleak, desolate, and depressing setting for any prison in the state in which bleak, desolate, and depressing is pretty much the norm for prison settings. Anne called me on behalf of her friend, the librarian at the newly opened complex at Buckeye. The facility was very large, but new and not totally occupied yet. It seemed that they had six libraries and no books. No books at all and no prospects of getting any, although they had a librarian. Could I help? The image of a library with a librarian and no books haunts me still. It seems, somehow, to represent the entire Arizona prison system as I have come to know it.

I made an appeal to my colleagues in the English department at the university: "It isn't Christmas, but we need it now" was the slogan I coined for the book drive. Hundreds of books began coming in. Tom Collins (that's his name) gave me nearly every book he had in his office when he retired. Others pulled many titles from their private libraries. Through Frank and Barbara Waters I met Ann Merrill from Taos, New Mexico. Ann started sending me books from her library and then talked the people at Moby Dickens, a spectacular bookstore in Taos, into donating the books they didn't sell.

Of all these books, some I used in my own workshops in the Tucson complex, some I sent to the Perryville women's prison, but the majority I sent to the prison at Buckeye to help fill up all those empty shelves. Later I shifted to sending most of the books to the Tonto Library at Safford, where Tamara Swerline, or "Marian the Librarian" as we called her, was rapidly building one of the best prison libraries in the state.

In December 2001, Janet Voorhees of the Lannan Foundation came to visit the Santa Rita workshop. In the course of our conversation I mentioned that I was gathering books for several of the prison libraries. All the prison libraries were limited, but some were so small they hardly qualified as libraries at all. Once I got a letter from an inmate who told me there was only one book of poetry in the facility's library. Janet said the Lannan Foundation had hundreds of new books, fiction, nonfiction, and poetry, that it would be happy to donate to the various prison libraries. Soon the boxes began to arrive from the foundation, and Operation Books became a major activity.

I have never tried to keep track of how many books we have sent into the various prison libraries. A conservative estimate would be seven large cartons every two months for more than four years—thousands of books. I have now included the Douglas prison and am sending them many cartons of new books a year as the books continue to come in from the Lannan Foundation. At any given time our small guest house, where I sort and box the books, looks like a bookshop that got hit by a tornado.

I have to keep reminding myself and pounding it into my head that we cannot assume all prison employees are alike, anymore than we can assume all inmates are alike. For years, judging by the libraries I saw, I took a dim view of prison librarians, although I realized they were working with very small budgets and extreme security restrictions. But I came to feel that they had no use for contemporary literature and knew nothing about it, and that they were dismissive of any poetry written since 1900. Then I met Tamara Swerline and my stereotype fell apart. I had already known that there were inmates who wanted to read Cormac McCarthy, Lucille Clifton, Alberto Rios, Terry Tempest Williams, W. S. Merwin, and the whole gang of contemporary writers from many backgrounds and cultures. When I brought their books into the workshop, the members devoured them.

Tamara Swerline is open to contemporary writing and welcomes it on the shelves in both her libraries. It gives me pleasure to stroll through either of the two libraries in the prison at Safford and recognize book after book that I remember sorting into a box I had marked "Safford." Operation Books has been totally successful, with only one serious glitch. Once while Mark Menlove and I were working fast, sealing cartons of books to be mailed, a pair of scissors we were using to cut the sealing tape somehow fell into a carton and we didn't notice it. The carton went off to Safford, "ATTENTION, Tamara Swerline," and was opened at the prison's central receiving warehouse where the scissors were discovered and we were all in deep trouble. Tamara took the heat, but I learned to be more careful when boxing books. Now I count the scissors before and after each operation. Like surgery.

The next surprise was a call from one of the counselors at the Rincon Unit in the Tucson complex. It seems there was an inmate there named Tony, good old Tony the barber, who had been active many years ago in the Cimarron workshop and had been on the editorial board of two issues of *Walking Rain Review*. Not only was Tony now at Rincon, but he had been very busy. He had presented the counselor with a list of twenty-six men who had signed up to participate in a creative writing workshop if I would come in and direct it. The deputy warden had approved. Would I come in?

Since the Manzanita workshop met from 9 a.m. to 11 a.m. on Saturday mornings, I arranged for the Rincon workshop to meet from 12:00 to 2:00 p.m. on the same day. The Arizona state prisons serve only two meals, breakfast and supper, on weekends, so our workshops did not interfere with anybody's lunch except Mac Hudson's at Safford on Sundays. He was in the workshop at Tonto from 11:00 a.m. to 1:00 and then sprinted to the Graham Unit to direct that workshop until 3:00, while I had an hour for lunch between the two workshops at the Tucson complex.

Eventually the Manzanita workshop began to shape up as new people came in with more talent. The Rincon workshop got off to a rocky start as well, but after a few months and a change of the meeting room, things began to improve. At the time of this writing both the Manzanita and Rincon workshops are as exciting as any I have ever directed, and each includes several terrifically talented writers. In addition, Mac Hudson and I have added another workshop in the Echo Unit, a minimum-security unit in the Tucson complex.

The high point of all these workshops so far has been the visit by Terry Tempest Williams, the famous writer from Utah. It was electric, mesmerizing. She asked the men to write about where they found beauty, and they produced great work. Her intensity, seriousness, and concern for these men and the situation they found themselves in was palpable. The following week one of the members of the workshop said, "Why don't you bring somebody like that in every week?"

"Because there isn't anybody else like that," I answered.

He thought for a few seconds and said, "Yes. I guess you're right."

One of the Rincon workshop members is serving a 125-year sentence for bank robberies in which no one was physically harmed. He's older than I am and has been in prison much of his adult life. We have many stories to share. We both know he will probably never get out of the prison alive, although he continues to petition for relief. I see no sign of self-pity or resignation in him. He still gets angry when he mentions his exorbitant sentence, and creative writing is very important to him, a link with the world he will probably never again live in. He is, in fact, one of the most cheerful and positive people I know. He has honored me with his friendship. When he comes into the workshop we always shake hands with great enthusiasm. He asks, "How are you, Professor," looking at my face for any sign of change and really concerned with the answer. "I'm fine, my friend," I say. "And how are you?" "The same," he answers, "always the same."

22

Until one has worked in prison for a while, it's hard to imagine how many unexpected "problems" can arise. For me, just getting in can be a big problem, probably the major problem over the years. Getting out, with the exception of a delay from time to time, has never been a problem. The old stale joke, "Don't wait dinner; they may keep me," has always been just that, a joke. There was never any danger of them keeping me since "they" who run the prisons didn't want me in the first place. The difficulty is getting in each week, getting into an institution whose right hand often doesn't know what its left hand is doing. What I have come to fear over the years is not the possibility of a riot or any danger from the inmates. I have come to fear incompetence, carelessness, laziness, and a lack of concern on the part of the staff of the prisons. Coupled with this is the fact that the state prisons are severely understaffed, and the guards, who are now supposed to be called "correctional officers," are underpaid and often badly educated and insufficiently trained no matter what we call them.

The result is a disaster waiting to happen, although it isn't always waiting. It happened January 18, 2004, at the Buckeye complex on Highway 85 in the desert between the Palo Verde nuclear plant and nowhere. That was a Sunday, and I drove from Tucson to Safford to direct the workshop at the Tonto Unit and conduct the first meeting of the workshop in the Graham Unit. It's close to 150 miles each way, and that morning an icy wind was blowing out of the northwest.

As I entered the Tonto Unit at 11 a.m., I sensed great tension and excitement. While I was getting ready to go through the metal detector, which included removing my belt, badge, and keys, the young male guard asked, "Have you heard any news?" He assumed, since I was coming from Tucson, I might know something he didn't.

"About what?" I asked blankly.

"Buckeye. The hostages," he said.

Seeing that I was totally ignorant of the situation, several of the guards filled me in. Their faces were tense and their tone was depressed. At 3:15 that morning two inmates at the Lewis Unit of the Buckeye complex, inmates with long records of violent offenses, in a botched escape attempt had assaulted several staff members in the kitchen and managed to take over a guard tower with two guards as hostages, a man and a woman. The tower was well stocked with weapons, ammunition, riot gear, and bulletproof vests, and it was built to be impregnable.

It wasn't the best day of all days for me to be starting up another workshop in another remote Arizona state prison, but Tamara Swerline had been working on plans for the new workshop for a long time, and the men would be waiting. Depression and worry hung in the air like the dust that was blowing everywhere. I thought about the cold wind that blows nobody any good. All the guards at the Tonto Unit seemed to go about their jobs a little more carefully because they sensed that two of their colleagues at Buckeye were in mortal danger because somebody had been careless. I felt this too, but the job I was there to do was a different kind of job. I had that to be thankful for.

First I would spend two hours in the Tonto Unit where I would be greeted by a rainbow coalition of eager writers who seemed to have only one thing in common. They all wanted to get their work published in *Walking Rain Review*. That was the kind of pressure I felt, but they knew that as the editor I was holding a royal flush and they couldn't beat it. They also realized that the whole thing was a learning process, and since I would cease to accept submissions for the next issue on the last day of March, they had to learn fast. They had heard the story, probably from Mac Hudson or Joe Barlow or even me, of how somebody asked me, "How come so many of your students have become successful and famous writers?" My answer was, "I used a whip." Actually, for writers in prison I have used about everything I could get my hands on, and the possibility of publication in a magazine as handsome and highly respected as *Walking Rain Review* is no mean goal for an aspiring writer.

"This piece is a distinct possibility for publication," I might say, "but it's almost twice too long and needs cutting and compression. It's cluttered. Go through it and check the ratio of adjectives to nouns. Too much fussy modification. Get in there with a hoe and weed it out. I'll consider it if it's severely revised."

Hearing myself say this I think, *What an asshole you are! Lording it over these guys who are doing the best they can and haven't had the advantage of your education.* But when the piece comes back, clean, clear, and publishable, I feel better. Then, seeing the writer's pride when it is published, I feel positively good about being an asshole. On January 18, 2004, with the hostages on everybody's mind, I wondered if the guards at Tonto were going to start the business about the radio again, but they didn't. They were distracted. The Tonto Unit, like the Manzanita Unit near Tucson, is made up of long, one-story concrete-block buildings, tall and with flat roofs, that form the perimeter of a huge rectangle. All the buildings are the same color—dark gray. In July or August when the temperature is 110 degrees, heat waves rising from the yard give the impression that the buildings are undulating, gently dancing like elephants. The ground enclosed by the buildings at Tonto includes a baseball diamond, several concrete basketball courts, a circular track, and much open space. The Tonto workshop meets in a room that is about as far away from the entrance to the prison and the visitation area as one can get. It's a big, echoing room attached to one of the living units, with nothing but concrete-block walls and metal furniture.

Its remoteness had never bothered me because I always feel secure with the men in the workshop, and this workshop was no exception. Some of the guards had been troubled by the arrangement. They wanted me to carry a radio. I didn't want to and told them I was too stupid and technologically challenged to know how to work the thing. They showed me how to work it and insisted that I carry it. Actually, I am capable of operating a hand-carried radio, but my objection to carrying one came from a different place. The guards carry radios. Their presence is usually announced by squawking static and routine messages they receive almost constantly. To carry such a thing would give me an identity I didn't want—too close to one of the brownshirts. They explained to me that I could turn the radio off so it wouldn't disturb the workshop, but that I could use it to call out in case of an emergency. All of this was obviously well-meant concern.

"What would you do" one of the young women reasoned with me patiently, "if a fight broke out in your classroom?"

"I would get out of the way," I said, "and the other men would break it up. I have been doing this for thirty years and a fight has never broken out in my classroom." They were not reassured. I didn't tell them that a horrendous fight broke out in one of my freshman classes at the university many years ago. As I arrived in the classroom a few minutes late, two young men were fighting over one of the coeds while she stood demurely against the wall watching the two men, both of whom she had been flirting with, pound each other mercilessly. She was very young and very beautiful, usually came to class barefoot, and her name was Linda Ronstadt. Linda claims she can't remember it, but I remember it distinctly, and I remember, after we got the fight stopped, one of her would-be suitors stalking off toward the men's room leaving a trail of little drops of blood from his nose.

At Tonto, realizing that I was losing ground in the radio argument, I fell back on plan B, which usually works in prison. I dropped all objections and agreed to carry the radio. I carried it once. The next time I came in they had forgotten all about it, and I sailed through the sally port without any mention of a radio. At the previous meeting, I had apologized to the men in the workshop for having the radio with me. They understood. The next time I came in, and without it, they just grinned. They knew the strategy I had used, having used it so many times themselves. Give in to the power you are powerless to resist, and wait. Things change. People forget.

The guards at Tonto on January 18 were listening to little transistor radios here and there throughout the unit, trying to get news of what was happening at Buckeye, where the two inmates with their two hostages found themselves in an impregnable prison tower, but trapped in it.

During intense and protracted negotiations in which even the governor became involved, the inmates eventually released the male guard on January 24, but held the female guard for fifteen days, during which both of them, one of whom had a history of sexual offenses, raped her repeatedly. Ultimately the two inmates surrendered, having been promised that they would be incarcerated outside of Arizona.

The panel appointed by the governor to investigate what is thought to be the longest prison hostage situation in U.S. history said that the situation "evolved out of a rich combination of complacency, inexperience, lack of professionalism, inadequate staffing, vague security procedures, poor training, lack of situational awareness, premature promotions, non-competitive pay, ineffective communication, malfunctioning equipment, high inmate-to-officer ratios, bad architectural design and myriad other causes." I guess that pretty well covers it. Stated more succinctly, the system was all screwed up.

When the report was made public, one of the panel members, former senator Herb Guenther, said the prison system was "a monster that is alive right now." Former attorney general Grant Woods described the administration of former director of the Department of Corrections Terry Stewart as "less than progressive in prison management."

The system got into its disastrous condition under the leadership of its two previous directors, Sam Lewis and Terry Stewart. After running the Department of Corrections, both of them went into the private prison business. Lewis appeared before the Committee on Public Institutions and Universities as a consultant to Dominion Leasing to urge the construction of a 500-bed private prison at St. Johns, Arizona. Stewart is a consultant to Advanced Correctional Management, a firm that recently submitted an unsolicited proposal to build the country's largest prison for women, a private prison with 3,200 beds, at Douglas. Plans for this project were initiated while Stewart was director of the Department of Corrections, "raising concerns about conflicts of interest and the use of inside information," according to an article in the *Arizona Daily Star* of August 3, 2003.

I am often asked what I think about private prisons, which have sprung up both in Arizona and more recently in Texas and Oklahoma, to which Arizona inmates are exported. What I think is that it's simply one more middleman, and the taxpayers are still footing the bill. And it's one step away from any real control of the state prisons on the part of the public. But then the public does not exercise any real control of the state prisons anyway. The public doesn't want to hear or know anything about them and pays no attention unless something sensational, like a major riot or hostage situation, attracts the attention of the media. The murder of one inmate by another doesn't even create a ripple.

Private prisons are in business in order to make money from prisoners. That's really nothing new. Communities like Florence, with huge prison populations, have become rich from tax revenues awarded them for each prisoner while the state pays for the prisoners' upkeep. Any prison is a business whether it is privately run or run by the state, since it hires and fires, has a huge payroll, and produces a product. Prison is one of the few businesses that can retrieve its product and market it again, in some cases many times. It's a business whether the prison is public or private, and the taxpayer is subsidizing it in either case because the state pays the private prison to house its inmates. Private prisons can be well run or badly run, just like state prisons, although the pressure to cut costs in a private prison is probably more severe than in a state prison.

My information from the inmates of Newton, a private prison in eastern Texas near the Louisiana border, to which many Arizona inmates have been recently sent, includes the following from a letter by one of them:

> Everything is green, green, green. We even had flowers in front of each dorm. They pulled them up last week though because they found an 18" pot plant hidden among them. There have been gallons and gallons of homemade wine, poker tables, 21 tables, sports books. In general this place is full of mischeif [sic]. . . . It has been nice to be in a place that isn't as oppressive as an AZ prison. There are even a pair of cats here, one of which just had kittens and already they are as much a part of this place as are the fences. The downside is that we are packed in here like sardines. Double bunked with a 3' living area. Very noisy and not conducive to writing, reading, or thinking.

The picture that emerges from this and other letters from the private prison at Newton, probably fairly typical of private prisons in the West, is what one might expect. The more inmates that can be packed into a prison, the more profit the private prison makes, since it charges by the head. Other than that, the administration doesn't care too much what goes on inside, as long as all the inmates, the sources of revenue, stay inside. Programs, beyond gambling and making booze, are not particularly evident. Rehabilitation is not a goal.

Presently there is much political controversy in Arizona concerning public versus private prisons, which seems to me to be a red herring. Clearly private prisons involve the possibility of political chicanery for profit, but so do the public prisons under corrupt leadership. We are terribly conflicted when it comes to our attitudes concerning prison, confused and helpless. We know there is something wrong with the system, but we don't know what to do about it except continue to provide huge amounts of money to support it, money we need for other things like the education of our children. We are afraid not to support it. The newspaper is full of horror stories. Television writers also churn them out, and they are graphic. We find it impossible to approach the problem rationally. We are afraid.

That we are conflicted is indicated in every statistic one can find relevant to our state prison system. Here are a few: Since 1978, spending for corrections has increased from 3 percent to 10 percent of Arizona's general fund. During the same period, spending for higher education in Arizona decreased from 19 percent to 12 percent. We are gradually starving our colleges and universities in order to support our prisons. All of them are educational institutions, but the kind of education provided is quite different.

Since 1978, the year Will Clipman and I started at Arizona Correctional for young offenders, Arizona's population has increased by 100 percent. During the same period, Arizona's prison population has increased by 1000 percent. I hate statistics as much, if not more, than anybody, but these have washed over me during the years, not as numbers, but as a daily awareness of escalating changes and frightening attitudes. I don't need to read the statistics; I see the embodiment of them each week. Maybe I and the people who work with me have been able to reach a few dozen inmates each year, but the system remains and has grown worse daily. Over the years I have grown old while the system spins more and more rapidly out of control, an industry that depends for its energy on the processing of living bodies. I have learned to be subversive in order to survive in it, while the system flourishes and is constantly renewed as it chews up the youth of America and spits them out as "the criminal element." Something has got to be done about the system, something far more dramatic than utilizing private prisons. The problem is that we *are* the system. We are the statistics, and nobody except us can change them.

We can point our fingers, often accurately in fact, toward the dysfunctional family, the nonperforming school, the city or county that provides little or no programs for its youth, the judicial system that caves in to social pressures, and the legislature with its mandatory sentencing laws. But pointing fingers is not going to do any good until we realize that *it's us*. It's us, doing our jobs and trying to get by, not always easily. Sometimes we can't sleep and we get up in the middle of the night and go into the kitchen and hear the refrigerator humming. Maybe we don't think about it, but the sound of that refrigerator humming is the sound of our lives, the sound of the great American middle class. It is the sound of our fear, a kind of steady low susurrus we can generally ignore except sometimes late at night. We check to make sure the outside doors are locked and the outside lights are on. *But we don't do anything else about it.*

We don't know what to do about it. Some of us vote for "get tough on crime" candidates in each election, but no matter how tough they are, nothing seems to change, and we begin to suspect it was just a ploy to get elected. We tell ourselves that our prison system is in the hands of highly trained professionals who know what they are doing. Then we find out that a young, relatively inexperienced female guard has been raped repeatedly *for fifteen days* by a mad man. This is the result of highly trained professional leadership in the prison? Perhaps what we need is more input from those who are neither so highly trained nor so professional. Somebody like us.

We are, after all, paying for this disaster of a system. Surely we have some right to do what we can to make it functional and effective. Surely we have some right to question its basic premises when we see it deliberately defeating any hope even the most promising inmate has for rehabilitation and a responsible, productive future life.

I believe that we, you and I, the concerned American public, can so alter the American state prison system as to make it obsolete within fifteen years, leaving only a fraction of the present number of inmates incarcerated, often in secure mental hospitals for those who are criminally insane and dangerous to society. The great majority of inmates in the state prisons today are neither criminally insane nor mentally ill.

First we have to get to know the prison system, and to know it is not to love it. We have to get into it some way, and it won't be easy, but I am proof that it can be done. We must go in as volunteers. It's the only way we'll get in. Not as religious volunteers, although they perform a valuable function, but as educational volunteers.

The computer expert could go in to teach computer skills. The plumber could go in to teach plumbing. The music teacher could go in to direct a choir or teach music composition. The graphic artist could go in to teach his or her skill, as could the journalist, the carpenter, the piano tuner, the photographer, the landscape architect, the dental technician, the chef, and on and on. If the prison administration objects to individuals coming in to teach particular skills, the individuals should ally themselves with powerful organizations that will "sponsor" them, although they work as unpaid volunteers. Churches, professional organizations, schools and universities, fraternal organizations, neighborhood associations, unions—there are hundreds of organizations that could act as sponsors to get volunteer teachers into the prisons. If the prison administration refuses to allow a qualified volunteer to come into the prison and teach his or her specialty, let them deal with the Mormon Church or the Teamsters. I guarantee that individual prison administrations will do everything they can to prevent volunteerism on a large scale. My experience has been that most of them will do whatever they can to prevent it on *any* scale.

The object of this massive move toward volunteerism is twofold. First of all it would help provide the inmates with marketable skills when they get out. Many former inmates return to prison simply because they do not have the skills required to make a decent living on the outside, and the prison has done nothing to remedy that situation. In many cases, of course, the former inmate would need further training on the outside, but the initial experience and success in prison would be an impetus to go on, to get whatever formal training was necessary. Also, the volunteer teacher, with his or her contacts in that particular specialty, might be able to steer the inmate emerging from prison to some kind of apprenticeship or transitional position leading to a secure future.

Most inmates, upon release from the Tucson complex, for instance, are dropped off at the bus station in downtown Tucson with $50 and, in many cases, nothing more than the clothes they were wearing when they were arrested, often representing the fashion of an earlier decade. If they are completing a second or subsequent sentence, they are given no money when released. For many of them, the only contacts they can call upon for temporary help are the ones that will lead them directly back to prison. Enter the volunteer who has already made contact with the inmate before his or her release and is fully aware of the former inmate's history. Such volunteers could advise and counsel the emerging inmates, to prevent them from making decisions out of panic. The idea that there is somebody in the free world who knows you and cares about your future, especially during the first few confusing weeks after years in prison, can often mean the difference between making it and not making it for the former inmate.

Sometimes it's just the accumulation of little things, as it is for all of us. Ken Lamberton told me that when he first got out of prison he had never seen a seat belt in a car and had no idea how to use one. He felt helpless, awkward, and inferior. This is the man whom I call now when I have a computer problem. He comes over, goes zip, zip, zip, and fixes it all. Yet after many years in prison he was unable to manipulate a seat belt. That's what prison does to people.

Another marked effect of massive volunteerism would be to make the prison system transparent, something it certainly is not at the present. Volunteers have eyes and ears and are usually not brainwashed by the prison administration. (Especially in the Tucson complex since we have a new intelligent and humane head chaplain in charge of programs.) More people on a prison yard who are not employees of the prison would have, I feel sure, a good effect on the prison administration, especially at its highest levels. Any system that has the power of life or death over millions of people twenty-four hours a day needs to be, above all, transparent to the public. And it needs a public that is concerned, vigilant, and *knowledgeable*.

A massive volunteer program to work with inmates within the prison and after their release would undoubtedly cut down on the recidivism rate and consequently lower the overall prison population, but it would not be enough. The prison problem needs to be attacked at both ends and the middle, all at the same time. At the front end, the loading end, many alternatives to incarceration are available, especially for nonviolent inmates, which includes the majority of the inmates in any state prison today. According to the Arizona Adult Probation Department, it costs roughly $4.50 a day for each person who is put on an electronic monitoring system, an ankle bracelet that reports the person's location and can determine that a convicted person is at home, at work, or at school. It costs $50 to $55 a day to house the same person in the county jail and even more, often much more, if he or she goes to prison. In spite of this, the Adult Probation Department in Pima County has dropped its electronic monitoring program because of massive cuts in its budget, thus causing the taxpayer to pay the higher figure for the offender to go to jail or prison. It's fiscal madness on a huge scale. It's also inhumane warehousing.

Other alternative programs like drug rehabilitation programs are always the first to have their funds cut in the sporadic belt-tightening movements that sweep through this and every other state. But the prison budgets are constantly increasing, and increasing at an incredible rate. It isn't merely a matter of priorities; it's fiscal madness again.

Of course we need to start these educational and rehabilitation programs earlier, in the schools and communities and with at-risk families, but we seldom have the money because we are spending every cent we can scrape up to support our existing prisons and build new ones as fast as possible. No country in the world incarcerates its citizens at the rate we do. We have now surpassed Russia, which previously held that honor at 690 incarcerations per 100,000 population. So we have now reached more than 700 incarcerations per 100,000 population as compared to England and Canada's 100 to 199, Germany and Japan's less than 100, and most of sub-Saharan Africa, also at less than 100.

And just who is it we are putting in prison, anyway? Do we know? Do we care? A recent study by Human Rights Watch reported in the *New York Times* concluded that "as many as one in five of the 2.1 million Americans in jail and prison are seriously mentally ill." That's 20 percent. These people need various kinds of care and treatment depending on the nature of their illness. What they don't need is to be dumped into prison, where their conditions deteriorate while they create problems, often serious problems, for the other inmates and the prison staff. Some of them merely need treatment and medication and could probably live in group homes in the free world. Some of them are truly mad and often dangerous and belong in secure mental hospitals. Many states do not have secure mental hospitals, and gradually the prison has taken over this function. But the staffs of the prisons are not adequately trained to deal with the insane even though the prison has now become the default mental health system.

Certainly the unwholesome nexus between the state legislature and the state judiciary needs to be examined. When legislators, in response to public hysteria and in a bid for reelection, pass draconian mandatory sentencing laws and demand longer and longer sentences for even minor drug use, they are simply filling the state's prisons with more and more inmates for a longer period of time. If the judges' hands were not tied by politics, and if the programs were available, many of these people could be sent to drug rehabilitation programs and kept out of prison where illegal drugs are cheaper and more readily available than on the streets, and where their drug habits will probably be confirmed.

I recently appeared on a lecture program with Dan Vanelli, who was the deputy warden at the Santa Rita facility during some of the years my creative writing workshop was functioning there. Dan is retired and does full-time missionary work in undeveloped countries. He said many interesting things, much of which I agree with. He said that the state prison system has long since given up any pretense of rehabilitating inmates. There was a time when rehabilitation could be one of the prison's goals, when the prison population was much smaller and inmates could be treated as individuals. But the crunch of numbers now makes such a goal impossible.

This sounded very reasonable when he said it, and I'm sure he believes it, but I can't agree. It seems too much like a justification for warehousing inmates. The time when rehabilitation was a goal had to be before 1974 when I began working as a volunteer in the prison. There was only one prison in the state then, and nothing in its history suggests to me that rehabilitation was one of its goals. The only goal I was aware of at Florence was security, and even that failed repeatedly. But the other part of Mr. Vanelli's statement might hold up under scrutiny. Any attempt at rehabilitation in the prison is hampered by sheer numbers. This is, of course, the old catch-22, the chicken and the egg dilemma that results in stasis. The prison can't rehabilitate because it has too many inmates, and its failure to rehabilitate is largely what's creating more inmates. The revolving door.

Although I don't buy Mr. Vanelli's argument, I am certainly aware that the sheer number of inmates affects any attempts to get control of the system and make it an effective tool for rehabilitation. Consequently, reducing the number of inmates drastically without endangering society should be a major, immediate goal. I believe it could be accomplished if sufficient public interest and attention were given to the entire process of incarceration. We have to admit that it's our problem, not the prison's, and the prison has to let us help solve it.

It's Saturday morning in mid-March at the Manzanita Unit. Still cold at 9:00 a.m., and the wind coming off the Santa Ritas has an edge to it, but by midafternoon, when I leave the Rincon Unit, it will be too warm for the sweater I'm wearing. I notice that the guards working out on the yard have on their heavy brown coats and those silly hats with the earflaps, while the inmates standing outside the chow hall to smoke are shivering in their flimsy orange jackets. I wish I had worn my coat, but it was so much warmer on the other side of the valley when I left the house that I didn't think I'd need it. I should know better by now. Except in the summer, it's always at least ten degrees colder out here than where I live in the Tucson Mountains.

I start across the yard toward the Education Building pulling my little two-wheel luggage carrier with a big plastic box attached to it with a bungee cord. The box is filled with writing pads, books, magazines, and pens. I don't think I could express how much I hate the awkward rolling affair. It turns over on the slightest incline and constantly nips at my heels. Getting it onto and off of the bus when I go to Rincon is a nightmare. Fortunately, at Manzanita I can drive right up in front of the facility, but manipulating the stupid thing around the metal detector is not easy.

A group of about thirty men, all in orange and walking two by two, are coming toward me on the sidewalk, headed for their dormitory after chow. There isn't room for all of us on the narrow sidewalk, but I know they will give way and let me pass, as they always do. Some make eye contact; some don't. Most respond to my "Good morning" or "Howdy." Some call me by name, although they are not in the workshop. One of them says, "Hey, Creative Writing, you need a longer handle."

Well I'll be damned. Maybe that's it. That's why this contraption is so hard to maneuver and keeps bumping my heels and turning over. Why am I the last to figure these things out? I have to be told by a complete stranger who happens to be passing, and a convicted felon at that. Oh, these men in orange. I've learned more from them than I ever taught them, and it's been good stuff. They never tried to teach me how to hot-wire a car or all that business with the spoon and the syringe. They have taught me to be patient; never to whine no matter what; to expect the worst and be happy if I get anything else; to be subversive in the face of unjust, cruel, or stupid authority; to be loyal, to be forgiving, to be kind. They have taught me that we are all law breakers and we are all victims of crime. They have taught me that growing old is no disgrace, but that a youth, wasted in prison, is a disaster.

This morning the guard is there to unlock the door and let me into the Education Building. It's good to get in out of the wind. Last week was even colder and I had to wait outside the building about fifteen minutes because the prison was shorthanded and all available guards were deployed in or outside the chow hall. But last week I had my coat.

I can usually tell what the week has been like for the men in the workshop by the way they come in and start assembling the tables together, jockeying to get the best chairs, and going through the books I brought in. It's a young group, filled with energy. They like each other, and some of the closest friendships and literary collaborations are cross-racial. They live in dormitories, which makes it possible for real friendships to develop. Some of them sit up late into the night, writing and reading to one another what they have written. Friday night is the most frantic and exciting night of the week because on Saturday morning they will read what they have written to the entire group, and Friday night is final polishing time and time to get up their courage to read a major new work. Sometimes as we go around the table and I ask each one if he has something to read, one will say "No" and shake his head, having lost his nerve, and his buddy will say, "Yes, he does have something to read. We worked on it half the night. Now you read it, wimp, or I'll read it for you."

Usually they come in all in a rush of talk and laughter, bantering with one another. High spirited, looking forward to some intelligent discussion in which their views will be listened to with respect. It makes working with them a joy. Today, however, things are different. They file in quietly, say "good morning" in a monotone, and get the long table set up almost in silence. *I'll wait,* I think. *It might not be any of my business. If it is, they'll tell me sooner or later.*

I pass out the sheets with their work on them. Lois has typed the work from their handwritten sheets, and I have made enough copies for everybody. Today there are only ten out of the usual fourteen. Noah has been rolled up, they tell me. Mark T. has been sent to a private prison in Oklahoma, and two of them are on a work detail in the kitchen. When they mention the private prison in Oklahoma, I say, "I thought they were sending people to Newton in Texas, near the Louisiana border."

"Now they've got a new one in Oklahoma," Mark Sanchez says. "I'm going. They're taking me." The room gets very quiet.

I'm horrified. Mark is the best fiction writer in the group, and undoubtedly one of the best fiction writers I've ever worked with anywhere. Each workshop has one member who holds it together with his intense energy and dedication to writing. Mark is that star for the Manzanita workshop. He is young enough to be my grandson, small, wiry, and looks like a little devil with his black hair cut short, a pronounced widow's peak, and huge expressive dark eyes that snap and flash when he talks. Mark is always pushing the technical envelope in his writing. He devours contemporary work and constantly asks me technical questions that are sometimes over my head because I've written so little fiction. He's been experimenting with point of view and interior dialogue, and he reads everything from Samuel Beckett to Cormac McCarthy. He has some college credits already, earned in courses offered at the prison. He has two years to go, and I feel sure that, with a little help from a Regents' Professor I know at the University of Arizona, he will be able to get a minority scholarship and study in one of the best creative writing programs in the country.

If he is moved to the private prison in Oklahoma, much like the one in Texas, it will probably all go down the drain. He needs the workshop. He needs the stimulation of technical and intellectual discussions with a teacher who is also a professional writer. It's obvious he doesn't think he can make it on his own yet, and I'm not sure he can either.

"But don't you have family here?" I ask. "They weren't taking anybody to Newton who had family to visit them here."

"Yeah, I've got family here. But it doesn't matter anymore. They say that at this new place in Oklahoma they're arranging for family visits on TV. Doesn't that sound like fun?"

"Even people in major programs are going," somebody says. "People who are just about to complete a class. They'll lose the credits. They seem to be taking people at random."

I look at Mark closely. His normally bright, expressive eyes are dull. His color is sallow and he seems listless. He's given up, I think. He isn't complaining. He's just quiet. He's been hassling with the authorities over this all week. His family members are writing letters. But he knows the system, young as he is. He's losing. All that incredible creativity, passion, intelligence. He won't be able to sustain it in some hellhole in Oklahoma. He will lose his whole support system, his family, the workshop, the crazy Regents' Professor who spends hours going over his work and is a ruthless critic, the professor's wife who turns his handwritten stories into professional-looking manuscripts, and his fellow writers in the workshop who encourage and admire him. He will lose it all. When he gets to the private prison in Oklahoma, there will be nothing but booze and drugs and gambling to take the place of all he has here, and he will arrive in despair.

I know why this is happening. It's pretty well spelled out in the February 20, 2004, issue of the *Arizona Capitol Times*, if one knows the history. Certain members of the state legislature who have bought into the private-prison philosophy of Terry Stewart and Sam Lewis, in spite of the fact that both of them had or have vested interests in the private prisons, are using the recent hostage situation to force the new director of the State Board of Corrections, Dora Schriro, to fill private prisons to relieve the overcrowding in the state prisons, in spite of the fact that neither Ms. Schriro nor the governor believe that such a solution is viable. But Schriro has caved in to the political pressure, probably because she has little choice, and is now sending prisoners as quickly as possible, helter-skelter, to the private facility in Oklahoma. Mark and many others are pawns in a political game with some highly unsavory aspects. Actually, they always have been, but it wasn't quite so obvious.

I make a note to call the head chaplain and ask him to intercede for Mark. I realize the chaplain doesn't have the power to affect the situation, but it's all I know of to do. I am sick to the core. For a few seconds I think I'm going to throw up. I've told myself hundreds of times: *Never enter a prison on an empty stomach*, but this morning I broke my own rule except for one cup of coffee that only makes things worse in my churning stomach. For me it's all happening again, just as it happened at the Tonto Unit in Safford when inmates began to be sent with almost no warning to the Newton private prison near the eastern border of south Texas.

One of them was Brian Potter, whose poetry in *Walking Rain Review* IX suggests his enormous potential as a writer. I feel about Brian Potter's poetry much as I felt about the poetry of Michael Martin thirty years before. The work is haunted, magical. It is very masculine poetry but written out of some irreparable damage or loss. With Michael Martin I knew what was behind most of his work. It was his father's body hanging in the basement when Michael discovered it. With Brian Potter I don't know what the central tragedy was, but I know it was there. He could have dealt with it and created unforgettable poetry, but I don't think he will now. I've lost him. I think he might lose touch with himself at the Newton private prison. Like Michael Martin, he may drift through the nightmare of the underside of America, maybe for the rest of his life

Last month I received a letter from Wei, the very young, very gentle Chinese boy who was in the Rincon workshop until he was sent to Yuma recently, rolled up without warning. Wei was raised in China and is a real scholar in the tradition of overachieving Oriental scholars. He was working on a PhD in physics when he was arrested. Even working in a second language he has been able to achieve shimmering brief prose pieces, bizarre and beautiful. The first part of the letter is:

Dear Professor Shelton,

Today turned out to be the most morale-raising and the most discouraging day since I came to Yuma.

Morale-raising because I was told that you sent me a book titled "We Stand Alone" by Wei Jingshen, one of the most famous democratic activists in modern China.

Discouraging because the authority told me they will send this book back. Here is their reasoning: I have had seven books in possession already, including a Merriam-Webster Collegiate dictionary, a paperback Webster dictionary (Your Christmas gift to us), a thesaurus, a two-volume New Shorter Oxford English Dictionary, and a two-volume Chinese dictionary. Therefore, I can not have more books unless I destroy or send out my reference books. Since these dictionaries are basic tools for daily study, I can neither destroy them or send them out.

I begged, entreated, implored to put one dictionary in storage to exchange for your book. Met with the most resolute refusal, and the threat to lock me in the "cage." I was in hopeless situation. This sergeant in charge had his implicit satisfaction. I can never forget the leer on his face while I explained in vain the value of reading.

Graciously, they allowed me to touch the book before they sealed it back to the envelope. Your simple words "Wei, we miss you. Richard Shelton" on the inside cover broke my last facial attempt at toughness. I cried . . .

Yours Sincerely
Wei

P.S. They are considering sending me to a private prison in Oklahoma or Texas. But I am not afraid, dear Richard, you have saved me before they might have destroyed me. I am singing.

Of course I have received no book, although the letter arrived months ago, and I don't expect to. This has happened before. I hope the books find their way into the prison libraries, but I suspect many of them find their way into the prison trash cans.

At the conclusion of the Manzanita workshop, I am surrounded with men who have questions or work to give me for next week, and Pedro, who will wait until everyone else has gone and then walk with me all the way to the gate, asking questions and trying to figure out how to improve his novel. I look for Mark in the confusion. He's at the door, about to leave. I make a gesture toward him. It may be the last time I will ever see him. I want to say something to him, something encouraging, but he's too smart for me. He knows that any encouragement I could give him would be false, and he doesn't want the last words between us to be a lie. He turns and gives me one look over his shoulder as he goes out the door. I cannot really describe that look. It includes the admission of defeat and great pride. It says, *I promise you I'll try, but I'm afraid. I don't think I can do it. You gave me hope. Why did you do that to me? Why did I let you?* Then he is gone.

Two of the men load the books into my cart, books that have been circulating for several weeks and are now going out. Pedro is waiting. I don't want to walk out with Pedro right now and greet the guard who will lock the door behind us. I don't want to tell Pedro what's wrong with his novel. I want to put my head down on the table in front of me and weep with a pain that will not be comforted and a rage I cannot express.

Notes

Chapter 2

"I'm willing to accept . . . in the Honor Compound." Ken Burton and Charles Schmid, "Charles Schmid: A Prison Life and a Prison Death," *Tucson Citizen*, December 30, 1978.

"They published . . . death row." Charles H. Schmid Jr., "Entente" and "Lady," *Inscape* 2, no. 4 (1972): 8–9.

"On January 2, 1974, . . . I somehow belong." Unpublished letter from Charles Schmid to Richard Shelton.

Chapter 4

Richard Shelton, "Certain Choices," from *Selected Poems: 1969–1981* (Pittsburgh: University of Pittsburgh Press, 1982), 170.

"And when, last month . . . ignore the law." Kim Smith, "Boy Says Guard Molested Him, Asks $1M from State," *Arizona Daily Star*, April 12, 2006.

Chapter 6

"As long ago as 1973 . . . would actually go down." Jessica Mitford, *Kind and Usual Punishment* (New York: Knopf, 1973).

"As the journalist . . . 'a blot on society.'" Scott Shane, "U.S. Leads in Prison Population," *Register-Guard National*, June 1, 2003.

"Marc Mauer, in *Race to Incarcerate* . . . 'for a white boy.'" Marc Mauer and the Sentencing Project, *Race to Incarcerate* (New York: New Press, 1999), 129.

"As detailed in . . . nerve center of the prison." Thornton Price III, *Murder Unpunished* (Tucson: University of Arizona Press, 2005).

"On June 22 . . . and Theodore Buckley." "Mass for Slain Guards," *Florence Blade-Tribune*, June 28, 1973.

Chapter 7

"Michael Mulcahy . . . within eighteen months." *Correction*, a documentary film by Michael Mulcahy (Independent Television Service, 2003).

Chapter 8

"I have before me . . . 'was also three inches.'" "Reporter's Transcript of Proceedings in the Matter of the Inquisition held upon the Body of Charles Howard Schmid Jr., Deceased, in the Justice Court of East Phoenix Precinct No. 1 County of Maricopa, State of Arizona, April 4, 1975, 3:00 o'clock p.m., Hon. Ben Arnold . . . Ex-Officio Coroner and a Coroner's Jury."

"I also have . . . and 'Dirty Dan.'" "Verdict in the Matter of the Inquisition Held Upon the Body of Paul David Ashley aka Charles Howard Schmid Jr., April 4, 1975."

Chapter 9

"I have a copy . . . 'not shown here.'" "High Wall Jammers," by Gary Lewallen, *La Roca*, June 1974.

"Some of its . . . as 'Stretch' and 'Red Dog.'" See Price, *Murder Unpunished*.

"In a letter . . . 'one good poem.'" Unpublished, undated letter from Paul Ashley to Richard Shelton.

Chapter 10

"According to . . . possibility of parole." Price, *Murder Unpunished*, 43.

"The particular circumstances . . . capacities for regeneration." W. S. Merwin, unpublished introduction to manuscript of "The Unfinished Man," by Paul Ashley, 1975.

Chapter 11

"In 1977 . . . were stabbed." R. H. Ring, "A History of Hard Time," in "The Convicted: A Special Report on Arizona's Corrections System," *Arizona Daily Star*, August 8, 1982.

"In his book . . . 'cycle without end.'" Price, *Murder Unpunished*, 69.

"He was serving . . . Cardwell refused." Background on Tony Serra is from James W. Clarke, *Last Rampage: The Escape of Gary Tison* (Boston: Houghton Mifflin, 1988), 119–25.

"So the anthology . . . nonliterary lives." *Do Not Go Gentle: Poetry and Prose from Behind the Walls*, ed. Stephen Dugan [pseud.] (Tucson, AZ: Blue Moon Press, 1977).

"Looking for Someone," by Michael Martin, in *Do Not Go Gentle*, 127.

Chapter 13

"There is a depth . . . unhealthy and diseased." Charles Dickens, *American Notes: A Journey* (New York: Fromm International, 1985), 99, 109.

Chapter 14

"I have a copy . . . fancy embroidery." *COSMEP Prison Newsletter* 5, no. 2 (Spring/Summer 1981).

"Devotions," from *The Listening Chamber*, by William Aberg (Fayetteville: University of Arkansas Press, 1997), 31. (By permission of the author.)

Chapter 15

"There is an anthology . . . in 1982." *The Promise of Morning: Writings from the Arizona Prisons*, ed. by W. M. Aberg (Tucson, AZ: Blue Moon Press, 1982).

"Workshops now exist . . . for Women." Jay Barwell, afterword to *The Promise of Morning*, 101–3.

Chapter 17

"Commenting on this . . . 'have been committed.'" Richard Shelton, foreword to *Wilderness and Razor Wire: A Naturalist's Observations from Prison*, by Ken Lamberton (San Francisco: Mercury House, 2000), xiii–xix.

"His 'Species Profile' . . . well written and informative." Ken Lamberton, "Harris' Hawks," *Bird Watcher's Digest* 14, no. 1 (September/October 1991): 50–54.

"Ken's article . . . in the magazine." Ken Lamberton, "The Ubiquitous Side Blotched Lizard: Profile of an 'Annual' Reptile," *Reptile and Amphibian Magazine*, September/October 1991, 42–45.

"The most recent . . . University of Arizona Press." Ken Lamberton, *Beyond Desert Walls: Essays from Prison* (Tucson: University of Arizona Press, 2005).

"In the recently . . . District of Columbia." *Invisible Punishment: The Collateral Consequences of Mass Imprisonment*, ed. by Marc Mauer and Meda Chesney-Lind (New York: New Press, 2002), 117–35.

Chapter 18

"Many years later . . . *Sing Soft, Sing Loud*." Patricia McConnel, *Sing Soft, Sing Loud: Scenes from Two Lives* (New York: Atheneum, 1989).

"Her novel . . . flattering light." Terry McMillan, *Disappearing Acts* (New York: Penguin, 2002).

Chapter 20

"Five percent . . . have a college degree." *Correction*, documentary film by Michael Mulcahy.

Chapter 22

"The panel appointed . . . 'myriad other causes.'" Barrett Marston, "Panel Finds Ample Blame in Prison Hostage Standoff," *Arizona Daily Star*, March 5, 2004. This is an article quoting the findings of Governor Napolitano's Blue Ribbon Panel on Corrections.

"When the report . . . 'alive right now.'" Phil Riske, "Napolitano Calls Prison Findings 'Outrageous'; Promises Clean Up," *Arizona Capitol Times*, March 12, 2004.

"Former attorney general . . . 'in prison management.'" Jim Erickson, "Mecham Should 'Clean Up Government by Firing Prisons Chief Lewis, Says Ewing," *Arizona Daily Star*, June 28, 1987.

"The system . . . disastrous condition." Phil Riske, "Prison Report Cites Poor Security, Low Pay," *Arizona Capitol Times*, February 13, 2006.

"After running . . . of August 3, 2003." Barrett Marston, "Az Gov. Refuses to Make Public Bids from 3 Companies Seeking 3,200 Bed Facility Deal," *Arizona Daily Star*, August 3, 2003. Sandrine Ageorges, "Former Dept. of Corrections Chief Involved with Firm Bidding to Build New Prison," *PrisonAct*, August 9, 2003.

"Since 1978 . . . 12 percent." *Correction*, a documentary film by Michael Mulcahy.

"According to . . . to jail or prison." Shane, "U.S. Leads in Prison Population."

"A recent study . . . 'mentally ill.'" Fox Butterfield, "Study Finds Hundreds of Thousands of Inmates Mentally Ill" [report on a Human Rights Watch study], *New York Times*, October 22, 2003.

Chapter 23

"It's pretty well . . . knows the history." Grant Smith, "GOP Lawmakers Demand Action on Corrections Overcrowding," *Arizona Capitol Times*, February 20, 2004.

Suggested Reading

Aberg, William. *The Listening Chamber: Poems*. Fayetteville: University of Arkansas Press, 1997.

———, ed. *The Promise of Morning: Writings from Arizona Prisons*. Tucson, AZ: Blue Moon Press, 1982.

Baca, Jimmy Santiago. *Martin; and, Meditations on the South Valley*. New York: New Directions, 1987.

———. *A Place to Stand*. New York: Grove Press, 2001.

———. *Working in the Dark: Reflections of a Poet of the Barrio*. Santa Fe: Red Crane Books, 1992.

Bruchac, Joseph, ed. *The Light from Another Country: Poetry from American Prisons*. Greenfield Center, NY: Greenfield Review Press, 1984.

Clarke, James W. *Last Rampage: The Escape of Gary Tison*. Boston: Houghton Mifflin, 1988. Reprint, Tucson: University of Arizona Press, 1999.

Dickens, Charles. *American Notes: A Journey*. New York: Fromm International, 1985.

Dugan, Stephen [pseud.], ed. *Do Not Go Gentle: Poetry and Prose from Behind the Walls*. Tucson, AZ: Blue Moon Press, 1977.

Lamberton, Ken. *Beyond Desert Walls: Essays from Prison*. Tucson: University of Arizona Press, 2005.

———. *Wilderness and Razor Wire: A Naturalist's Observations from Prison*. San Francisco: Mercury House, 2000.

Magnani, Laura, and Harmon L. Wray. *Beyond Prisons: A New Interfaith Paradigm for Our Failed Prison System*. Minneapolis: Fortress Press, 2006.

Mauer, Marc, [and] the Sentencing Project. *Race to Incarcerate*. New York: New Press, 1999.

Mauer, Marc, and Meda Chesney-Lind, eds. *Invisible Punishment: The Collateral Consequences of Mass Imprisonment*. New York: New Press, 2002.

McConnel, Patricia. *Sing Soft, Sing Loud: Scenes from Two Lives*. New York: Atheneum, 1989.

Mitford, Jessica. *Kind and Usual Punishment*. New York: Knopf, 1973.

Moore, Daniel G. *Enter without Knocking*. Tucson: University of Arizona Press, 1969.

Mulcahy, Michael. *Corrections* [documentary film]. Independent Television Services, 2003.

Price, Thornton W., III. *Murder Unpunished: How the Aryan Brotherhood Murdered Waymond Small and Got Away with It*. Tucson: University of Arizona Press, 2005.

Rossi, Richard Michael. *Waiting to Die: Life on Death Row*. London: Vision, 2004.

Schlosser, Eric. *Reefer Madness: Sex, Drugs, and Cheap Labor in the American Black Market*. Boston: Houghton Mifflin, 2003.

Serge, Victor. *Men in Prison*. Translated, with an introduction by Richard Greeman. London: Writers and Readers Publishing Cooperative, 1977.

Tannenbaum, Judith. *Disguised as a Poem: My Years Teaching Poetry at San Quentin*. Boston: Northeastern University Press, 2000.

About the Author

Richard Shelton is a Regents' Professor in the Creative Writing Program at the University of Arizona, Tucson. He is the author of eleven books of poetry and the nonfiction memoir *Going Back to Bisbee*, winner of the Western States Award for creative nonfiction and now in its tenth printing. In 1974 he established a writers workshop in the Arizona State Prison at Florence. That program, over the years, has expanded into many prison workshops, four of which are currently operating with the support of the Lannan Foundation. Dozens of books by graduates of this program have been published. He is the editor of the journal *Walking Rain Review*, which features the literary work of those who have been or are incarcerated in Arizona state prisons.